ANGER MANAGEMENT

The Ultimate Anger Management Self Help Guide:

How to Take Complete Control of Your Emotions, Make Your Relationships Thrive, and Tame the Lion Inside of You for Good

4 BOOKS IN 1

1) **PERSUASION TECHNIQUES**

2) **THE SECRET OF MANIPULATION**

3) **DARK PSYCHOLOGY**

4) **ANALYZE PEOPLE**

TABLE OF CONTENTS
PERSUASION TECHNIQUES

INTRODUCTION 10

WHAT IS PERSUASION? 15

METHODS OF PERSUASION 23

HYPNOSIS 41

DARK NLP 65

COVERT EMOTIONAL MANIPULATION 78

BRAINWASHING 98

DECEPTION 107

CONCLUSION 166

TABLE OF CONNTENTS
THE SECRET OF MANIPULATION

INTRODUCTION..172

WHAT IS MANIPULATIVE BEHAVIOR......................176

VICTIMS OF MANIPULATION 179

HOW TO USE DARK PSYCHOLOGY TO MANIPULATE OTHERS 206

MANIPULATION TECHNIQUES.............................233

IDENTIFYING MANIPULATOR TYPES 248

THE MOST POWERFUL MIND-POWER TOOL 264

MASTERING YOUR EMOTIONS 274

CONCLUSION 316

TABLE OF CONTENTS

DARK PSYCHOLOGY

INTRODUCTION 324

WHAT IS DARK PSYCHOLOGY? 326

THE FOUR DARK PERSONALITY CLASSIFICATIONS 352

TECHNIQUES OF DARK PSYCHOLOGY................... 361

BRAINWASHING TO STOP BEING MANIPULATED.... 403

UNDETECTED MIND CONTROL............................ 410

THE POWER OF PERSUASION............................. 416

UNDERSTANDING DECEPTION 435

SPEED READING PEOPLE 454

CONCLUSION... 462

TABLE OF CONTENTS

ANALYZE PEOPLE

INTRODUCTION 476

WHY ANALYZE PEOPLE 479

ANALYZING PERSONALITY PEOPLE 490

BODY LANGUAGES 501

EFFECTIVELY ANALYZING PEOPLE THROUGH THEIR WORDS 548

PERSONALITY AND BIRTH ORDER 562

PERSONALITY TYPES AND PATTERNS 576

THE ART OF ANALYZING HUMAN BEHAVIOR 593

CONCLUSION 623

PERSUASION TECHNIQUES:

How to Stop Being Manipulated. Learn the Method and The Secrets of Manipulation and Persuasion. How To Influence People With Mind Control techniques.

© Text Copyright 2019 – Jason Halpa

The content contained within this book may not be reproduced, duplicated or transmitted without direct written permission from the author or the publisher.

Under no circumstances will any blame or legal responsibility be held against the publisher, or author, for any damages, reparation, or monetary loss due to the information contained within this book. Either directly or indirectly.

Legal Notice:

This book is copyright protected. This book is only for personal use. You cannot amend, distribute, sell, use, quote or paraphrase any part, or the content within this book, without the consent of the author or publisher.

Disclaimer Notice:

Please note the information contained within this document is for educational and entertainment purposes only. All effort has been executed to present accurate, up to date, and reliable, complete information. No warranties of any kind are declared or

implied. Readers acknowledge that the author is not engaging in the rendering of legal, financial, medical or professional advice. The content within this book has been derived from various sources. Please consult a licensed professional before attempting any techniques outlined in this book.

By reading this document, the reader agrees that under no circumstances is the author responsible for any losses, direct or indirect, which are incurred as a result of the use of information contained within this document, including, but not limited to, — errors, omissions, or inaccuracies.

INTRODUCTION

Consider your audience in phrasing your message. The way you address college students must be different from the way you address senior citizens. You may also have to modify the different genders.

Let us use the example of health products once again; weight loss products to be precise. When introducing such products to women, you can emphasize the need to look good in cute dresses, avoid stretch marks, acquire a bikini body and so on. These are issues that are close to their hearts.

Men may not respond as effectively to a message phrased as such. The word 'fat' seems not to sound as atrocious to men as it does to women. If the old clothes don't fit, how about just get others a size (or 3) larger? And don't even get started about the beach. They'll comfortably spot their beer bellies, shirtless, and enjoy their holiday without a care in the world. They insert 'big' before their name and actually make it sound cool. Thank you very much, Big Austin.

See? A message that was well-received by the women

goes in and out for the men. Perhaps the way to get men to listen in this case would be to hit below the belt, quite literally. Tie your products to sexual health. Sexual prowess, to be exact. The idea that they can be beasts (or close) in bed can get them eating oats and celery sticks in no time. Or whatever else you suggest.

If you're speaking to a creative, such as an artist, do not drown them in analytical figures. Spare that for the business executives. These ones are fascinated by numbers, they say they don't lie. Creatives thrive in hearing how ideas will come to life.

You must carefully choose which detail to exemplify depending on whom you're speaking to. These are just a few examples of personalizing the message depending on the receiver. The principal goes beyond the business world to other facets of life. You should now be in a position to do the same depending on your situation.

When people do not positively receive your message right away, you have to be prepared to say it time and again. Sounds like nagging, right? Not necessarily. Think of politicians campaigning for political posts. They campaign for months, speaking to people every day, essentially repeating the same message over and over. Should they lose that particular election, they return the following one and continue expounding the reasons they believe they're best placed to represent the people. Former President Abraham Lincoln lost 8 separate elections before he was elected to the highest office in the land.

There is something about a man (or woman) who asks without ceasing. One who refuses to back down. The persistence convinces people that he has ideas that will make an impact on their lives. Even the most stubborn of them end up listening.

How can you remain persistent without being a nuisance? Keep paraphrasing the message. Say things differently. Add some more details each time. Develop a demo or prototype. Collect relevant statistics. People respond better to something they can see as opposed to plain words. Give the listeners time to process the information, then communicate again. Keep knocking on that door, and eventually, it'll be opened one way or the other.

To make others see your point of view, you have to communicate with conviction. Your verbal and body language makes the first impression and determines the perception of the listener towards you. Whether you're giving a speech, speaking to a small group of people or to a single person, confidence is key.

How do you portray confidence? Body language first. Walk with your head high. Maintain steady eye contact. Shake hands firmly. This will make people want to hear what you have to say. Listen attentively when it's the listeners turn to speak. Nod periodically.

Confidence carries an aura of energy that is instantly transferred to others. It motivates and excites them about your ideas. They can see that you're totally sold on the idea, and this will increase their curiosity and make them want to try it.

Make your listener see that there is a limited time. This is a strategy mostly used in marketing. What do they tell you? Hurry while stocks last! Offer valid for the first 100 buyers! Buy today and get a discount! In most of these sales, the stock is not limited as they want to make you believe. They know a sense of urgency works. They manage to convince you that it'll be a privilege to be among the first buyers and receive a certain offer. And it works.

Still, on marketing matters, make sure you

demonstrate that other people have shown interest or given good reviews of your ideas. In this age of social media, you can rely on the response that you're getting online as proof of interest.

Begin by posting your idea online on multiple platforms. You can sponsor an advert in which you're in a position to so that more people can view it. As is the case with interesting ideas, it goes viral. Scores of people will view your pictures, watch your videos or read the articles. Even better, they share the content and just like that; it's exposed to a larger audience. Fortunately, social media platforms keep track of it all. Numbers sure don't lie. Use those hits, likes, shares, follows and comments in your next pitch. People are drawn to ideas that have fascinated other people. They don't want to be left behind, they want to be part of the excitement too.

WHAT IS PERSUASION?

When we discuss manipulation and persuasion, it usually comes down to a difference of intent. For instance, is the person who is persuading you to do something that will benefit both you and them? If so, that's the classic win-win scenario, and we could say that persuasion was used to help you come to the right decision.

But what if the same person gets you to do something that benefits him, but leaves you worse off? That would be characterized as manipulation, and that type of persuasion happens all of the time, too. You may have done it yourself without really realizing it, and not felt too good about it afterward.

Persuasion can be used for all kinds of purposes, both good and evil. People can manipulate you into giving them your money, your time, your faith, your talent, and provide you with nothing in return. Or they can persuade you into giving of all of these things and leave you better off in the end. And sometimes, the lines aren't so clearly drawn.

What I will attempt to show you in this book is just how persuasion happens in various parts of your everyday life, how persuasion can be used to help you get what you want, and how to recognize persuasion techniques that are used on you. Ultimately, everyone makes their own decisions. By being aware of persuasion techniques, you can more successfully analyze your motivations and make sure that what you are doing benefits both you and others.

Today's Pervasive Persuasion

Persuasion is also an important topic today because we are contacted by more and more sophisticated methods of persuasion than ever before. Persuasion comes at us in all forms, at a velocity never even possible previously. I'm sure you can guess the cause of this increased persuasion. That's right! It's called The Internet.

Never before have people had direct access to the tools of mass communication. You can pick up your smartphone and start broadcasting live right now, with just a few clicks. You can start typing and send your views to millions of people around the world. Or you can post a picture of that adorable thing your cat just did to your partner to brighten their day at work. And all of the people you are reaching can get that information instantly because they probably have a smartphone or computer or screen nearby that they are looking at, and you have access to that network. This type of reach and access was unheard of only a decade or two ago. Today, this connection is commonplace and growing.

But do you ever take time to decide how the words and pictures that you consume play a part in what you think, or what the motives were behind sending them to you in the first place? Much like a loaded gun in the hands of someone who doesn't know how to shoot, persuasion techniques can sometimes have unintended consequences that can be devastating. If you don't realize what the warning signs are, or how you can protect yourself from those consequences, and make sure you aren't unintentionally harming yourself.

The Principles of Persuasion

Since that book, many researchers have created experiments to test these theories with surprisingly consistent results. The bottom line is that we humans seem to be hard-wired to behave in certain ways given certain circumstances. Using various methods to trigger those responses that we want, we can cause the outcomes that we want.

The 6 Principles of Persuasion

Reciprocation

Give something to get something, right? Remember the story of the chicken who planted grain so that her chicks could eat? She asked for help to sow the grain, to keep the field clean from weeds, to harvest the grain and finally, to make the bread. She asked her neighbors and friends to help, but in the end, no one was interested until the bread was hot and ready to eat. Since her neighbors had not given her anything in the form of help, she was not inclined to give them any of the final product.

That give and take is the first principal of getting along in life, and it's known as one of the foundational principals of persuasion as well. Reciprocity merely means that if you give someone something, they are more likely to give you something in return.

Commitment and Consistency

We, humans, have a "reality" surrounding us at all times. I put this "reality" in quotes because it is a reality of our creation.

Our brains have an innate ability to tell stories, and we tell ourselves stories all of the time. We tell ourselves stories of the type of person we believe we are, and how we behave feeds into that story. When presented with a choice, you make that choice based on the story of who you are. One of the options looks "right" to us because making that choice is consistent with what we believe a person like us would do.

Social Proof

This core persuasion principle is also sometimes referred to as Consensus. Social proof feeds directly from the previous storytelling of Commitment and Consistency. We have told ourselves a story of what we believe we are, what we stand for, and the kind of person we are. To reinforce that story, we look at how other people behave for Social Proof of how people like us should react in a particular situation.

Now more than ever, the Internet has created countless places where we can go for this type of reinforcement. Some of that reinforcement is legitimate, some not so much. All of it is used as a powerful tool for persuasion, as we'll find out going forward.

Authority

Now once we have decided on the type of person we are and we've assembled with the kinds of people we believe reinforce that identity; the next step is to seek out knowledgeable people to reinforce what we've told ourselves to be true. That's where the idea of Authority takes hold.

As sane people, we are likely to take the advice of people who appear to have more knowledge about a subject than we do. That is certainly necessary. No one can know everything, not even with smartphones and Google just a tap away. We seek out the advice of people who know more about a subject than we do. We'll talk more about using this in persuasion later.

Liking

Liking is one of those core principles that seems

obvious, but yet it needs definition since it is at the hub of all types of persuasion. Liking, simply put, means that you are much more likely to be persuaded by someone that you like.

If you don't like someone, are you going to take their advice? Probably not. We humans are wired to make snap judgments about almost every situation we get into, and one of the simplest decisions to make is whether we like someone or not. Every person you meet triggers a feeling instantly of comfort or wariness. This was a survival skill in the early days of our evolution, and it still holds sway today, as we'll see.

Scarcity

Speaking of evolution's early days, our final persuasion principal is an obvious holdover from the early days of staying alive. Scarcity makes things more valuable to us, so when something seems like it is limited in quantity, we are more likely to want it.

Sand is commonplace; gold is not. Which would you rather have? Or more to the point, what does all humankind want more? It most certainly used to be food that was so valuable, so that early man found ways to preserve food when it was abundant so that it would be around when food got scarce.

Survival depends on specific resources that can be in short supply, so humans are naturally prone to try and save and hang on to that which is not always available. Since this is core hardwiring in our brains, we'll see that this is an often-used method of persuasion today.

METHODS OF PERSUASION

For some people, the art of persuasion comes easily. You can watch them talk to almost anyone, and it seems like they will always get the response that they want from the other person. On the other hand, there are those people who may have the best message in the world who couldn't convince anyone, even their closest friends, to do something. No matter where you fall in either of these groups though, with a little bit of practice and hard work, you will be able to learn how to use persuasion to your advantage.

In terms of the process of using persuasion, there will usually be three parts that you need to follow including:

The communicator, or the medium used as the source of persuasion

The persuasive nature of the appeal

The audience or the target person that the appeal is going to be sent too.

Each of these elements needs to be accounted for

before you try to use persuasion on a higher level. It is always a good practice to look around you and check to see how many instances of persuasion are going on in your daily life. Some of these are going to be overt, but many of them are going to be pretty subtle. This can be great training for persuasion because you will be able to employ the same kind of tactics. Let's take a look at some of the options that you can use when it comes to good persuasion and using the right techniques.

Using the Aristotelian appeals

So, the first option that we are going to look at is the Aristotelian appeals. Aristotle is well-known and is actually one of the most famous persuaders of all time. He believed that there were three main ways that a person could approach thing when they were trying to use persuasion to change the opinion of the other person.

Ethos

The first appeal that one could use was ethos, which is going to focus on things such as trust, integrity, and character. This appeal is going to focus on the reputation of the person and some of the things that they may have done in the past, or even how others think about them today. There are many people who value their reputations, and they will work hard to maintain them, especially if the person is in a high office or in the public eye. This is not a bad thing to care about your reputation.

As the persuader, it is fine to show off some character because this shows that you are a human like everyone else and you can even show off some of the flaws that you have. The trick here is that you need to only show off flaws that are pretty small, ones that the target audience will not see as a big deal, but they do need to be large enough that they show that you are still a person who has some good values and even virtues.

You need to be credible as well if you would like to be persuasive. People are much more likely to believe what you are saying if you are seen as a credible person, someone who is seen as an expert in their chosen field. If you would like to get started with persuading other people to act in a specific way, then you need to start cultivating the right impression with good virtues, small flaws, and by showing that you are an expert in your field.

Pathos

The second appeal that you should work on is pathos, which is when you evoke the emotions of the other person. You will want to find some way to excise the other person, to get their interest in some way. This can often be done with storytelling or even by referencing situations where injustices were done at some point. You can add in some ethos to this by condemning these actions and describing how your values fall into the matter.

If you are working on this appeal, it is important to use the right linguistics. Language is going to be your most important tool for getting the emotions involved. A good speaker will always be able to pick out the right words to get their message out there. For example, they know how to use words that will amplify or subdue the situation based on the results that you want to get.

This can be hard to learn in the beginning, especially if you do not consider yourself to be that great of a speaker. But the next time that there is a big pollical debate or speech going on take the time to listen to the words that they are using. This will help you to see how the words can bring out the right emotions that the communicator is looking for.

Logos

And the third appeal that you can use when it comes to persuasion is logos. This is when you are going to use logic, rational explanations, and even evidence to help support your claims. Some people do not respond that well to the emotional side, and they may feel that anyone who is using their values and integrity are only doing so to make a sale. These people are probably going to do the best with logos, being told logical information that they can look up on their own to verify before they make a decision.

This does not mean that you cannot go through and make some changes to the wording and try to convince these people still. You can always bring the most prominent features to light, or if you know the person, at least bring out the features that are going to appeal to them the most. This is not a license to lie to them about the things that you are doing and saying, but it doesn't hurt to show your argument in the best possible light.

Foot in the door

We talked about this one a bit earlier, but it can be one of the most effective persuasion techniques that are out there. This one allows you to ask for a bigger favor after you have already been granted a smaller favor, especially if they are related in some way. You may start off with something that is pretty small, such as just borrowing a cup of sugar from your neighbor. Your neighbor will probably be fine with this because it's not that big of a deal and most people, as long as they have it on hand, will have a cup of sugar to share with you.

Now that you have asked for that cup of sugar, you may take it up a notch. You may then ask if they have some butter and eggs that you can borrow as well. Since they have already lent you some sugar, they figure it is not a big deal to lend you some more things a well. And the persuader can just keep going, perhaps asking if the target would mind baking the whole cake for them in the end.

If the persuader had started out with asking the neighbor to make the cake, it is unlikely that the neighbor would have agreed. The neighbor might say that they are busy or that they really do not know how to make a cake that well. But since the persuader started out with something small, something that would be silly not to help out with, and then slowly built up from there, the neighbor may eventually feel a sense of obligation to get the work done at this point.

This method can be used in many different persuasion circumstances. The trick is to always start out with something small, something that you think the target will be willing to help you out with. Then you will slowly build yourself up until you get to the bigger thing that you would like them to have in the long run. You may have wanted the target to start with the bigger thing, but if you went there first, you would have completely missed out on the sale.

Reversal tagging

Another option that you can use is known as reversal tagging. This is a trick that uses simple and subtle sentence phrasing to get an agreement, or at least compliance, from the target in general. It is going to use two opposing structures inside the sentence, the first part being an affirmative statement and the second one will be a tag question.

The premise here is that you will make the initial statement to open the line of questioning, but you will add on the tag question so that the target has a binary choice for answering. This will help you to reframe the response so that it sounds like they agree with you the whole time.

For example, you may say something like "You like this house, don't you?" to your spouse. There are a few ways that they can choose to respond to this. If they say "Yes, I like this place" you would respond something like "As I thought, you like this place." On the other hand, if they give you a different response, such as "No, I don't like this place," you can simply turn it around and say "As I thought, you don't like this place."

Statements like the one above are designed to have a negative reversal element to them. If you do them in the proper manner, the statement will hide the command because it becomes a rhetorical question because it will first tell the person what they should be thinking, but then it inserts the question that will offer a level of disagreement, even though it implies that the disagreement is not wanted.

The key to this method is to ensure that the first statement is pretty strong because it is going to be the main persuasive component. This kind of technique is also useful when you are trying to convince the other person to take an action on something, rather than just agreeing with you. It is the same principle, but this time you will state out your negative first before taking a long pause and then adding in the tag question. For example, you could say something like "You aren't able to do that.... Are you?" this implies that the person is not able to do something and it is going to evoke them to respond in a way that will prove you wrong.

Reverse psychology

This is something that you have probably heard about in the past because it is a psychological tactic that is often used when you want to get the other person to take an action. However, if you are not good at performing this tactic, it is going to seem pretty obvious, and it will not work the way that you would like it to. This tactic is basically going to get somebody to do what you would like by suggesting that they do the opposite in the beginning. It is going to be the most effective if you can evoke an emotional response because it will stop the person from thinking rationally through their decision.

This is a principle that can work well with those who like to have control, such as rebellious people or those who just like to do the opposite of what they are told to do. It is often called reactance theory, and it will describe the scenario where a person feels like they are losing control of things and they are going to try to grab that control back by doing the exact opposite of what they have been asked, even if it is not their best interest to do so.

Cognitive dissonance

Have you ever been in a situation where you know that something seems a bit off about it, but you cannot figure out why it doesn't feel right? When there isn't something quite right about a situation, it is going o set off some dissonance in the mind and will trigger the person to try to make it all right. People who have OCD will often know this feeling because they will notice when little things are out of the normal.

If you can change things up a little bit, you may be

able to convince the other person to act in the way that you would like. They may feel that their reputation is falling a little bit, that they are missing out on something, or so much else. You can then step in to offer them a solution, an easy to way to change things back to normal, and they are more likely to jump right at it.

Counter-attitudinal advocacy

It is pretty common for people to state a view on something, or even to support an opinion, even if that is not something that they really believe themselves. This isn't necessarily that deceptive because the things that people choose to do this with are usually small or they have the best intentions. For example, it is common for someone to tell a little white lie because it will help to protect the feelings of someone else. When this happens, we are attempting to reduce the dissonance that we caused by saying that our actions are still noble.

Whether you think that telling a little white lie or doing something similar is acceptable or that you think honesty is the best option is irrelevant because you can still use this human tendency to your advantage when you are persuading others. This is a common technique to use when it comes to cults or even gangs when they are trying to change the beliefs of others to justify their behavior.

When you are using this as a persuasion principle, you are going to be tied in with what is known as incremental escalating requests. What this one means is that you are going to offer the target with some small rewards so that they are not really going to attribute this new behavior to some changes. Over time though, the effect is going to keep escalating until it reaches a point where they are doing something that is really different compared to where the behavior started.

A good way to practice this is by getting those you know to go along with you on some small points, but these small points need to have an eventual goal of persuasion that you would like to accomplish. These points need to all be small enough that the internal justification for agreeing with you is not that big of a deal and the other person is not going to resist you or have a lot of questions in the process. Over time, if you have done this properly, the beliefs of the other people should change to fit with yours.

Perceived self-interest

If you ask anyone, they often believe that they are generous and pretty caring creatures. No matter how much most people believe this though, as humans we are really a self-serving species. There have been a lot of studies done on this over the years, and it has been proven over and over again. Even altruism is a self-serving act because it does help the grantor to feel good about themselves in the process.

The idea behind this technique is a pretty simple one to work with, but you will be spending your time on perception. If you can convince your target that they are doing something that is in their best interest, whether that is true or not, then the target is much more likely to go along with the whole thing. This can be really apparent when you are trying to persuade someone who is higher up than you.

For example, you may work with your boss, and you can say something like "I see my job as making you more successful." This can help to endear a new employee to their boss because even if you are getting some of the credit along the way, you are showing that the majority of the limelight is going to go to your boss along the way, and their self-interest is really going to like this.

This one is known as disrupt-then-reframe, and it is similar to offer biasing and Russian front. The idea with this one is to put out a statement that is completely far away from the ideals and belief of the target right from the beginning. This is like making an offer to the other person that they are not really likely to accept. After they have rejected your offer, you are going to do a follow up that is more rational, something that your target is more likely to go along with, especially since they are still comparing it to your first offer in their heads. Of course, the second suggestion that you make is usually going to be the one that you wanted to persuade the target to in the first place.

It is similar to reverse tagging, but it is going to include a longer statement. The aim here is to disrupt the other person is thinking and then show them that you can still be rational in the process and that you want to work with them to a better goal. Since you are working with them, and the second request is not so ridiculous compared to the first one that you made, the target is much more likely to go along with what you are suggesting.

Hurt and rescue principle

This principle is going to be based off evoking some discomfort or fear in the person from the start. When the person is assessing their options for a solution, you will be able to offer the perfect solution in the form of the thing you want to persuade them to. You need to be able to manufacture a level of discomfort here first and being crafty enough to make this work can be hard.

Since you are trying to bring in some fear or discomfort with your target, you do need to be a bit careful with this option. It is not a good idea to come off as aggressive or intimidating in the process because this will just turn the person away from you completely.

For example, you may work with someone and say that you have noticed that their performance has dropped off recently and that there may be an issue with their funding getting cut off because of it. Now that the other person is worried about what is going to happen with their funding and their job, you can come in as the one with a solution. You may say something like you have convinced them to not do that just yet as long as the other person can start meeting their performance metrics again.

Of course, you will need to go through and change things around to work with the thing that you are trying to sell or the thing that you are trying to persuade the other person to do. But the point is that you will start out by adding in some discomfort or fear for the target before providing them with the solution that will make things all better.

Trial ballooning

Another option that you can use is known as trial ballooning or trial closing. This is the starting point, and it is relevant whether you are the seller or the buyer in the negotiation. The idea is to start out with the final solution that you would like to end up. You will just put that information out there and see if the thing works.

With this tactic, there is nothing wrong with going a little bit big right from the beginning. Being the one to make the first offer in this kind of exchange will usually put you in the worst position because you have shown all of your cards and this is why it is so important for you to go as bold as possible. When you start out with an aggressive offer, it will provide the anchor that is needed to help you get a good deal. The other person is going to bring you down from that anchor spot so going high helps you to get closer to your goals.

And you never know, your big offer may not seem so bad to the other person, and they may be willing to just give in right from the beginning. If the other person is really in a hurry to come to a resolution, they will really take this balloon offer, and you will come out ahead.

Auction model

This strategy is a good one to put in place if you are working with more than one buyer at the same time. Otherwise, it is not going to be the best one. With this method, you want to play one of the parties against the others so that there is a buying frenzy and it is more likely that the price is going to be driven up, no matter what you are trying to sell.

It is human nature to be competitive, and when they are faced with some opposition to something that they would like, their primitive instincts are going to come out. Possession seems to be an innate for most of us, especially if we haven't gone through to rationally appraise the real use for the item ahead of time. The persuader will be able to use their advantage, getting all the buyers in the deal to jump on board and try to pay more than the other person.

As you can see, there are a lot of different techniques that you can use when it comes to being successful with persuasion. The one that you will choose often depends on the goals that you have in mind, what you are trying to persuade the other person to do, your comfort level, and how hard the other person will be to persuade. Try a few of them out and see which one works the best for you.

HYPNOSIS

What Is Hypnosis

There have been many definitions about what hypnosis actually is. Hypnosis has been defined by the American Psychological Association as a cooperative interaction where the hypnotist will give suggestions to the person, he picks which he or she will respond to. Edmonton said that a person is simply but in a deep state of mind when in undergoing hypnosis. Hypnosis is therefore when a person enters a state of mind in which a person finds himself or herself vulnerable to the suggestions of a hypnotist. Hypnosis is not new to us because many people have seen it in movies, cartoons or actually been to magic shows or performances where participants are told to do usual acts and they do it. One thing is for sure that, some people do believe that hypnosis actually exist and would do anything to avoid being a victim while others believe that its fiction.

Induction

Induction is considered as stage one of hypnosis. There are three stages in total. Induction is aimed at intensifying the partaker's expectations of what follows after, explaining the role they will be playing, seeking their attention and any other steps needed during this stage. There are many methods used by hypnotists to induce a participant to hypnosis. One of them is the "Braidism" technique which requires a hypnotist to follow a few steps. This technique is named after James Braid. First step would be to begin with finding a bright object and hold it in your left hand and specifically between the middle, fore, and thumb fingers. The object should be placed where the participant will be able to fix his or her stare and maintain the stare. This position would be the above the forehead. It is always important that the hypnotist remind the partaker to keep his or her eyes on the object. If the participant wonders away from the object, the process will not work. The participant should be completely focused on the object. The participant's eyes will begin to dilate and the participant will begin to have a wavy motion. A hypnotist will know that his participant is in a trance when the participant involuntarily closes his or her eyelids when the middle and fore fingers of the right hand are carried from the eyes to the object. When this does not happen, the participant is begins again being guided that their eyes are to close when the fingers are used in a similar motion. Where therefore, this puts the participant in an altered state of mind he or she is said to be hypnotized. The induction technique has been considered not to be necessary for every case and research has shown that this stage is not as important as previously had been known when it came to the effects of induction technique. Over the years, there have been variations in the once original hypnotic induction technique while others have preferred to use other alternatives. James Braid innovation of this technique still stands out.

Suggestion

After Induction, the next stage that follows is the suggestion stage. James Braid left out the word suggestion when he first defined hypnosis. He however described this stage as attempting to draw the conscious mind of the partaker to focus on one central idea. James Braid would start by minimising the functions of different parts of the partaker's body. He would then put more emphasis on the use of verbal and non-verbal suggestions to begin to get the partaker into a hypnotic state. Hippolyte Bernheim also shifted from the physical state of the partaker. This well-known hypnotist described hypnosis as the induction of a peculiar physical condition which increases ones susceptibility to the suggestions by the participant. Suggestions can be verbal or one that doesn't involve speech. Modern hypnotist uses different form of suggestions that include non-verbal cues, direct verbal suggestions, metaphors and insinuations. Non-verbal suggestions that may be used include changing the tone, mental imagery and physical manipulation. Mental imagery can take two forms. One includes those that are delivered with permission and those that are done none the less and are more authoritarian.

When discussing hypnosis, it would be wise if one would be able to distinguish between the conscious mind and unconscious mind. Most hypnosis while using suggestions will try and trigger the conscious mind other than the unconscious mind. While other hypnotists will view it as way of communicating with the unconscious mind. Hypnotists such as Hippolyte Bernheim and James Braid together with other great hypnotists see it as trying to communicate with the conscious mind. This is what they believed. James Braid even defines hypnosis as the attention that is focused upon the suggestion. The idea that a hypnotist will be able to encroach into your unconscious mind and order you around is next to impossible as according to those who belong to Braids school of thought. The determinant of the different conceptions about suggestions has also been the nature of the mind. Hypnotists such as Milton Erickson believe that responses given are normally through the unconscious mind and they used the case of indirect suggestions as an example. Many of the nonverbal suggestions such as metaphors will mask the true intentions of the hypnotist from the conscious mind of the victim. A form of hypnosis that is completely reliant upon the unconscious theory is subliminal suggestion. Where the unconscious mind is left out in the hypnosis process then this form of hypnosis would be impossible. The distinction between the two schools of thoughts is quite easy to decipher. The first school of thought believe that suggestions are directed at the conscious mind will use verbal suggestions while the second school of thought who believe that suggestions are directed at the unconscious mind will use metaphors and stories that mask their true intentions. In general, the participant will still need to draw their attentions to an object or idea. This enables the hypnotist to lead the participant in the direction that the hypnotist will need to go into the hypnotic state. Once this stage of suggestion is completed and is successful, the participant will move onto the next stage.

Susceptibility

It has been shown that people are more likely to fall prey of the hypnotist tactics than others will. Therefore, it will be noted that some people are able to fall into hypnosis easily and the hypnotist does not have to put so much effort while for some, getting into the hypnotic stage may take longer and require the hypnotist to put quite the effort. While for some even after the continued efforts of the hypnotist they will not get into the hypnotic state. Research has shown where a person has been able to reach the hypnotic state at some point in their lives then it is likely that they will be susceptible to the hypnotist's suggestions and those who have not been hypnotized or it has always been difficult for them to reach that state then it will be likely that they may never be able to reach that hypnotic state.

Different models have been established to determine susceptibility of partakers to hypnosis. Research done by Deirdre Barrett showed that there are two types of subjects that considered being more susceptible to hypnosis and its effects. The two subjects consist of the group of dissociates and fantasizers. Fantasizers are able to easily block out the stimuli from reality without the specific use of hypnosis. They day dream a lot and also spent their childhood believing in the existence of imaginary friends. Dissociates are persons who have scarred childhoods. They have experienced trauma or child abuse and found ways to put away the past and become numb. If a person belongs to this groups finds him or herself day dreaming then it will be associated in terms of being blank and in creation of fantasies. These two groups will have the highest rates of being hypnotized.

Types Of Hypnosis

A hypnotist can use different types of hypnosis a participant. Each of them will use different ways and will help with certain issues. Some types of hypnosis will assist in the area of weight loss while others will be used to help a participant relax. The types of hypnosis are discussed below.

Traditional hypnosis

This type of hypnosis is very popular and used by hypnotists. It works by the hypnotist making suggestions to the participant's unconscious mind. The participant that is likely to be hypnotized by this is one who does what he is told and does not ask many or frequent questions. If one was to self-hypnotise themselves, they will do this by using traditional hypnosis. Like we have said this type of hypnosis is very popular and this could be attributed to it does not require much skill and it is not technical. The hypnotist will just have the right words and just tell the participant what to do. This might pose a problem to the hypnotist where the participant is a critical thinker and is able to analyse a given situation.

Neuro-Linguistic Programming (NLP)

This type of hypnosis gives the hypnotist wide criteria for the methods they can use in the process of hypnosis. The hypnotist is able to save time during the process as the hypnotist will just use the same thought patterns as the one that is creating the problem in the participant. If it is stress for example, the same thought pattern causing this stress will be used to counter the stress. The different types of NLP are discussed below.

NLP Anchoring

To understand how anchoring works, think of a particular scent. The first time you had that scent you were going through some feeling which the unconscious mind attached these feelings to that scent. Through this, the scent will become the anchor for those particular feelings. Every time you heard the scent, those feelings come rushing back triggered by the unconscious mind. This type of NLP has been useful to hypnotists in the process of hypnosis. If for example you won a prize or some money, the hypnotist will try and recreate those feelings you had when you won the prize. While recreating these feelings, the hypnotist will ensure the participant does an action during this process. Each time the subject does the said action, they will be reminded of those feelings.

This type of NLP can be used to motivation a person to accomplish their goals for example if they are trying to be healthier or trying to lose weight. The hypnotist will create a positive anchor that is in line with the mental image of the participant. The mental picture will be that of a sexy slim body. This image will be used as the motivator to start losing weight.

NLP Flash

This technique should only be done by a certified professional because it is considered to be very powerful and used to alter thoughts and emotions around the unconscious mind of the participant. It is considered helpful to persons who experience chronic stress or are addicted to a substance. Here is what the hypnotist will do; he or she where a person is addicted to a substance instead of it causing some feelings of happiness the act will now cause feelings of pain. Where the person had chronic stress, the cat will bring a sense of relaxation. Those addicted to substances such as cigarettes and alcohol will now feel pain when they take these substances which then can effectively assist them in getting over their addiction. While those undergoing chronic stress will find this technique also very useful as it helps them relax because stress can be very harsh to one's body. They will be able to know what causes their stress and redirect them to cause feelings of relaxation instead. NLP flash has been effective in getting rid of conditioned responses found in the mind of the subject. A practical example will be a person who enjoys drinking alcohol in events. Whenever this person is at an event even where no alcoholic drinks are being served, he will associate every event to alcohol. When this person goes through NLP Flash, they will be to separate these two events from each other. This means the person will be able to enjoy an event without thinking about alcohol and will be effective when trying to quit consuming alcohol.

NLP Reframe

This is the third type of NLP that can be used in hypnosis. It aims and works well in helping the participant change the way they behave. The hypnotist, for this work, should be able to comprehend that there is in fact a positive outcome when the behaviour is changed. The focus on the outcome is critical as this is the reason for using this form of NLP in the first place. Despite this, the behaviour chosen to achieve the outcome is not as important. The process involves the hypnotist trying to engage with the unconscious mind of the participant. The end game is to get the unconscious mind to be responsible for the participant's new chosen behaviour that will help in achieving the secondary gain. This new behaviour will then be more acceptable to the conscious mind of the participant.

Ericksonian Hypnosis

This type of hypnosis uses stories and metaphors. This hypnosis uses stories and metaphors to create ideas and suggestions in the unconscious mind. This hypnosis is very effective and powerful but the only downside it has it is that it requires someone whose experienced and trained for it to work and be effective. What is the reason behind its efficacy? The reason underlying is that it is able to eliminate any resistance to the suggestions of the hypnotist. The metaphors used will be of two types. The first is called isomorphic metaphors. This is a common metaphor that gives steps to the unconscious mind by presenting s somewhat story to the participant that in the end will have a moral ending. The unconscious mind will be able to link the elements coming from the story and the element of the problem situation. An example of a story with a moral ending is the famous story of the 'Boy Who Cried Wolf'. This story was told to children to warn them about what would happen when they continuously lie. The children being told this story will be able to link the telling of lies and the boy who is mentioned in the story. They will be able to see that lies can bring problems and that the child will willingly stop lying to avoid problems. The other metaphor is the intersperse metaphor. Here the command explained in the story is not easily understood by the participant outside their unconscious mind.

Hypnotism is a state of consciousness that involves the focused attention together with the reduced peripheral awareness that is characterized by the participant's increased ability to respond to suggestions that are given.

Major Myths of Hypnotism

Myths are untruths or exaggerations regarding the

definition, process, and purpose of something. I will list some myths along with their refutations about hypnotism.

Is Hypnotism Sleeping?

No. The hypnotic trance is a modified state of consciousness called the Alpha state. In this state, other than physiological sleep, there is strong electrical activity in the brain due to the very high level of concentration that the subject is performing. Simplifying hypnosis to the maximum, we can define it as monoideism, that is, absolute focus on the imagination.

Hypnotism Is Conditional

A trusting partnership between the hypnotist and subject is required, so if the subject does not want to be hypnotized, they will not be. In the old days, it was said that the hypnotist became the operator of the mind of the hypnotized subject, but I would say that the hypnotist is another facilitator of the trance. He bridges the conscious mind and the unconscious, thus allowing the subject to access a state of consciousness which allows the subject to experience the full potential of their own mind.

Hypnotism Works

If this is true, 100% of the people who can pay attention are mentally weak. After all, if you "dream awake", have fun reading a good book, "travel" listening to an interesting story, or go to the movies and get emotional about them, you go into a trance.

Have you ever encountered a person who has a lost, seemingly distracted look and when you catch her attention, she takes a little fright? This person is not distracted, in fact, she is hyper-concentrated, that is, in trance.

The truth is that once in a while, our brain "hibernates" for a few minutes to save energy. Have you ever wondered if you needed to be aware of everything you do all the time? Consider someone who drives a car, when he was learning, he found it all complicated – steering, gears, brakes, throttle, clutch and all at the same time!

But now, he operates so unconsciously (or automatically) that he even commits himself to reckless talking on a cell phone while driving.

Basically, if a human being is able to concentrate and obey the instructions, he can be hypnotized.

The Hypnotized Subject Will Do Whatever the Hypnotist Says

The human mind is not "mother's house". There are particular moral principles of each person and these principles are obeyed and protected by the subject's unconscious mind. Thus, it is true to say that a hypnotized person will do nothing against their moral principles (religion, family, values, physical integrity), that is, if you would not perform an action while "awake", you will not do so while hypnotized.

The Hypnotized Subject Will Tell All His Secrets to the Hypnotist

Hypnotism is a Physiological Phenomenon

It is a legitimate neuro-physiological phenomenon, where brain functioning has very special characteristics, such as muscle relaxation, anesthesia, dilation of the pupils, and memory enhancement.

During the trance, there are actually changes in the brain and this has already been confirmed in a study by examination of volunteers using an encephalogram. Perhaps in mysticism, there is a little hypnosis, but in hypnosis, there is nothing mystical.

Can a Person Not Return From the Trance?

Back from where? You're not going anywhere. The advantage of being hypnotized is that you can travel the whole world without leaving your body, just with your mind.

Finally, hypnosis is a safe method for both entertainment (street, stage) and clinical applications (hypnotherapy and the like). If you believe in God, see the ability to be hypnotized as a divine gift for your self-improvement, but if you do not believe in a deity, see hypnosis as a very powerful tool that nature has given to the human being to accelerate positive changes in life.

Hypnotism Techniques

There are 3 main techniques of hypnotism used in clinical treatment. Clinical hypnotism, that is, hypnotism performed in the office by a trained professional, can follow different methodologies or concepts, depending on the line of work of the hypnologist. Today, we will present the three most known lines and their main characteristics:

Conditional Hypnotism:

Created and patented by Luiz Carlos Crozera, conditional hypnosis is a technique used to rid the patient's mind of blockages that directly interfere with his physical and emotional health.

In this technique, deep body relaxation is done so that the patient has a decrease in his brain frequency and, with the purest mind, can be led by the hypnotist to the traumatic records that accompany him. At this point, the professional removes the registered emotional charge, disassociating the trauma from the given situation.

Upon returning from the trance, the patient already has an important behavioral change when faced with what caused him anguish. Thus, the hypnotist uses the post-hypnotic suggestion, a technique that executes the commands inserted during the trance, in order to achieve the best possible results. In conditional hypnosis, the patient does not interact with the hypnotist.

Eriksonian Hypnotism:

In this technique of clinical hypnosis, described by the American psychiatrist Milton Erickson, the patient is suggested to seek within himself new learning that leads to a reformulation of thoughts and truths. Thus, the patient is led to the trance and suggested to relive, in a metaphorical way, the situation that causes him pain and suffering but with a completely different outcome, aiming for the trauma to be forgotten.

The idea is not to change what has been experienced, but to give other responses to the trauma since it is believed that the patient has all the resources necessary to solve his own problems.

Classic Hypnotism:

This method is mostly in disuse because it presents less efficient results than the other methodologies. Classic Hypnosis consists of searching in the memory of the patient for the facts that bring him suffering and making him understand that it is part of the past and should no longer reach the present.

How to Hypnotize Someone Without Them Knowing

Have you ever heard of a method that many claims to be able to achieve through repetitive motions, with the help of pendulums or finger movements, which allows them to stay in a state of trance? Is it possible? Well, some people believe so. Texts produced in Egypt in 1550 BC show evidence that older people already used these practices.

Well, the name of this method is hypnosis and, in fact, this is a psychological state, which brings together several phenomena that occur in our mind, and which can produce different impacts. It can be conducted by a voice and has been used as an instrument in the treatment of different diagnoses.

While there are those who believe in past lives and those who do not, it is true that hypnosis can cause the patient to return to a certain age. For example, hypnosis may return someone up to an "x" age, when he may have contracted some kind of trauma.

Let's look at a situation to illustrate: A patient is in a hypnotized state. The doctor puts his hands on the patient's arm and warns that he is applying an ointment, when in fact, he is not applying anything, he just touches the patient's hands. Despite this, the patient has the feeling that the doctor is actually applying an ointment, even being able to smell the ointment as it passes through a positive olfactory hallucination. The patient, who is hypnotized, really believes the doctor's words.

Another example is the case of a patient who smells a scent. When they smell the gunpowder, if this smell happens to be strongly associated with when they were 10 years of age, then the patient can regress until the age of 10 to try to solve some kind of childhood problem. Not everyone is able to perform this practice because a badly done hypnosis session can cause great harm. This is because hypnosis is not restricted only to the return to time but also the treatment of certain psychological problems, which can be aggravated if not treated by a specialized professional. For this reason, only those who have technical knowledge of the use of hypnosis should practice it.

How to Hypnotize a Person

However, if you would like to learn this technique in

order to know the principles of hypnosis and then go deeper into the subject, follow this step-by-step guide:

The first thing to do is to make the person quite relaxed. Sitting comfortably and getting ready for the session in peace is a good start. It is not good to lie down because it can lead to sleep and prevent hypnosis from reaching the person's mind.

The second step is to start speaking very slowly so that the person pays attention to your voice and begins to relax at the same time. Then you can use a pendulum (swing the pendulum at the height of the person's eyes) or your own finger, making repetitive movements also at eye level. You could also use the moving image of a spiral. Continue the movement until you see the person become half asleep.

Ideally, the person should not close his or her eyes. One way that helps create concentration is to blink and focus the mind on what is being said. Talk about certain things, slowly, that cause you to relax and ask the person to imagine a feeling of warmth and comfort all over their body.

You need to always be in touch with the person who will be hypnotized. Ask him to take a deep breath and breathe out slowly through his nose. Ensure that the participant always stays relaxed during the hypnosis.

Ask him to imagine himself levitating and also to pay attention to all parts of his body, trying to perceive any discomfort or pain starting with his head and working downwards. Tell him to let the pain go away. Ask him to repeat this kind of thinking for each part of his body.

As soon as you realize that the patient has reached a state of relaxation, have him imagine a spiral staircase. He should fully visualize this thought and go down the stairs. With every step he takes on that ladder, he must feel he is moving ever deeper into his thoughts. A few steps later, as many as you think necessary, let the patient know that there is a door at the end of the staircase and that it is time for him to cross that door.

The person must open the door and enter the next environment. Direct the person to imagine that this environment is a room, which can be decorated in any way that he would like to imagine. Then direct the thoughts of the person saying that he should look in this room for a place to sit.

Say you will count from 1 to 10 and that, in the end, the participant will be in a deep state of hypnosis. This is the time to ask the questions that will bring the patient to the result that you want to extract from that experience. This is also the time to cause sensations by the suggestion of taste and smell, among others. For example, you can ask him to find some chicken in this room and eat it. The hypnotized person will actually believe and feel the taste of eating the chicken.

After the experience, let him know that he will wake up in a few moments. Ask him to rise from the place where, mentally, he is sitting and walk back down the same path. When he reaches the last step, he will be awake and relaxed. Then count to three and say wake up!

Remember that this experience needs a lot of care and attention to be put into practice. After all, there are proven cases of poorly done hypnosis practices that have caused mental problems in patients. Therefore, seek the guidance of a professional!

DARK NLP

In the 1970s, psychological researcher John Grinder, coined the term Neuro-Linguistic Programming (NLP) for a mind controlling method to change our conscious thoughts and behaviors as desired. Neuro (mind/information) Linguistic (language/words) Programming (learning/control), simply put it's the art of learning the language of your mind to generate satisfying results. NLP is a lot like a User Manual for the brain, to help you communicate the goals and desires of the unconscious mind to the conscious self. Imagine you are in foreign country and craving chicken wings, so you go to a restaurant to order the same but when the food shows up, it ends up being liver stew because of a failed communication. Humans often fail to recognize and acknowledge their unconscious thoughts and desires because a lot of it gets lost in translation to the conscious self. NLP enthusiasts often exclaim: "the conscious mind is the goal setter, and the unconscious mind is the goal getter". The idea being your unconscious mind wants you to achieve everything that you actually desire but if your conscious mind fails to receive the message, you will never set the goal to achieve those dreams.

NLP was developed using excellent therapists and communicators who had achieved great successes as role models. It's a set of tool and techniques to help your master communication, both with yourself and others. NLP is study of human mind combining thoughts and actions with perception to fulfil their deepest desires. Our mind employs complex neural networks to process information and use language or auditory signals to give it meaning while storing these signals in patterns to generate and store new memories. We can voluntarily use and apply certain tools and techniques to alter our thoughts and actions in achieving our goals. These techniques can be perceptual, behavioral and communicative and used control our own mind as well as that of others.

One of the central ideas of NLP is that our conscious mind has a bias towards a specific sensory system called the "Preferred Representational System (PRS)". Phrases like "I hear you" or "Sounds good" signal an auditory PRS, whereas, phrase like "I see you" may signal a visual PRS. A certified therapist can identify a person's PRS and model their therapeutic treatment around it. This therapeutic framework often involves rapport building, goal setting and information gathering among other activities. NLP is increasingly used by individuals to promote self enhancement, such as self reflection and confidence as well as for social skill development, primarily communication.

NLP therapy or training can be delivered in the form of language and sensory based interventions, using behavior modification techniques customized for individuals to better their social communication and improved confidence and self awareness. NLP therapists or trainers strive to make their client understand that their view and perception of the world is directly associated with how they operate in it, and the first step toward a better future is keen understanding of their conscious self and contact with their unconscious mind. Its paramount to first analysis and subsequently change our thoughts and behaviors that are counterproductive and block our success and healing. NLP has been successfully used in treatment of various mental health conditions like anxiety, phobias, stress and even post traumatic stress disorder. An increasing number of practitioners are commercially applying NLP to promise improved productivity and achievement of work oriented goals that ultimately lead to job progression.

Now, let's look at how NLP works. John Grinder, in association with his student Richard Bandler, conducted a research study on techniques used by Fritz Perls (founder of Gestalt therapy), Virginia Satir (Family therapist) and Milton Erickson (renowned Hypnotherapist). They subsequently analyzed and streamlined these therapy techniques to create a behavioral model for mass application in order to achieve sand reproduce excellence in any field. Bandler, a computer science major, helped develop a "psychological programming language" for human beings. On the basis of how our mind processes information or perceives the external world, it generates an internal "NLP map" of what is going on outside. This internal map is created based on the feedback provided by our sense organs, like the pictures we take in, sounds we hear, the taste in our mount, sensations we feel on our skin and what we can smell. However, with this massive influx of information, our mind selectively deletes and generalizes a ton of information. This selection is unique to every person and is determined by what our mind deems relevant to our situation. As a result, we often miss out on a whole lot of information that can be immediately noticed by someone else right off the bat and we end up with a tiny and skewed version of what is really occurring. For example, take a moment and process this statement: "Person A killed person B", now depending on our circumstances and experiences we will all have our own version of that story. Some might think a "a man killed a woman", or "a lion killed a man" or "a terrorist killed a baby" or "John Doe killed Kennedy" and so on and so forth. Now, there's a method to this madness, whatever story you came up with, realize there is way you got to that story which was driven by our own life experience. Our mind creates an internal map of the situation at hand and then we compare that map with other internal maps from our past that we have stored in our mind. Every person has their own internal "library" based on what is important or relevant to them in accordance with their personality.

Did you ever feel that once your conscious mind makes you aware of what you want to do or gain, suddenly the universe seems to be propping up signs that could help you find your way to get what you want? For example, one day you wake up thinking I need to take my family on a vacation. You go on with your day the same way as you have been for days or weeks, but you suddenly notice a poster on an exciting trip to Florida on your way to work, that you later learnt from your coworker has been up for over a month now. You suddenly see that close to that same Starbucks you visit every day, there is a big travel agency that you had never paid attention to. When browsing the Internet, you will suddenly see travel ads all over your Facebook or ads from Airbnb popping up on your YouTube videos. Now all these may come across as coincidences, but the matter of the fact is those things or signs had been there all along but your mind deleted that information or perception because they were not relevant to you. So as your conscious mind starts connecting the dots between your wishes and the reality of the world, you start picking up on new information that may have already been in plain sight, but you are only tuned into now.

What Is Dark Nlp?

Your personality profile also plays a major role in what information your mind chooses to exclude and what is processed. People who are more focused on security, they are constantly assessing their situation to determine whether its safe for you or not. On the other hand, people who are more freedom oriented, they tend to think of their situation in terms of options and limitation with no focus on safety at all. Your personality determines what and how you update your mental library and ultimately the meaning you add to these internal maps. For example, a kid looking at a roller coaster is thinking only about the fun of traveling through open space in a cool looking ride and given the opportunity will easily and fearlessly jump on the ride, because his personality is not security oriented. But an adult who is able to focus not only on the fun and excitement of the ride but also it's safety and potential hazards, will think twice before making that same decision.

Here are some prominently used NLP techniques:

Anchoring

A Russian scientist, Ivan Pavlov, conducted an experiment on dogs by repeatedly ringing a bell while the dogs were eating and concluded that he could get the dogs to salivate by the ringing the bell anytime, even when there was no food present. This neurobiological connection observed in the dogs, between the bell and salivation is called a conditioned response or "anchor". Thus, the process of creating a perceivable sensory trigger to the state of how you feel is called Anchoring.

Try this yourself! Think of a gesture or sensation on your body (pulling your earlobe, cracking your knuckles, or touching your forehead) and associate it with any desired positive emotional response (happiness, confidence, calmness etc.) by recalling and reliving the memory when you actually experienced those emotions. The next time you are feeling stressed or low, you can trigger this anchor voluntarily and you will notice your feeling will immediately change. To strengthen triggered response, you can think of another memory when your felt the desired emotion and relive it. Every time you add a new memory to the mix, your anchor will become more potent and trigger a stronger response.

Content Reframing

This NLP technique is best suited to combat negative thoughts and feelings. With the use of this visualization techniques you can alter your mind to think differently about situations where you feel threatened or disempowered. Simply view the negative situation and reframe it's meaning into something positive. For example, let's say you just broke up with your long term girlfriend or boyfriend. You will most likely be hurt and in pain. But you can choose to reframe the end of your relationship with empowering thoughts of being single and new potential relationships. You can choose to focus on the lessons you learnt from your past relationship and how you can implement them to have an even better relationship in future. Thus, by simply reframing the break up, you can feel better and empower yourself.

This technique has massive appeal in treatment of post traumatic stress disorder and for people who have experienced child abuse or are suffering from chronic or life threatening diseases.

Rapport Building

Rapport is the art of generating empathy in others by pacing and mirroring their verbal and non-verbal behaviors. People like other people who they think are similar to themselves. When you can subtly mirror the other person, their brain will fire off "mirror neurons" or "pleasure sensors" in their brain, which make them feel a sense of liking for you. You can simply stand or sit the way the other person or tilt your head in the same direction as theirs or the best of all, just smile when they smile. All these cues will help you build rapport with the other person. The social significance of rapport building cannot be underscored. Strong personal and professional connections lead to a happier and longer life.

Dissociation

The NLP technique of dissociation guides you in severing the link between negative emotions and the associated trigger. For instance, certain words or phrases may instantly bring back bad memories and make you feel stressed or depressed. If you can successfully identify those triggers and make an effort to detach those negative feelings from it, you are one step closer to healing and empowering yourself. A slew of mental health conditions like anxiety, depression and even phobias can be effectively treated with this technique. It can also be used to positively deal with difficult situations at home and work.

Future Pacing

The NLP technique of leading the subject to a future state and rehearsing the potential future outcomes so as to achieve the desired outcome automatically, is called Future Pacing. It's a type of visualization technique or mental imagery, used to anchor a change or resources to future situations by imagining and virtually experiencing those situations. A skilled manipulator can lead their victim on a mental journey into the future and influence the responses occurring when the future unfolds. An expert NLP user with prominent Dark Psychological traits may cognitively transport their victim into the future and suggest outcomes while monitoring the victim's response to eventually get their own desired outcome into the psyche of the victim.

Influence and Persuasion

This is definitely the most ambivalent NLP technique and houses a gray area between Dark Psychology and Psychotherapy. NLP is primarily focused on eliminating negative emotions, curb bad habits and resolve conflicts, another aspect of NLP deals with ethically influencing and persuade others. Now pay attention to the word ETHICAL here.

One of the prominent psychology therapist to participate in Grinder's original research on NLP was, Milton Erickson, leading hypnotherapist and founder of the "American Society for Clinical Hypnosis". Erickson was so adept at hypnosis that he could literally hypnotize anyone anywhere and communicate with people's subconscious mind without needing hypnosis. He helped construct the "Milton Model" of NLP, designed to induce trance like state in people, using abstract language patterns. According to the Milton Model, using artfully vague and deliberately ambiguous sentences will trigger the person to search for meaning of what they hear from their own life experiences and fill in the details subconsciously. This powerful tool can be used to not only ethically influence and persuade people but also help people deal with some deep seated negative emotions, overcome fears and increase their self awareness.

COVERT EMOTIONAL MANIPULATION

Today, the greatest battles are not fought on battlefields, but in our minds and hearts!

And one of the biggest and strongest reasons for an inner battle is psychological manipulation. The biggest problem with psychological manipulation is not only the fact that we are often not prepared to deal with it but also the way we respond to it. And then, our greatest enemy, beyond the manipulator/oppressor, will become ourselves!

One of the main characteristics of psychological manipulation is that the manipulator (who can be a father, a mother, a brother or sister, a romantic partner, or a friend) exercises great control and power over us. And in that instant, our life becomes a real hell and we live in tremendous anguish.

However, it is crucial to know that we are not, and should not be, impotent in this situation and that there are various ways of combating these techniques of psychological manipulation.

The first step is to achieve consciousness, that is, to become aware of these techniques. Take a closer look and learn more objectively how your handlers "work" so you can protect yourself in the future. There are several Manipulation Techniques. See some of them below:

Psychological Manipulation Technique 1: Emotional Blackmail

Emotional blackmail is one of the oldest and most used manipulation techniques employed by human beings. But how does this work exactly?

Many people succumb to this trick because they feel they have no choice. At this point, phrases such as "If you really cared about me, you would do this for me" are very common and make the manipulated person feel "forced" to make decisions that they do not really want. The target will make them anyway just to please the person who manipulates.

To avoid this manipulation technique you will have to develop a strong sense of your own self, and this involves knowing who you are, what your responsibilities are towards others, and who your true friends are. Usually, manipulative and blackmailing people tend to stay away from people with strong and solid personalities. Always remember: you always have a choice and it is you who decides what you do with your life and how you want to react to the world.

Psychological Manipulation Technique 2: Focus on Negative Aspects

Some people like to put a "brake" on another's ideas and brilliant projects by emphasizing everything that could go wrong with them. These people often push him to doubt his projects and all the good things they would bring if they were put into practice. And at these times, the manipulators offer an endless list of questions that will only serve to create and raise doubts in their target's mind and heart.

For example, if you are telling someone you are thinking of traveling somewhere for a month to relax or go on vacation, and if for some reason that person does not feel comfortable with the idea, they will probably react to your news by talking about the immense travel hazards and the endless number of negative things that can be expected at the airport, etc., etc.

At such times, if there is no apparent reason for such a

reaction from the other person. If you are comfortable with your decision, bearing in mind that it will not harm you or others, choose not to listen to them and follow through with what you have decided.

Do not be overly swayed by this negative thinking pattern because if we think about something a lot, we attract it. That is, if you put it in your head that something bad will happen and focus on it excessively, it is very likely to happen because the thought has life and is a great magnet.

Psychological Manipulation Technique 3: Teenage Rebellion

Unfortunately, sometimes the manipulative person adopts a childlike attitude as a response to his decision, or something you have said to him.

For example, you want to leave your home and live independently. At first, it may even seem like everyone is happy and comfortable with your decision. But with the passage of time, as soon as you start looking for the perfect apartment, things start happening one after another. Some kind of personal crisis occurs in the family, your mother or father suddenly (re) starts smoking, etc. These are adult people, but they adopt the behavior of a teenager and rebel against the idea.

The easiest way to deal with this is to make them see that their efforts in trying to make you give up are worthless and that you will go ahead with your decision.

At first, it can be very difficult and hard for you, especially if you have been exposed to this type of psychological manipulation for a long time. But as time goes by, it will become much easier and you will see that even the people who manipulate you will come to respect you much more.

Psychological manipulation can be done throughout life, but always remember that you have the power to break this vicious cycle and above all, remember that only one person can change your life: You!

Love and life together can be sources of well-being, pleasure, and support or a dead end in which you feel suffocated and as if you are in the dark. The worst is that in many cases, these can be combined in a single day. Both feelings and problems begin when the relationship shifts rapidly and you find yourself immersed in a constant storm of feelings. This mainly happens to those who do not know how to escape such situations.

Many people are immersed in insane and toxic relationships in which they suffer psychological abuse of various kinds. They receive continuous damage to their integrity and their honor and levels of disrespect that when seen or heard from outside seem crazy, but to the person who is now accustomed to suffering, does not even produce a minimal reaction in their daily lives.

Love is not an excuse to hide the emotional pain that another person can cause us, and it is our responsibility to ourselves to learn how to defend our rights and enforce them. Beyond your own insecurity, the parental patterns that you picked up in your childhood, and all the mechanisms of self-deception that you are capable of activating so as not to see reality, at the bottom of your being, you know how to differentiate what is right and what hurts you. That said, sometimes we need someone to tell us in a neutral and unbiased way that we have the right not to put up with what we know we do not deserve. Next, I present a list of the main techniques of manipulation in unhealthy couples.

Manipulation to maintain social control: This technique usually begins in a very subtle way. The couple criticizes friends, family, work colleagues and anyone in your social circle until they can completely annul the other's social network in such a way that the only source of effort and social support is the couple. This is manifested through jealousy: "If you really love me, you would prefer me over your friends" etc.

Emotional blackmail: This mechanism is famous for being used between pairs of individuals. It is also widely used by almost everyone and you likely know it very well. It is about using phrases to handle guilt and repentance as a tactic to get something or as an impediment so that the other does not do something or does not abandon the manipulator. The manipulative person usually uses phrases like: "If you do that, it means you don't love me", "I do not want you to suffer, I would never do that to you", "I want the best for you, even if you let me destroy my life", "If you let me die", etc.

Mental manipulation techniques: These are the most creative and there are many types. The manipulator frequently attempts to put the other person into some type of debt to them or does things that have a lot of intensity so that the victim feels a commitment to that person. These phrases help explain the main idea and are things the manipulator will often say: "Only someone who loves you very much will do this for you", "No one will love you like me", etc. It is also a manipulation technique to mentally "vaccinate" the other person to things people in their environment might say by mentioning things like: "Your family hates me, but they do not know what love is", "They will speak ill of me, they will tell you that this relationship does not work", or "It's convenient, but I love you like nobody else", etc. These phrases echo in the head of the manipulated person and confuse and influence their behavior.

Intermittent reinforcement guidelines: This manipulation technique is designed to get the couple to overestimate the pleasant moments that the other- the one who manipulates-offers. For this, what he does-whether consciously or unconsciously-is to have arguments and fights over small things so that afterward, there is reconciliation and more intensity is created in the relationship. This technique is very addictive because of the pleasant stimuli, reconciliation, that appears after the unpleasant stimuli. This is as addictive to our brain as one of those slot machines because the couple is totally unpredictable and the person ends up living in a world of fights waiting for each reconciliation. The person usually thinks "I suffer, but I know that everything is going to be fixed".

In the psychology of learning, we call it "intermittent reinforcement patterns", it is a simple mechanism: Fight-suffering-tears / reconciliation-passionate love-sex- and start again for a new fight. Periods of peace and "Honeymoons" start becoming less and less frequent and become shorter in duration. This mechanism is so powerful that if the person leaves the relationship, he will miss it and it will create self-esteem problems. It is also difficult for the abandoned person to forget the other. The addiction is established when the subject continues to play despite losing because he has the memory in his head that he once won, so he will continue to insist on continuing even though the prizes are minimal compared to the effort to "play".

Techniques designed to reduce self-esteem: This type of technique usually appears once the social network of the other person has been damaged and now the couple is the main or only support system the person has. It is usually based on insulting, criticizing, ridiculing, weaving a network of lies before third parties about that person, giving no rewards to things and initiatives that the other has by discounting their importance, diminishing their merits or pleasing actions, and focusing conversations on everything that person does wrong or lacks. The most common are phrases like "I would be better off without you" and "Without me you are nobody".

Another very frequent way to diminish self-esteem is to make the other person feel guilty by using criticism and shame with phrases like "I did not expect that from you", etc. The manipulator may also adopt an active role in the victim's life, making decisions for them or taking care of many activities that require effort. This causes the victim's coping mechanisms for facing life to be less and less effective because they get used to the comfort of being with someone who does things for them and solves problems. This technique can cause the person to feel that they must depend on the other person in some important aspect or even for less important things such as making purchases, making food, keeping household accounts, etc

Stereotyped Roles: This technique is based on playing specific characters within the couple. The most frequent within the couple is usually: The role of the savior, victim, or persecutor. The person with the role of the victim usually manipulates with expressions of jealousy, crying, and stimulation of emotions of grief in the other person. The role of the savior is the person who seeks in the couple someone to protect, seeking recognition for it. The persecutor is usually vigilant, critical, and points out all the mistakes of the other person.

Self-destructive acts: This manipulation mechanism consists of anything that a subject does that cause physical or psychological damage to themselves. The aim is to produce in another person a feeling of guilt, grief, and emotional blackmail. It can also be breaking a material object in the victim's presence, self-coupling, or doing it in front of another person who knows the victim so that it reaches their ears. These self-destructive behaviors create strong feelings of guilt and make it difficult for the person to disassociate from the manipulative partner. The manipulator may even say things like: "If you leave, I will kill myself."

Compulsive acts aimed at revenge and the creation of

fear: This consists of doing things that the person knows will hurt the other to continue emotional intensity. This mechanism is also aimed at keeping the relationship together because it generates strong feelings of fear of possible reprisals or negative consequences of deciding to leave the couple.

These are some of the main techniques used in unhealthy relationships to maintain control in the other person. In spite of living in a continuous battle and suffering, such relationships usually last for years before they are perceived as harmful enough to warrant leaving, even though the two parties that make up the couple usually suffer very intensely.

If you have identified with the behaviors discussed above, surely you have suffered psychological abuse and may even use that same pattern on your partner. People are like mirrors, we reflect everything that surrounds us and it is common that in this type of unhealthy relationship both parties are exercising some kind of manipulation.

It is not about looking for the guilty party or attempting to demonize the other. In a relationship, all the participants contribute to the result and end up feeling the consequences in one way or another. In an unhealthy relationship, nobody wins or is better than the other and in most cases, people simply do the only thing they know how to do and project their own problems on the other person. Therefore, understanding the dynamics of the couple is one of the most important means we have for personal development. Finally, we each have an important lesson to learn about ourselves; if we are able to discover it before the link is completely broken and if both are open to change, it would be possible to perform couples therapy. Although in most cases, emotional breakdowns are so painful and the destruction in different areas of the lives of the people involved in the relationship is so extensive that ending the relationship is more likely. Reconciliation is often seen as difficult as there is a need to invest in a personal change to continue with that partner.

Between the banks of pain and pleasure flows the river of life. Only when the mind refuses to flow with life and stagnates on the banks does it become a problem. Flow means acceptance, letting come what comes, letting go what is meant to go.

Persuasion is never without moral implications but in

dark persuasion moral implications are just not the determining factor. There are many other factors which are more important than being morally correct. The smartest thing about a dark persuader is that in their circle they would be the most selfish person but would show and seem that they are least selfish. They would get exactly what they get, without the other person knowing or even realizing.

The other thing that a dark persuader does is knowing about the weakness of others. This helps them in extracting words, presents, and gifts which they can take or give according to their advantage and situation. For example, if an employer knows that he has illegal immigrants working in his company, he can always lower his wages as per his choice as they know that they cannot work anywhere else in the country.

Dark persuasion can vary from small to very large scale, such as a kid asking his elder brother for all the ice cream he has to a leader trying to ask for help in war to defeat another country. So, to determine dark persuasion it is always vital to understand the different personalities and their circumstances.

Covert manipulation is even worse than manipulation,

in this, the manipulator tries to use the emotional vulnerability to their benefit. They would strive to their best so that they can know about your goals, strengths, weaknesses, fear, family, etc. So that they can use all of these factors to make you feel low and weak. It is said to be underhanded methods of control. It operates under your level of conscious awareness. The bad part of it is that the victim is not even aware that they are being manipulated, that is the reason it becomes prime for you to know about the manipulation games that these people use, which we will discuss later in coming chapters.

Covert manipulation is very dangerous as it is so subtle and underhanded that it takes a long time before you can make out that you were being manipulated. According to research, it was also found that there are few manipulators with such sharp skills that they are called puppet masters, you would without even knowing become their puppets, so it is important for you to know their signs so that you can take the actions accordingly. They would make you feel that you are doing according to your own wish but the truth is that you do that only what they ask you to do.

Sometimes you might feel that something is wrong but you would not be able to analyze that someone is trying to manipulate you. In covert manipulation first thing which is prime is that you should ask yourself if you are being manipulated? As covert manipulation is adverse and has a negative effect on us, so it would be easier for you to understand that you are being manipulated.

It is significant for you to understand a few characteristics of a covert manipulator, so it becomes really easy for you to spot them if they are around you-

Lying- They would lie straight in your eyes and you would not even get to know that they are lying. They would tell you twisted truth or half-truth which you might or might not get to know later. If you ever have any doubts on the other person about the truth, you should always double-check the information so that it does not hamper your relationship or work.

Backhanded compliments- This is something they are best at. Covert manipulators are great in giving backhanded compliments. They would give compliments as you did it in a great way although you are so weak and low in confidence, still, you handled it well. You cooked so well, although you do not cook for me often. These compliments make you feel even more embarrassed and awkward, where you do not even know how to react. In such cases, the best thing is to ignore or giving them the taste of their own medicine by replying in the same way.

Mirroring- The coincidences would be extravagant. They would agree to all your points, likes, dislikes, taste, color, etc just to impress you or to be with you. When they want to take benefit from you they would agree to all your things and choices. Once they get what they wanted everything would change. You would feel that the person has fully switched. So, you should always beware of the person who agrees to whatever you say without keeping their point of you, it straight away means that they are trying to be manipulative.

Rationalization- This is something many people would do to cover their lies or fault. They would cook new stories to cover their flaws such as the reason why you did not tell that you had a girlfriend before me, the reason they would give you would be like I did not want to lose you by telling this or I did not know how you would react after listening to this, etc. Thu they would have answers for all the lies, so make sure that you know and follow your gut feel to analyze if he is saying right or just faking it.

Hurried Intimacy- This is a very alarming sign of a covert manipulator. They would very quickly tell you about their goals, achievements, passion and past and what ask you the same things. Once you open up with them, they would use this information to control and manipulate you. Therefore, you should always be wise enough to understand when to share the information and how much information to share. They would be very quick in proposing for marriage and talking about the future but you need to be careful before telling your weaknesses.

Playing the victim- This is another thing they do to gain your sympathy. Just to gain your love and attention they would lie to you to any extent. They might say that their childhood was very bad as the parents were not good, etc. Just to get more love and care from you. They might make any stories for your love and care, so always know the past first before you get so much involved.

Silent Treatment- Leaving room or house for a couple

of hours, would not engage in any activity, etc. They also hide behaviors or start avoiding you so that you realize it is your mistake or you start the conversation. They keep the concerns unspoken within them which is a dangerous sign too.

Belittling- They do react weird such as rolling the eyes, scoffing, mocking, teasing, etc. They do not even respect others point of view or abilities, and they always want another person to feel low and always try to demean them. You should always maintain a distance with such covert people who are jealous of your success and feel bad seeing you rise.

Word Play- A covert manipulator very well knows what you want to hear and would please your ears by saying that. They know how to put a convincing statement, paint the picture well and also to induce an emotional reaction in front of you. Not only this, they are great it talking double meaning things, they would mean something else but say it in a different context. For example, please marry me I will change your life. This can be in any aspect positive or negative. So be precise and clear while talking to a covert manipulator.

Finance controller- Covet manipulator not only restrict

by playing with your emotions they are also good in controlling and gaming with your finances too. For example, accessing your account but denying access to their account, taking things on loan in joint names without even asking you, running up debts, borrowing and not paying, etc. These are very tricky things which you should be careful about and take a step in time before they make your account nil.

These were the few characteristics of a covert manipulator which you should be diligent about so that nobody can take advantage of you or humiliate you.

BRAINWASHING

In this guidebook, brainwashing is better discussed in psychological terms and how it is associated via social influences. Talking about social influences, it is the collective approaches used for influencing or changing other people's beliefs, attitudes and behavior toward something. Be that as it may, brainwashing could actually be characterized as a social issue in a severe form since it functions at changing the perspective of a subject without the subject agreeing to it.

To carry out a successful brainwashing, the subject has to be totally isolated and dependent since it has an invasive effect on the subject. This explains why most cases of brainwashing happen in prison camps or totalistic cults. The agent or brainwasher needs to gain complete control of the subject. He or she must be in absolute command of their subject's sleeping patterns and eating habits whilst satisfying the other vital needs of the subject, and none of these happen without the knowledge of the brainwasher. While the procedure takes place, the agent seeks for ways to break down the subject's entire identity, so it doesn't work right anymore. From the moment that identity is broken, the brainwasher strives to exchange it with the desired attitudes, beliefs and behaviors.

The idea of brainwashing is not generally agreed upon by everybody. If it works or not isn't certain yet, as many people have different opinions about it. Some psychologists believe that if the right conditions are in place, brainwashing a subject is possible. However, the entire task is never as severe as portrayed in the media. Several definitions of brainwashing exist which makes it really tough to know the consequences of brainwashing on a victim. Most definitions require the presence of some form of threat to the physical body of the victim for it to be called brainwashing. In line with this definition, most practices carried out by extremist cults would not be regarded as real brainwashing since physical abuse was absent.

The remaining definitions of brainwashing make use of control and coercion with no physical force, while aiming at getting the subject to change his/her beliefs. Whichever definition it is, pundits agree that even with all the conditions in place, the results of brainwashing lasts for just a brief moment. Experts also agree that the former identity of the victim is never erased totally with the experience; instead, it is sent into hiding and re-surfaces when the new identity is no longer forced upon the victim again.

Robert Jay Lifton presented fascinating opinions on brainwashing in the 1950s after observing prisoners of the Korean and Chinese War camps. During his studies, he concluded that his subjects (prisoners) went through several stages in brainwashing. These stages start with an attack on the victim's self-concept and conclude with a supposed change in beliefs of the prisoner. Lifton defined 10 steps for the brainwashing process in the prisoners he studied. These steps are:

Attack the subject's identity;

Force guilt on the subject;

Force self-betrayal on the subject;

Reach a breaking point;

Offer the subject leniency if they change;

Compulsory confession;

Point all the guilt in the intended direction;

Liberate the subject from supposed guilt;

Move into harmony;

A last confession before a rebirth.

These steps must be carried out in a completely isolated area. What this means is that all the regular social references the victim is used to coming in contact with are not available. Furthermore, mind clouding schemes like starvation and sleep deprivation will be utilized in order to speed up the procedure. Even though this may not be what's obtainable in all cases of brainwashing, there' is often the presence of some kind of bodily harm. This makes it difficult for the subject to think critically and independently like they usually do.

Different Techniques Of Brainwashing

As we now understand, brainwashing doesn't occur overnight but is usually a series of actions taken simultaneously over a period of time, which eventually results into a changed personality. Perception and behavior change, sometimes to such an extent that the victim becomes unrecognizable to their friends or peers.

The techniques used and the speed with which the personality changes depends on many things, but most of all on whether the target is being subjected to brainwashing against their will (in which case they'll naturally resist as much as they can) or whether they don't know they're being brainwashed (e.g. in cults) and believe all the ideas being impressed upon them are their own and that they themselves are making the decisions. This could be deemed successful brainwashing, as the victim is unaware of what's occurring.

Most common overt and covert brainwashing techniques:

- **Repetition and nagging**

    It's hard not to start believing something or at least begin doubting one's self if someone is constantly repeating the same thing over and over every day, for months or even years.

- **solation**

    It is easier to control someone if they have no access to sources of information which conflict with the brainwashing material. If the target talks to someone about the ideas being imposed upon them and other people understand what's happening, they may scupper the chances for a successful brainwash. This tactic is often witnessed in abusive relationships, where one partner doesn't want the other to communicate with friends or family incase their motives are uncovered.

- **Blind obedience**

This prevents the victim from thinking for themselves.

- **Responsibility**

One central brainwashing technique is to make someone feel responsible for their faults and the things that go wrong in their life. If they make mistakes, do something poorly, or if things don't go according to plan, making them feel responsible leaves them feeling negative emotions such as guilt and shame, which lowers their defenses and opens them up for manipulation.

- **Guilt and fear**

These are used extensively as part of an overall

emotional manipulation plan. When a huge guilt complex is imposed, we start believing we're deserving of any resulting punishment.

Self-brainwashing techniques:

Identify a negative thought pattern

Identify a negative thought or belief that's been holding you back. How long have you felt this way? Can you connect the programming to any early life experiences? Are you aware of how this belief has affected your life? What do you think your life would have been like if it weren't for this negative thought pattern? Do you believe you are what others tell you? What skills or abilities do you wish you had?

Acknowledging the damage

Be aware of any negative emotional, mental or physical harm this thought pattern has done to you, then make the decision to do something about it. Negative programming can be reversed, but it takes time, so be prepared to work on this issue for a long time if need be.

The Power of Suggestion

Much of our negative thinking comes from suggestions

we take in from others. Think of how many times someone has spoken to you negatively, said you were fat, stupid or unintelligent? Eventually, when these suggestions are heard repeatedly they tend to became our reality.

We can reverse such damage by purposefully taking our suggestions onto a more positive path by consciously choosing positive beliefs. Whatever flaws you believe you have, they can often be reversed. One such way is to constantly tell yourself what you'd like to become, by verbally affirming (or thinking) how successful, healthy or confident you are. Eventually, with commitment, these suggestions can come true as our actions and behaviors gradually begin to follow the constant positive reinforcement we're feeding ourselves.

Repetition

Repetition is successfully used in self-brainwashing. Consistently reinforce positive thoughts about yourself or your self-image by repeating confidence-boosting words and affirmations throughout the day. If it helps, use sticky notes on your desk, inside your car, on the fridge, and other places where you'll often see them.

Or, try chanting short phrases such as, 'I am smart', 'I am successful', 'People like me' or whatever you're trying to change.

DECEPTION

It is about time we moved onto our first form of mind control: deception. You will see a lot of similarities between deception and manipulation as you continue reading. One of the reasons is that both are types of covert mind control systems, so, the aims and processes are somehow similar. Again, manipulative people are known to deploy a lot of deception so as to achieve their goals.

What Is Deception?

Deception is identified as the act of misleading, promoting an idea, concept, or belief that is false or simply hiding the truth. If someone is 25 years old and says they are 30 years old, they are committing the act of deception. As humans, we deceive others a lot of times. Even the people we consider as honest deceive others or themselves several times a day, according to various studies. Deceiving others may not necessarily be a bad thing as it can help to avoid negative situations. In society, some lies can be used to maintain proper functioning as long as no negative consequences arise from the deception. For example, if the police announce that they will conduct swoops on places frequented by idle youth so as to keep them off the streets yet fail to do it; we can refer to this as a necessary form of deception.

In the context of our book, however, we are talking about the dark type of deception which has the potential to cause harm to other people. Therefore, we can add to the definition of deception as the act of concealing the truth and making people believe in falsehood for selfish benefits while exposing them to harm. So, if a child lies about being chased by a dog as the reason for coming late to school, they are not exposing the teacher to any harm. Even if the deceit was discovered, it would only spell more punishment to the student. When we are talking about harmful deception, it is the one where the agent promotes falsehood to gain an advantage over their victim. If such deceit is detected, it risks harming the subject more than the agent.

Let us have an example of harmful deception.

A story is told about three elementary school kids who were at a park on a night in the 1980s when police were called about a woman who had been found raped and badly beaten. Upon getting to the scene, the police took the woman to a hospital as others went searching inside the vast park for any clues or suspects. At the far end of the park, they saw the three young boys sitting under some trees while sipping booze and laughing. Without conducting any proper inquiries, the police immediately arrested the boys on the assumption that they had committed the offense.

At the police station, the leading investigator wrote a statement claiming the boys were found near the unconscious woman and were laughing about the matter when the police found them. The woman had suffered severe trauma to the head that led to memory loss and inability to speak well. Therefore, she could not confirm or deny whether the three boys were her attackers. The only evidence that existed was semen on the woman's undergarments and the fact that the boys were at the park on the same night of the abuse. Unfortunately for the boys, the judge believed the police and imprisoned each of them to 25 years in jail.

10 years later, a man approached the judge who had

convicted the boys and confessed to having attacked the woman. At this time, DNA technology had emerged. Upon comparing the DNA on the semen found on the woman with that of the man, they matched. He confessed to having been on a revenge mission after the woman walked out on their marriage. The young men were set free after spending 10 years in undeserving incarceration.

Upon further investigations, it was found that the police officer who had lied about finding the boys near the woman and laughing at their actions had been under pressure to reduce crime in his area of work. To prove his effectiveness, he had lied about the young boys. This act not only deceived the judge into jailing the innocent men but also proving to his superiors and community that he was an effective officer. The judge apologized as the officer was sent to prison.

From this story, we can see that deception aims at tricking and fooling the other party for personal gains. We can assume that if the officer were not under pressure to prove his worth, he would not have lied about the boys. To him, the crime at the park presented itself as an opportunity to redeem his career without caring about the consequences that his actions would have on the victims.

It is also evident that dark deception may take some time before it is discovered. At times, it may not, at all. However, in the event that it is discovered, it leads to devastating consequences for both the victims and the offender. In this case, the three men had been suffering for a crime they did not commit. Even though they were set free, the 10 years they had lost were not going to be recovered. The judge, too, felt guilty of sending the innocent kids to jail and had to apologize. The perpetrator, too, was affected in that he was punished for deceiving the justice system.

In summary, deception in the context of dark psychology benefits the deceiver more than the subject. The deception can be used to create a relationship between the two, allowing the deceiver entry into the subject's mind. Once a relationship is created, the deceiver starts exploiting their victim and extracting their benefits.

Primary Components Of Deception

Manipulators such as liars are aware that trust is the strongest bond that can exist between two people. Therefore, they usually create it between them and their victim before they initiate their mind control process. On the other hand, when the victim trusts the deceiver, this act is equivalent to dropping the guard that prevents them from being controlled without their knowledge. If we can go back to our story, we know the judge trusted the investigating police officer. In the judge's mind, police officers are sworn to be truthful. As such, when he was told that the boys were found near the unconscious lady and that they had been laughing about their actions, he was bound to believe it. In short, the officer had betrayed the trust and influenced the judge's mind.

The saddest part about deception is that it utilizes the trust to harm the victim. This makes it very painful for the victim when they realize it. In a way, they perceive themselves as having been fooled and actually assisting the agent in taking advantage of them. Trust, like many emotions, has the ability to convince people to do things which they would not do if it had not existed. For example, in e-commerce, people purchase things on a pre-order basis. This is mainly because they trust the companies that offer products such as Apple. If apple were a new company with no reputation online, people would not pay for items that they have not seen or touched. This trust is what deceivers use to access their victims and control them as they wish.

Evidently, trust is the emotion that enables the agent to control the victim. The victim believes in the deceiver and might even base future plans on the deception. All this time, everything the deceiver will be saying or doing is false. Another thing the deceiver is aware of is that the trust can be ruined in case the subject finds out that they have been lied to. Therefore, they need to be good at turning things around so as to reduce their chances of being found out. More characteristics of deceivers are listed below.

The Process of Deception

The overall concept of deceit is to propagate a false sense of reality, such as a story so that the target believes it and then later doing something totally different. That said, the process of deception can be divided into three parts, as explained below:

The Objective

Before finding their potential targets, deceivers first

come up with the end goal (objective) in mind. For instance, a con artist decides what they want to get from someone. It might be money, a valuable item, or personal favors. Their type of objective is critical in the entire deception planning process. Once they have the end goal in mind, they work backward to find out what needs to be done to achieve it.

Identifying Potential Targets

Once the goal is set, they go to identifying the most vulnerable type of people. Just like animals in the wild prefer the most vulnerable prey such as the young, aged, sickly, injured or weakest, a deceiver is also very careful when choosing his or her prey. Back to the example of the con artist, assuming their goal is to steal credit card details from someone, they might prefer going for older people who are not conversant with online purchases. An elderly person is easier to deceive on the internet than a young one.

Studying the Target

Once the deceiver has identified the potential target,

they start the process of studying them. The aim here is to figure out the target's vulnerabilities and strengths. These include their capabilities, strongest emotions, capabilities, beliefs, preconceptions, social and family status, and so on. If they are successful in "predicting" the vulnerability of their targets, they know exactly where to hit so as to improve their efficiency. At this stage, they move in to create trust as the technique to reduce suspicion and gain control of the target's mind.

Settling on the Best Technique

The final stage of the deception planning process is to formulate the story or the most appropriate form of deception.

This four-step process might appear like it takes weeks or months to plan, but it can even be made in a few minutes. A good example is when a bully wants to steal another person's property. Although the planning process might take a few minutes, it adheres to the above template.

The Trojan horse Story

Let us use the story of the Greek Trojan horse to understand this process better.

The Greeks had attempted to invade and destroy the Troy (Trojan) City for close to a decade without any success. When it finally dawned on them that invading Troy was not going to be easy, they decided to apply a different strategy. This strategy was going to involve mind control. At this point, we can easily decode the objective of the Greeks as invading Troy and winning the war.

Next, the Greeks decided to lure the Troy army by faking retreat. They knew that by retreating, the Troy army would assume the war was over and drop their guard. This was seen as the best plan as opposed to their previous ambush method, which had failed for a decade. At this point, again, we see the Greeks identifying their target's vulnerability.

The third step was studying the target and creating trust with them. To earn the Trojans' trust, the Greeks decided to "gift" them with a symbol that would represent their withdrawal. The gift was a large wooden horse that could house a number of Greek soldiers inside. When the Trojans saw the horse, they were happy and believed the Greeks had given up victory in their favor. To add to the manipulation, the Greeks sailed their ships away.

As the Greeks sailed away, the Trojan army moved the wooden horse into their city. Unknown to them, the horse contained some skilled Greek soldiers. That night, as the city slept, the soldiers jumped out of the horse and opened the city gates. The ships had also come back, and the entire Greek army ambushed the city and destroyed it. We can say the Greeks had settled on the technique of diversion or, to some extent, dazzling. Eventually, they achieved their goal.

Detecting Deception

Detecting any form of mind control, leave alone deception, can be hard owing to the wit of the toxic people as well as the carefully planned processes they use. Most of the time, the deception will show up once the goal has been achieved or if the deceiver missteps and blows their cover. Otherwise, if the liar is a good one, they will juggle with the subject's mind until they have achieved their objectives. Therefore, detecting deception can be difficult since there are no accurate or reliable indicators that can detect when deception is happening.

As hard as it might seem to detect deception, there might be a few loopholes that present themselves during the process. According to psychologists, deceiving others can place a large load on the perpetrator since they need to keep their covers perfectly hidden. To some extent, they need to fight with the notion of deceiving themselves while trying to control their subjects. The risk of missing a single step and making the subject suspicious usually overwhelms the deceiver. Therefore, at some point in the deception process, hints might be dropped, albeit subconsciously. Some of the clues are verbal, while the rest are non-verbal such as body language.

Aldert Vrij, a scholar who studies deception, there are no specific tell-tale signs that may suggest that deception is happening. There may be a few clues, though, but they risk being confused with other traits that represent different ideas. Therefore, the surest way to tell if a manipulator is using deception is when they are caught.

The lack of definite methods of detecting deception does not mean we should ignore potential signs that may indicate something fishy is happening.

Psychologists have come up with several verbal and non-verbal clues that can occur during the process of deception. Let us have a look at some of them.

Characteristics of Deceivers

They are Manipulative

Deceivers are known to be manipulative people. They can switch between situations and personalities so they can persuade others, through covert force, to fulfill their selfish goals. A normal lie does not require a person to pre-condition the other so they can succeed. Rather, words or actions, usually not pre-planned, are used. However, a pragmatic deceiver displays manipulative traits. In a relationship, for instance, the lover who is always forcing the other to change their ways so they can be satisfied is more likely to be a deceiver. Frequent lies usually build up to chronic manipulation. In short, a person who displays a manipulative character is an obvious deceiver.

They are Good Actors

A person who is good at deceiving others is a definite actor. Acting is the process of putting up a false show, either physically or psychologically. A good actor can arm themselves with false behaviors or stories to convince their subjects. For example, a healthy person can feign illness and ask the public or their friends for money to seek medical attention. If they are not good actors who can change their voices, looks, and mood, they risk not convincing others to give them money. On the other hand, if they put up convincing shows, they can easily win sympathy.

They are Intelligent

It takes a lot of intelligence to convince the human brain to perceive reality in a manner that it would doubt in normal circumstances. Crafting an effective plan after observing a person for a short or long while is a tough task. However, deceivers are swift at decoding human behavior. They can predict the outcome of situations before they happen and plan accordingly. Intelligence is also required when dealing with the cognitive load which they carry. It helps them to overcome this limiting factor without leaking their plans and/or intentions.

They are Confident

Confidence is one of the most attractive and convincing human traits. Confidence is the ability to approach people and situations without fear or doubt. When someone comes up to us smiling and speaking fluently, we are more likely to listen to them. Conversely, if someone tries to talk to us, yet they are inaudible or shy, our attention and interest are lost. That said, a deceiver tries to be very confident when making their moves to minimize suspicion and improve their overall appearance. They seem to have satisfactory answers to everything. Confidence is very important to them because they also need to overcome their conscience, which might discourage them from taking advantage of others.

They are Eloquent

Liars are either born with eloquence, or they practice it. They are said to be smooth, natural performers. During an interaction, they take charge and make the moment as lively as possible. They speak without stammering or hesitating even when talking about false things. Deceivers come off as excellent listeners as they know people are attracted to those who give them an ear. When it is their turn to speak, even after some doubt is cast, their wordplay is powerful to the extent that it can make a lie to be acceptable. "Ers" and "Uhm" are never part of their vocabulary.

They are Keen

Unknown to us, we have an innate gift of detecting suspicion when we have done something wrong. For instance, if we lie about our ages, we watch out for clues which may hint that the other party is not taking the lie. Some clues might be raising their eyebrows, looking at us from head to toe or throwing a sarcastic statement which seeks to doubt. Similarly, deceivers are overly keen. They know how to read verbal cues and body language. This skill is used to evaluate their progress, know when to change a narrative, or abandon the mission in general.

They have a Sharp Memory

You have probably heard the saying that the disadvantage of lying is that you must force yourself to remember everything. One of the betrayers of deception is giving contradicting statements from what one had previously stated. A keen subject can detect a deceiver if they notice a conflicting narrative. To overcome this shortfall, deceivers have adapted by developing a sharp memory. If someone asks them about something they had said previously, they give the exact sentiments. This single trait alone makes it hard for them to blunder and very hard for outsiders to detect their fallacies.

They Speak Half-truths

The high intelligence that deceivers possess increases their prowess at misleading people. They understand that fabricating a lie from scratch is hard and is easier to be detected. Therefore, they resort to bending truths. A half-truth is more convincing as part of it can be verified. It also translates to less cognitive load since they only need to fabricate part of the story. For example, a retail store might announce a sale where they have slashed the prices of vegetables. While this might be true, they might as well be selling the vegetables cheaply since they are of inferior quality. To them, they have no remorse for selling bad groceries as long as they prevent losses at the expense of the customers.

They are Expressive

A deceiver is bound to be someone who can express an idea in a way such that the recipient has no room for questions or doubts. They are good with detailing and articulating issues because a narrative that has no loopholes is easier to adopt. The expressiveness is deployed at their first interaction with the target as a way to create a good first impression. First impressions influence the way we see others. As such, if they make it worthwhile at first interaction, they make the target easier to influence due to their good image.

False lovers are examples of expressive people. When asked why they love someone, they provide juicy reasons which convince their innocent others.

They are Rapid Thinkers

The other trait that is commonly seen in liars is the ability to think fast. This is especially true with the deceivers who hunt for victims in public or when they have limited time. They have to come up with effective plans in the shortest way possible before their subjects disappear or become suspicious. Similarly, they also display rapid thinking when they are cornered or forced to make impromptu explanations. Some of them are professionals in the art of deception that they can come up with the most convincing statements in a short while.

A good example of rapid thinking is deployed by salespeople. During their marketing sprees, they can meet with potential customers who ask all sorts of questions. For instance, a lady intending to purchase a watch might ask, "Is this one waterproof?" The salesperson, aiming at securing a deal, rushes to respond, "Yes, Madam. Not even air can get inside. Our bosses use these watches, and I'm only selling it to you because you are dressed like a boss!" Such trickery easily wins the trust of the client who might get home only to find the watch is the opposite of everything they were told.

They are Decent

There is a funny but unfair observation in psychology that attractive people are more likely to be trusted than their average-looking counterparts. The deceiver of today comes off as a chivalrous gentleman or well-groomed lady. Humans are used to "bad" people possessing hard looks or being unfriendly. This is an outdated notion because deceivers have evolved into the charming people we meet online, the needy children we pity, the beautiful women we find with flat tires around the corner and the same people whose glowing faces we see the first thing in the morning. The deception begins with the creation of false trust.

They are Cold-blooded

Empathy is the innate feeling, which limits the extent to which we can get when interacting with others. If we place ourselves in their shoes and have a feel of what bad actions would have on them, we naturally react by not doing them or by making it up to them. Deceivers are a different breed. They do not experience any guilt or remorse when they harm someone. This is partly because they know emotional reactions can hinder their plans, and, in addition, because they are masters at suppressing their emotions. Their dark sides are exposed when they are caught or after they have achieved their objectives.

For example, a man might seduce a lady, pretending to love her. After some time, the lady gets pregnant, and the man abandons her since he did not genuinely love her, but used her for sex. He may ignore her advances henceforth and turn abusive in a way the lady would not have anticipated before the pregnancy. It is at this time that she sees his true colors; which are that of a psychopath.

Deceivers, as it is evident above, possess a lot of admirable traits. They package themselves in a manner that disarms suspicion while earning them instant trust. These traits make them very hard to detect. All the same, most of their characteristics are false, meaning they can drop them accidentally; exposing their malicious intents. It is important to consider that while a person might portray one or more of these characteristics, they do not automatically qualify as deceivers.

Areas of Our Lives where Deception Is Common

People deceive each other every day. Lying and cheating are acceptable human traits if they are controlled. However, just like everything else, if overdone, deception can ruin our interpersonal interactions and cause far much bigger problems in society.

Everywhere there are humans, deception must exist. That said, we shall list some of the areas in our lives where a deception is a common event.

Social Media

Social media is a virtual community that unites the entire world through internet connectivity. It allows people to create their preferred profiles and interact with the rest of the world using them. The aspect of social media, which makes it a commonplace for deception to occur is that a person can use false information to set up a profile. When this happens, the people in his or her circle think they know the real person when, in reality, they do not exist. False information such as incorrect age, wrong gender, inaccurate place of origin, race, profession, and much more is easily provided. Therefore, the people who interact with such a person are deceived into believing they are interacting with a genuine person.

The other way that social media can be deceiving is when people use engineered images and videos to create a better impression of themselves. They might attract other people with whom they eventually meet up beyond the virtual world. To the shock of many people who meet this way, they find that the people they meet are totally different from the ones they had seen online. Such interactions end up being disappointing, and one party feels cheated or taken advantage of.

Romantic Relationships

Deception thrives exponentially in romantic relationships because of the number of emotions invested in them. The high connectivity means that when one partner decides to deceive the other, they can do it easily without being detected. One of the most common forms of deception can happen when one partner talks their lover into initiating a romantic partnership, yet they are not genuinely in love with them. They might be pursuing hidden agendas such as sexual or financial benefits. Toxic lovers may even manipulate their partners just to play with their feelings.

Another occurrence that is not new in love bonds is cheating. This is the situation whereby one partner has extramarital affairs. They go out with third parties while keeping their loves in the false belief that they are faithful. In such circumstances, the partner who is being cheated upon is being deceived. Their trust has been won and used to gain an advantage over them such that they cannot realize that their lovers are sleeping with others.

Criminal Justice System

Deception in the criminal justice system begins with the interaction between law enforcers and suspects. When the suspects are arrested, they always try to convince the police that they are innocent to avoid the trips to the police stations. At this point, they may try to twist the truth to prove their innocence; which they sometimes succeed in doing. For example, an overspeeding driver might lie to a traffic officer that they were rushing to pick their wives or kids who have collapsed in the house. Owing to this high-risk situation, the officer might believe them and set them free.

The second level in the justice system where deception is a frequent visitor is during court sessions. Lawyers are the main culprits here. They are paid by criminals who know too well they are guilty of their crimes to try and save them from incarceration. Depending on the presentation of facts and countering the prosecution, hardcore criminals such as murderers and fraudsters might end up returning to society. In such instances, the lawyers are said to have deceived the prosecution and assisted a criminal in getting away with a crime.

On yet another level, criminals in jail understand that if they displayed reformed behavior, they could be paroled way before the end of their sentences. To achieve parole, they use disguise to create the impression of reformed prisoners. Some of them are lucky enough to fool the prison systems. Once out of jail, they can drop their fake personalities and return to lives of crime.

The Military

We have all heard stories of how armies in the two World Wars deployed an array of mind control tricks to get leverage over their opponents. One of the tactics we know of was the use of decoy tankers and planes to throw enemy troops off balance. An army would send a platoon of fake tankers and planes towards the enemy. When the enemy responded, the army would approach them from a different angle and ambush them. This amounted to the use of diversion to deceive their enemies.

Militaries are also the kings of camouflage. Everything from their backpacks to gear and vehicles, planes, and infrastructure are all made to blend in with the environment. Camouflage enables them to hide their presence when they do not need attention. In the World Wars, armies were known to cover their tankers and trucks with jungle-green canvas to conceal them from enemy planes. In this way, they played the absence trick on them.

E-commerce

Electronic markets are the most preferred shopping avenues on the planet as at today. People enjoy the comfort of making purchases online and having their goods delivered to their doorsteps. However, this efficiency also comes with a cost.

First, there is the risk of being defrauded. An online shop might pretend to be genuine and market itself online. When a customer makes a purchase, though, they take their money but fail to honor their side of the deal. Fraud is a form of deception. A scenario like this means the buyer trusted the vendor with their money, but the vendor was not genuine all along.

There is another emerging trend where online vendors are advertising items, but upon purchase, the clients realize they have been shortchanged. For instance, you might come across a lovely pair of gold-coated shoes going for an unbelievably low price. Upon ordering them, however, you have a pair of doll shoes delivered! Well, it is the very same pair that you saw online, only that they never said they were doll shoes. Camera angles and editing were used to make the impression that they were average human shoes.

Drug Abuse

Did you know that over 60% of all drug users were introduced by their acquaintances? Now you know! We can make an assumption that most of those influenced were asked to "take a puff," "just one jab," or "try one for the road" only to wake up one morning and find that they were regular smokers or drunkards. The influence of this type qualifies as deception because if the person did not consent to try them out but was seduced or coerced, it was against their will. Concisely, they were cheated into trying them out, and that ended up as being the start of a never-ending road to dependency.

The Media

The media is one of the biggest influencers in the world. Under this umbrella term, we have music, advertisements, films, papers, magazines, and news. The list is endless. Since we depend on information from the media to plan our lives, we subconsciously become their puppets.

If we look at the issue of fake news, they can cause panic, misinform the masses, or cause civil unrest such as clashes. Unfortunately for us, we tend to blindly absorb everything we are fed by news sources. The issue of fake news took headlines after the 2016 election of US President Donald Trump. Some newspapers claimed he would deport all non-Americans while some claimed his supporters were attacking non-Whites. This led to protests and minor skirmishes in some major states like New York, Oakland, Seattle, Philadelphia, and Chicago. Years after his election, the news came to pass as false. The media had deceived the Americans.

The deceptive influence of music cannot be overlooked. In recent times, it has been observed that the lifestyles displayed by musicians can be misleading to some audiences. Young people, who are the most affected, believe everything they see in the videos is true. They try to live like the musicians and when they fail, negative cognitive effects such as low self-esteem and depression kick in. As such, we can quantify some music at potential deceiving.

Communication

Last but not least, we have communication in terms of interpersonal relationships. Unpleasant conversations like gossiping and shaming are composed of false information about other people. Deceivers can use badmouthing to talk foul about others with the aim of painting them in a bad light. If the receivers of false information believe in it, the victim of the gossip or shaming gains a negative but false reputation; making it be deception. Deception of this kind makes use of lies and diversion to achieve its mandate.

Now that we have covered the traits that a manipulative individual seeks and their reasons, let's review how you can spot manipulation to avoid becoming their next victim. As you can see, a manipulator excels in applying psychological techniques that are meant to build relationships, only with a sinister twist, to achieve their goals. It is important to be aware of their subtle tricks and there a few more overt aggressive signals that you want to be on the lookout for. To protect yourself from becoming a puppet, you will have to pay attention to these signs that are the earmarks of a manipulative individual.

Psychology Tricks Used for Persuasion

When you are with someone, pay attention to their conversation habits. If most of their conversation is based around words that are mainly focused on their own life, their own experiences and they do not ask questions about you or your interests, then they are potentially manipulative and self-centered. These individuals always talk about themselves, brag a lot, making sure to keep the topic on their life, their "accomplishments", on what they are doing and how they are feeling. This is a power play for getting you to completely focus your attention on them. This is essentially baiting the hook, they want to be sure you are thinking about them and their situation, not yourself and your needs when they make the "ask".

The manipulative individual can be charismatic, charming and even flattering, which disarms the unknowing victim. When the off chance occurs and they do ask how you are, they do not listen to your answer. They will smile convincingly, even leaning in to appear interested, but it becomes evident they were not listening when they are unable to recall the details of your response. They will often blow past anything you say moving on to other topics or direct the conversation back to themselves. This is telling of their insecurity and insincerity.

They pretend to be interested in what you are saying to them without contributing to the conversation. They will stand with their arms akimbo, gesturing towards you with an open hand, they will nod at what you are saying to feign agreement. This nodding and open hand is a physical cue that there is a request coming. The core goal in their mind is to find a way to slip in what they want. They will look you up and down or hold eye contact for an unusually long period as a method of subconsciously controlling you. They will place themselves within close quarters to you because body proximity tends to influence others, using body language coupled with the "mirroring" technique is a sure-fire method of reeling a victim into their game.

A manipulative person is someone that wants something from you. You will find them presenting themselves in a pleasing fashion, being overly complimentary in conversation and always telling you what you want to hear. They always seem outrageously excited to see you or be around you. They will be charismatic, charming and will use flattery knowing that buttering you up and sweet-talking you will gain them favor in your eyes. They are softening you up to ask you for a favor or pitch you an idea.

They will often couple asking for a favor with the promise to return the favor. They will suggest their ideas to you while expressing there is an emotional benefit to you by fulfilling their request. When they finally make their desired goal known they use a "slick salesman" type of psychology by implying that, if you do their bidding, there will be some sort of value or reward in it for you. If you listen to what they are saying you will realize that they are making requests and following them with statements that are meant to convince you. The statements will usually be designed to convince you that helping them will be a good idea for you or improve your situation somehow. It is a good idea to evaluate their proposition to determine if you both will benefit from, or if this is just the manipulator's sly way to get your cooperation.

A manipulative person will be very kind and generous

at first and say nice things about you, everyone wants to be approved of. The manipulator knows this and will use that in their favor. The person who is seeking manipulate will do so with good deeds. They will do something that appears nice and generous, but only if they stand to gain attention and a good reputation from it. Remember that manipulation can be hidden behind kind gestures, but their acts of generosity and gifts are bribes to make them look good in front of other people. These actions are usually coupled with an outward display. You will notice they behave differently when they are alone with you and no one is watching. They may amplify this "good deed" psychological manipulation technique with guilt. This person will never let you forget what they did, they will bring it up, reminding you and will continue to drain you in repayment for the one or two times they did something for you. This creates a rinse-repeat cycle of manipulation by continuously wanting repayment for obsolete or past behaviors, rather than focusing on the current dynamics of your relationship.

The manipulator will exaggerate and lie to get what they want. They will repeat the same stories over and over, with details varying each time but the main subject is always them. They will tell stories that are flattering to themselves, put them in a good light or are filled with false self-praise. They will tell complicated stories of being victimized that are filled with "poor me" rhetoric to gain sympathy from you. They will often say that they are ill or hurt to avoid responsibility. These manipulative and dysfunctional people do not communicate directly usually resorting to falsehoods, lies and elaborate stories that will pull on your emotions and compel your help, gain attention and even do their work for them, which is their desired goal.

The manipulator has another psychological tool that they employ to avoid working, praise. They will praise you for the kindness you possess so they can influence you to do what they want, and they are playing upon your good qualities. They will tell you how "nice" and "helpful" you are, then ask for something, knowing now that they have complimented your charitable helpful nature you are likely to do what they ask. They will commend you for having a skill or ability, with the underlying goal being they want you to live up to this talent. This is so they can get something out of you. They will say things like "You know you are a great writer. Can you help me draft my speech?" or "You are so good with people. I am putting you in charge of the dinner party, you'll do a better job." They make a flattering statement placing the thought in your head that you are "better" at something they are, then switch quickly to asking you do them a favor or volunteering you to fulfill a task you never asked for or that was their responsibility, to begin with. With these bait and switch techniques, the idea is to give you high praise regarding your skill at something, encourage your self-confidence, and then redirect the conversation toward asking you to do something they just do not want to do.

You might also be manipulated by someone through them leaning on your helpful nature. The manipulator will take advantage of you by asking for your "help" with something they do not want to do. The manipulative individual knows that people love to help others and teach others about something they possess knowledge in, they will use this to their benefit. You will also find the manipulator pretend to be "less than" in some particular task, saying that they are "not good" at something or that they just "do not know how" to do it, relying on you to do it for them. This type of manipulation can prove to be equally undermining as they may not admit to your helping them and many times will even take credit for a "job well done" by you.

A manipulative person will pressure you into deciding right away, not permitting you time to review your schedule or your feelings when responding to a request or appeal. They will give the matter a false sense of urgency, they will crowd your space not permitting you time to yourself to think about their actions and they expect you to immediately decide or satisfy their need. They do not ever question their actions and may have a delusional belief that they are correct to pressure you. They think they are the only one who knows what to do and may even reason to themselves that you should see that they are right. The only goal they have is to get you to do what they want, and they will play upon your emotions to achieve this end. The only goal they have is to get you to do what they want and will often make you feel guilty if you do not.

Notice that a manipulative individual will not take "no" for an answer to any request or demand they make. They will continue to belabor the point until you give in to their demands They play upon your feelings through shame, guilt, and obligation. This is especially true if they are a partner, family member or friend. They may say things like "I helped you when you needed it " using your shared bond or history to make you feel the weight of obligation. They may attempt to pressure you by questioning your loyalty to them with statements like "How can you tell me 'no', you're my sister?" or "If you loved me, you would do this for me. " They will resort to enforcing relationship history to supplant your decision "We have been friends for such a long time I think you would want to help me with this." They will cry, wheedle and sometimes become loud or aggressive if you tell them you are unable or unwilling to do what they want. An aggressive manipulator will often make their demands with loud demonstrations in public, forcing you to give in to their wants just to avoid embarrassment.

A passive-aggressive manipulator will "pout" like a child when you do not give in to their desires. They will eye-ball you while giving you the silent treatment and if you attempt to approach them regarding their behavior, they will often say they are "not mad" or just ignore you altogether. They will resort to "pay-back" tactics when you do not give in such as failing to do something they had promised to or letting you down in some fashion as a method of retribution. This type of manipulative individual will pull the "disappearing act" or "ghost" you which is another one of their top psychological punishments if you do not give in to them. They will break or fail to show up for plans, do not respond to your calls and ignore your messages as a way of making you suffer for not doing their bidding.

This type of manipulative person will also employ gaslighting as a method of getting you back if you do not comply with their demands. You will find them making back-handed comments such as "That was a really great meal, too bad you don't always like that." or "I think it would be a great idea for you to go for that promotion, if you were more skilled at Marketing you would definitely get it." They will infer support while slyly inserting a statement or comment that is meant to insult you or attack your self-confidence. They will make fun of you and ridicule you and when confronted they will say they are "joking" or that you are being too "sensitive".

There is a dark side to gaslighting that can really push an insecure person into anxiety, depression or neurotic paranoia. This is when the manipulator will tell you something that really hurts or insults you to get back at you for not doing what they wanted. Then when confronted they say things like "I never said that. You're crazy." or "You are misinterpreting what I said, why would I say that to you?" This gas-lighting can extend to behaviors and actions as well with the manipulative person lying about their actions or telling the victim that they are not recalling the incident clearly and often will supply a completely fabricated version of the event. These aggressive attacks are designed to bully you into giving them what they want so you can avoid their punishment in the future.

Be aware, if you find yourself saying things like "I don't want to upset them." or "I will never hear the end of it." when contemplating saying "no" to someone or not responding to their request then you are probably being manipulated. Gas-lighting is one method of control, insults bring your self-esteem down making you easier to manipulate, but there are many subtle phrases that you will hear from someone that is trying to influence you into meeting their demands.

Phrases Manipulative People Use

We have reviewed the methods of psychological influence that employ phrasing to encourage others to see our point of view. Those methods of communicating that make others feel comfortable with us, like the "similarity" strategy, which can quickly bond us to others making them feel connected with us. But the manipulator will also use subliminal phrases that negatively influence us eliciting shame, guilt and sometimes even fear to force our hand and making us give in to their demands.

Many manipulative individuals will employ the dependency technique to psychologically influence others into doing what they want. This is the person who always seems to be in crisis or need of a helping hand. We explored this earlier when looking at the Dependent Personality Disorder, and it is not surprising to see this can be a manipulative technique as well. The phrases that are associated with dependence manipulation are designed to make you feel guilt or shame if you do not do what the manipulator wants.

The manipulative person will use emotional circumstances to make you feel guilty. They will ask you for help, make a request or demand that you be there for them in some circumstance and when you are unable or unwilling to meet their needs they will resort to guilt-inducing statements. They will use phrases like "If you don't do (request), I can't do this", "You don't care about me", "I would do this for you" or "If you don't (request) then I have no one else to help me." The main theme of these statements is that they make you feel responsible. The subliminal point the manipulator is making here is that they are dependent upon you meeting their request for things to go well for them. They want you to know that if you do not comply with their demand it will somehow be your fault that things do not work out for them. This type of manipulation is supposed to make you feel guilty because they are completely dependent upon you. They pretend to be weak and powerless, enforcing the idea that you must not let them down.

When you give in to this type of manipulative individual, they will often have you overextend yourself or go out of your way for them no matter how inconvenient it is for you. If you do not give in to their unreasonable demands, they will never let you off the hook. This person does not see that you have a life or might not be comfortable with their requests, they cannot accept that you just might not want to do what they want. Much like a petulant child, they will continue to bring up how you "Let them down" or "Were not there for (them)." The manipulator will use this as ammunition in future situations. They will remind you of your "failure to be there" for them in one situation using that instance to guilt-trip you into giving in to them later regarding something else. They will often replay these same "let down" statements repeatedly, leveraging the guilt, no matter how many times you meet their demands afterward.

Many of these manipulative techniques that are re-used will often lead you to feel less-than and insecure, which will fuel the manipulator's tactical strategy of getting you to become co-dependent upon them. The manipulative person will use absolute terms combined with gaslighting to push your emotions an obtain what they want. They will remind you that you failed in one respect or another in their opinion saying statements like "You ALWAYS do this to me" or "You are NEVER there for me" these absolute terms are meant to convey their dependence on your support and make you feel shame for the perceived offense when you do not give in to their manipulation.

Another technique that the manipulator uses is the blame game. This is a broader play upon their philosophy that you are responsible for their actions and the circumstances in their lives. They will blast you with blame for something they did with comments like "Look what you made me do" or "If you weren't always in the way I wouldn't have dropped this." They will make you responsible for how events they are involved in turn out saying something like "If you had been there this would have gone a completely different" or "This wouldn't have happened if you had helped me." This type of manipulation is very arbitrary and will be thrown at you no matter what the real circumstance is. This is the blame game technique that many who are hard-wired for manipulation are apt to display.

They will often turn a situation around with statements like "I did do (that), but only because you did (this)" twisting it back on you or someone else, "If they did not do (that), I wouldn't have had to" indicating their actions are appropriate responses to the actions of someone else. The manipulator does not ever take responsibility for their own actions or the circumstances they are involved in. They believe that everything that goes wrong is the fault of someone else.

How to Tell if Someone is Lying to You

One of the manipulator's best weapons for deflecting responsibility is lying. The manipulator will flat out lie to avoid taking responsibility for their actions or any circumstance they have created. They will lie about things they have said to you, the things they have said to other people about you and will even lie to themselves. This type of individual has such a large capacity for denial that they will sway the opinion of others with their fabrications and even come to believe their own excuses after repeating them so often.

But how can you tell if a manipulator is lying to you? There are a few clear signs that you are being lied to, especially when someone is trying to manipulate you. You can start with their vehement use of absolute words such as "I would NEVER do that", or "I SWEAR" when they are denying something. They generally will accompany these types of statements with feigned indignation, but you will notice that there is no honesty in their eyes, so watch for this micro-expression. If they are lying to you, they will not blink. The manipulator will look you in the eye and when they lie their eyes will not blink and then right after they complete the lie you will notice they blink rapidly several times. This is due to their nervousness in their knowledge that they have just lied to you.

Other physical signs that will let you know that someone is being untruthful with you are small body movements and excessive fidgeting. A good portion of the conversation especially when lying they cannot look you in the eye. You will see them looking down and looking away when they speak to you, especially if giving you an explanation or falsely promising something. They will blink slowly and then pull their head back or tilt it to the side before responding to avoid looking you in the face. They may touch their face, or their ears pointing to evasiveness.

When confronted they will respond with an answer that is vague like "I don't know", and "I don't remember". They may respond with very detailed and elaborate stories, or they may give you an answer that when pressed again the response changes or is inconsistent. Look for simulated facial expressions such as a smile that does not reach their eyes or crying that does not produce tears. Look for the crease between their eyes and pay attention to their jawline muscle, because if it tenses this indicates they're under stress. Look for small ticks or twitching while you are speaking to them or nervous laughing. They pull away, exhibit very controlled and limited body movement. They might cross their arms, or their legs, zip up their jacket or button their sweater. Ask an unrelated and unexpected question, then repeat the same statement or the same question you started with. Notice if their response changes. Ask them to repeat their story in reverse. When a person is lying, they cannot repeat the same contrived story backward.

Another way to spot a lie is if the person gets angry with you when their response is fraught with hostility it is a good sign, they are not telling the truth. They may just respond in an obnoxious tone. If you are dealing with a very manipulative person who is lying to you, they will resent that they are being confronted by anyone. They may have an indignant outburst of anger, be aware this may be a very loud and demonstrative outburst, so be cautious when you are dealing with someone like this. When confronted with their lies they may react with completely disproportionate anger. You may be asking them something simple like "Did you see my laptop?" and find them responding in a loud voice and aggressive manner, railing at you that they are "Not a thief! How dare you assume that I would take it! I don't know where your stupid laptop is!" Look for this steam roller technique as it is the manipulators' way of bullying you into believing them.

Signs Someone is Using Psychology to Manipulate You

It is important to realize that the manipulative individual will use any means necessary to get you to fill their need for attention, gain control and do their bidding. This type of individual thrives off controlling another person and will use their body language and manipulative wording to obtain the control they are seeking. There a few combined actions and phrases that will let you know when someone is using psychology to manipulate you. Once you have learned the combination of persuasion methods they employ, you will be less likely to fall into their trap.

There are many reasons that someone will try to persuade you, like when they are suggesting to you or requesting your help with something. When the individual is sincere there is an open dialogue. Their honesty will be expressed in their facial expressions and that sincerity will reach their eyes. Possessing relaxed body language and facing you directly, they will wait patiently for your response.

The opposite is true when you are being manipulated by someone who only wants you to comply with their desires. The manipulative person will demand that you give them an immediate response when they ask you to do something or when they request anything from you. Their body language will be tense while feigning altruism and their smiles will not reach their eyes. They will place their bodies in very close proximity and engage in prolonged eye contact, especially when providing a directive or making uncomfortable demands. The combination of these subliminal signals is meant specifically to intimidate and pressure you.

Flattery is another method that a manipulative person will use to persuade you to do their bidding. The individual that uses this method to encourage another to give in to them will often combine it with warm gesturing and a lot of eye contact. This person will "mirror" you and use the "similarity" strategy. This person will engage in polite banter asking how things are with you. They appear to listen intently to your conversation leaning in and looking you in the eye. They will let the conversation go on and when presented with the right opening, will almost too quickly reply with "I feel the same way" or " I completely understand how you feel", they will be quick to make the sympathetic identification with you to gain your favor. Then when the moment is ripe they will slip in "By the way, I was wondering if" or "You know that reminds me, I have been meaning to ask you" You will be able to spot their insincerity when their request or favor immediately follows their exclaiming how they feel the same way as you. This is a unique method of psychological manipulation and may take a while to pick up on because you will have been engaged in conversation with them for a few minutes before they will make their true intentions known. A big key to spotting this particular method of psychological manipulation is that this person will seem almost too happy to see you when approaching you as if it has been years since they have seen you and you are the only person in the world. This over-excited greeting pattern is designed to make you feel special and warm you up to them immediately.

Another method of manipulation is displayed by anger. They may begin by asking you to do something for them but more often, than not they just tell you using words like "I want you to" or "you had better do this." This is usually characterized by intense demands, aggressively repeating the demand or request and implying that there will be a negative result if you do not give in. This person will yell at you and sometimes become physically agitated. You will see their neck muscles straining and their face contorting in an ugly fashion as they tell you what they expect you to do for them. This person will not be attempting to identify with or flatter your abilities hoping to gain your favor. This person will be domineering, loud and obnoxious, basically just telling you what to do. This direct bullying tactic is very evident and if you are being treated in this fashion you should never engage and definitely, do not give in to the demands of this manipulative individual. Avoid this confrontation and remove yourself from their presence swiftly.

The exact opposite of the aggressive manipulator is the needy request. This type of manipulation is displayed in the manner of hopelessly needing your help and is often accompanied by the sad face, big-eyed plea or begging to get your help with something. They will often display depressed body language with slumped shoulders and a drooping head. They will ask you for your help in an almost whining voice indicating they are desperate for your help. This person then uses the psychological method of imploring you repeatedly to help them, to get you to do what they are asking. They say things like " Please" and " I really need your help with this" but the red flag that this is a manipulation tactic is once you give in, they are suddenly fine. You will notice their body language abruptly shift and they will perk up. This will make you feel good because they are no longer sad, and they are because you have given in to their demand. This person will use this method repeatedly once they find it has the desired result, so watch for it.

The last method is as we must discuss is gas-lighting. This person will have a history of employing demeaning and insulting comments that degrade you and destroy your self-confidence. They will say rude and unacceptable things to you and then say they are "only joking" and that you are "too sensitive." This is a method they will use on you repeatedly and then they will follow with statements like "C'mon you know I'm only kidding, I love you" or "Jeez, it's just a joke! You're my best friend we joke with each other all the time." The psychological technique to notice here is that by tearing you down they are building themselves up and making them appear somehow superior in your eyes. This method is to encourage you to give your power to them. If they are the "alpha" in the relationship you will naturally do their bidding in every situation and not even question it. They know this and it is a method of manipulation they have used successfully all their lives.

You will notice this person speak the same way to everyone and never admits to it. This is the person that will say " I never said that" or " That is now how I said it" and then conveniently change their statements around. This is the person that in a tense situation or disagreement will remain calm and cool when you get upset at their obvious lying. They may even laugh at you when you point out they are not recalling their statements or actions correctly. They will say things like "You are crazy" thereby making it appear you are out of control. They often combine this with the silent treatment telling you they will not speak with you until you "have pulled yourself together." This is a major psychology play after they have insulted you, offended you or wronged you in some fashion and is often combined with statements like "you are blowing this way out of proportion" or "you are overreacting." This is said to undermine you and make you doubt your memory of the entire event or conversation. This is a sinister method that once used on you successfully, may even be amped-up with the manipulator telling you an entirely different version of the events, expecting you to believe their version because your memory is inaccurate. Gaslighting becomes a very common and powerful psychological control tool when you are in a co-dependent relationship with a manipulative individual.

Power Persuasion Techniques Used in Manipulation

Unfortunately, when you are dealing with someone on a personal or professional level that is manipulative their psychological methods of persuasion are almost always being used to their advantage in every situation. These persuasion techniques become second nature to the manipulative individual and make them comes across as a powerful person when they are using them. These skills of persuasion have been finely honed with their success demonstrated repeatedly to the manipulator. We must keep in mind; this individual may not even know that they are using these methods of communication to manipulate you. The use of these techniques is instinctive because they have given the manipulator an edge in their social communication and obtained for them all their goals. Just like an athlete that has built up his muscles to achieve the win, the manipulative individual has become very skilled in using these power persuasion techniques to achieve their aim. We are going to look at a few of these power persuasion techniques and why they work with the goal being that you will be able to spot and put a stop to this controlling behavior.

The first technique that a manipulative individual will employ is avoidance. This is when you find you are asking a question and they reply with a question, or when you are speaking to them about something, they will switch the topic over to you. Many times, they will redirect your thoughts, they will flip questions back on you or start asking you an unrelated question. They will point out something you did instead of responding to you or dealing with the subject you are addressing. They always say the right thing, truthful or not to end the line of questioning pointed at them They will accuse you of behaviors that are aimed at making them feel bad when you attempt to make it clear that they have done or said something that has made you upset or has you concerned. It is not beneath them to say things like "You are a liar". They will flat out deny their actions and fight for the last word every time, just to win their point.

The cold manipulator who is seeking control over a sensitive individual will say things like "You are selfish", "You don't care about me", You are so cruel" or "You are so cold and uncaring" to upset your emotional balance and make you feel guilty. You will often be accused of doing the very thing that they did by making accusations like "Well you did this and you know how much that hurts me" the point will be to make you see they are being treated worse and distract your attention from the calculated way they have behaved. They will augment these statements as you move further into conflict by indicating to you that you could not possibly understand how much worse you made them feel rather than admitting what they have done to you. This avoidance of responsibility is a common practice for the manipulator as they are never at fault in their own eyes.

They use these attacks on your character knowing that you will relent with your direction of thought or stop questioning them. They will say things that paint you as a hurtful and heartless person so you will focus on showing them that you have the opposite positive qualities. They also use this weapon combined with guilt to keep you locked in a dysfunctional cycle of communication. By flipping boundaries around and accusing you of being selfish, unsupportive or cold, the manipulator will achieve their goal and have you scurrying to meet their needs.

They will use your sensitivity and breed insecurity in you to destroy your self-confidence and gain a foothold in your life. They want to be the only person that you will trust and turn to and they want to be the center of attention in every instance. They do this by presenting themselves as your confident while feeding you information that is offensive, destructive and designed to hurt you. They will often instigate disharmony by telling you something unkind that someone "allegedly" said about you under the guise of caring about your feelings, like "I'm sorry, I shouldn't tell you this, but so and so said " then drop a nasty or insulting comment another has said. Then they will follow it up with reassurance such as "don't worry, I have your back, I know you are not like that." seeking to divide you from others.

Another power persuasion technique used by the manipulator to undermine your self-confidence is their use of left-handed remarks. They will ask you a question like "I would never wear something so garish, but it looks good on you." or " Have you lost weight? You were really 'porking-out' there for a while." or highlight that "you look better than the last time" they saw you, inferring you looked ragged or worn prior. They will point out your vulnerabilities or something they know you feel insecure about and then follow that up with a statement affirming how much they like or care about you.

Another method they will use in pushing their agenda is forcing you into actions or activities that you may not want to do by implying it is for "your best interest" or "it will be good for you". They will use statements like "You know I wouldn't steer you wrong" or needle you with questions like "Don't you trust me?" This sort of power persuasion technique can be used perfectly to hold you back from trying new things or believing in yourself. When combined with implied constructive criticism it is very persuasive, the manipulator will say things like "I only want what is best for you" or "You know I'm always looking out for you" implying that they are holding you back or checking your self-confidence as a way of protecting you.

The thing to keep in mind with these power persuasion techniques is that they are designed to undermine you, make you feel uncomfortable and cut you off from supportive friends and family. The manipulative individual has the aim of becoming the only person you can "count' on so they can have that as a bargaining tool in the future to get you to do what they want. One of the key goals of the manipulator is that they want you to replay the hurtful things they say to you in your head. This will enable them to exert continued control over you because you will want to prove yourself to them.

The manipulator is seeking to get a response out of you, preferably they want you to defend yourself. The manipulator thrives off drama, discord, and dysfunction. This heightened emotional state that they place you in fuels their desire for complete focus. The result is that you are doing two things: one, you are completely fixated on them while neglecting yourself and two, when you are defending yourself you are in a state of emotional fatigue with the round and round arguments. This gives them leverage in every situation as they know eventually you will give up completely and they will "win" the battle. They will feed off your sense of being overwhelmed, your anxiety and your frustration. They will use these emotions to further convince you that you are not supportive enough or compassionate.

This will invariably lead you to display the opposite to the manipulator, giving in to their demands, no matter how outlandish they are or how inconvenient to you. The main powerful persuasion strategy being applied here is our universal need to be liked and held in esteem by others. People want to be known as helpful, kind and generous. They want to be considered good neighbors, reliable colleagues, and supportive friends to those they care about.

CONCLUSION

Finally, I am glad you made it to the end of this book. By now you would have mapped out a plan with the techniques provided in this book on how to manipulate, influence, persuade, and change people's minds. We all have different ways of doing and saying things and knowing the right way to do them will help you win when people are involved. This book contains secret techniques and step-by-step methods in which you can trigger people's emotions and be in charge. I have written this book in a very simple and easy manner so that a beginner and an expert can equally benefit from it.

Manipulation, persuasion, naked influence, and the art of reading people's mind are concepts that will aid you in getting the end result you want to see. They all have some basic differences between them, but the similarity between them is that they are all a form of human communication. As humans, we are easily changed by what we see and listen to each day. These three concepts all involve getting another person or people to do what you want. In this book, I talked about their meaning, some modern-day examples of how they are used, and techniques you can use to successfully put them in good use.

Also, I want to congratulate you for showing an interest in a subject like this. Only a few people will want to understand the social skills involved in manipulating, persuading and influencing others. Most people are interested in learning other social skills but neglecting these arts that I have talked about. Manipulation, influencing, and persuasion manifests wherever we go: starting with spouses that are attempting to change the unpleasant behavior of their partner to a mother that is trying to convince her child to eat broccoli. It is used by teachers who try to shape their student's mind to choose the best path of their career; leaders that motivate their followers to get involved in noble causes; and people who help others overcome hurdles, solve their problems, accept challenges, and rise above the struggles. These people are all using the art of manipulation, influence, and persuasion. This shows influence moving from one point to another in an ethical way. Remember don't hurt others in the process of using it. Always use these techniques out of respect for the other person.

Again, I want to use this opportunity to say thank you for staying with me throughout the book. I know it's a challenging one but at the same time, you will agree with me that it is exciting. I believe you have gained a lot and will be using the techniques shared in this book carefully to get what you want. Reading this book won't be enough, you have to be practical with these techniques and have a genuine will to carry them out effectively.

THE SECRET OF MANIPULATION

The Techniques Of Persuasion And How To Analyze People Guide That Allows You To Take Mind Control.

© Text Copyright 2019 – Jason Halpa

The content contained within this book may not be reproduced, duplicated or transmitted without direct written permission from the author or the publisher.

Under no circumstances will any blame or legal responsibility be held against the publisher, or author, for any damages, reparation, or monetary loss due to the information contained within this book. Either directly or indirectly.

Legal Notice:

This book is copyright protected. This book is only for personal use. You cannot amend, distribute, sell, use, quote or paraphrase any part, or the content within this book, without the consent of the author or publisher.

Disclaimer Notice:

Please note the information contained within this document is for educational and entertainment purposes only. All effort has been executed to present accurate, up to date, and reliable, complete information. No warranties of any kind are declared or

implied. Readers acknowledge that the author is not engaging in the rendering of legal, financial, medical or professional advice. The content within this book has been derived from various sources. Please consult a licensed professional before attempting any techniques outlined in this book.

By reading this document, the reader agrees that under no circumstances is the author responsible for any losses, direct or indirect, which are incurred as a result of the use of information contained within this document, including, but not limited to, — errors, omissions, or inaccuracies.

INTRODUCTION

A manipulator is very good at talking about what's wrong and sowing doubt in the minds of others. He speaks only by generalities; he does not know how to listen and does not take responsibility for his words or actions. Finally, he preaches the false to know the true and prefers what is "foolish" to what is clear and simple.

Recognize the Type of Relationship He Has With Others

Whatever we do, it's never good enough. He knows or does better than others. He does not give any compliments, but always finds the small details that allow him to say that it is not perfect. The manipulator often destroys insidiously and cannot help but criticize. He would like to control everything, but since he can't do that, he shows his power by pointing out the weaknesses or mistakes of others. If we are proud of what we have accomplished, he will find a pretext for belittling us and devaluing us. When a parent adopts this type of behavior with his child (or a leader with his employee), he destroys the trust of his victim.

He Is Not Interested in Others

When the manipulator is concerned about any problem, his entire family must be in tune with his emotional state. Wife, husband, or children know that you have to become transparent so as not to attract anger. But everyone also knows that the manipulator always ends up finding a pretext to unload his fury. He's an ego crusher who knows everything better than everyone else. He always has an adventure, a story, or an anecdote more impressive than yours to make you think that you are small, lousy, or uninteresting.

He Is Surrounded By People Who Live in Fear and Failure

At work, with friends or family, we enjoy living in a pleasant atmosphere. Of course, there are times when there is conflict, screaming and arguing, but overall people know how to talk to each other. They trust each other and feel free to live and to do business.

When there is manipulation, the atmosphere is heavy

and people do not dare to speak to each other anymore. People isolate themselves in their suffering. Teachers know that when a child becomes isolated and self-contained, they are no longer involved in class and communicate with difficulty. This is a sign that something serious is happening (usually related to the abuse).

In the world of work, one can be certain of the presence of a manipulator from certain symptoms:

- People feel wrong
- The atmosphere is thick and heavy
- There is a lot of absenteeism and sick leave
- The new employees do not stay, and the old ones try to leave
- There are a lot of rumors and gossip
- People watch each other, are jealous of each other, and accuse each other
- People feel more or less strongly because of a lack of direction
- Decisions seem to be made on an ad hoc basis

- Promises are not kept

- Clans form and clash

- Work results drop or remain desperately low

- The staff is de-motivated and no longer believes in anything

- Projects rarely or hardly succeed

To impose his power and knowledge, the manipulator removes what works well and imposes complex and "silly things" that work poorly or which greatly disrupt the activity of all. He invests his energy in vain enterprises, and he frequently gives unjustified reproaches. He gives his opinion on everything and makes others doubt themselves by saying "nonsense" with the utmost confidence.

CHAPTER 1

WHAT IS MANIPULATIVE BEHAVIOR

The word manipulation is used primarily in our language with two senses, on the one hand, to refer in a general way to the handling that is carried out on various elements, utensils, which precisely require from those who employ them a finished knowledge and expertise. This is because they are objects that have in their functional structure an absolute consistency in the action they generate or perform when used.

And on the other hand, we use the term to designate that person or group, which using various characteristics that it has, such as the authority or power that it has in moral, social or political matters, uses it to get that person or group to not issue or express individual opinions, so that they do or not such or that thing.

That is, manipulation is what seeks to direct the opinion and thought of the other, nullifying their free will and their innate freedom, to orient it towards the end that best suits the manipulator.

On the political level and also in the contexts of mass media, manipulation, turns out to be a common currency that will have the purpose of getting the population or a sector to promote a political ideology or program, or to buy a particular product or service, among others.

It is worth mentioning that this conviction is carried out through a methodology in which the subtle prevails, and various effective persuasion techniques are put into practice , so that, of course, the recipient does not find a direct order or obligation to do something or think in such a way, but rather that the message in question decodes it as an opportunity or as the best alternative you can choose for something to be successful, among other options.

Although many strategies can be put into practice, among the most common are the appeal to emotions, the good ones, such as love, friendship, and also those that are feared, such as fear, or anguish.

And on the other hand, it is common to use the figure

of a person with authority in some aspect to exercise manipulation, mainly because that power that is recognized will be able to dominate or manage the opinions and actions that the manipulator wants to control.

CHAPTER 2

VICTIMS OF MANIPULATION

Just as predators have several traits they often all have, so to do their targets. The people that predators choose to target are typically chosen methodically, seeking out those who are least likely to rebel or try to fight back from any sort of manipulation. They can identify potential targets at a glance, needing little more than seconds to pass judgment on whether that person should be pursued with shocking accuracy. They can tell based off of body language, clothing, situations, interactions, and more, who will be able to serve them best, and they frequently act upon it. Here are some of the most common traits people who find themselves victims of manipulators often have.

Lacking Confidence

Due to lacking confidence, an individual can be quite easy to steamroll. Looking for body language that marks someone as lacking confident is a surefire way for predators to identify an easy target. Those who lack confidence are not likely to put up any sort of fight, either if you attack physically or emotionally. In lacking confidence, the predator can be sure that the individual also lacks the ability to defend boundaries or him or herself. When someone comes across as self-confident, he or she exudes an air of someone not as willing to put up with any sort of manipulation without a fight. Those with confidence will fight back when they feel wronged, violated, or hurt, and would have no qualms walking away from a relationship because they trust their own judgment.

By seeking someone lacking confidence, a predator goes after the easiest possible target to get whatever is desired, whether it is physical affection, arm candy, money, a home, a sale, a vote, or even just the feeling of having dominated someone else. The predator is able to boost his or her own ego through completely taking over another person's life and making decisions for the person. They may want someone around that will always defer to them, allowing them a position of power, even if it is undeserved or unwarranted. They may want someone to make them feel better about themselves, and someone with low self-confidence is likely to do that.

Sometimes, however, predators will go out of their

way to identify someone with higher levels of confidence, as they see it as a game. They make it a challenge to so thoroughly break someone with high confidence that the target allows them to dominate the situation. This predator is doing nothing more than toying with the target and seeks nothing but self-gratification from doing so.

Have Something Desirable

Sometimes, personality has nothing to do with being targets. Sometimes, predators go after someone because they have something the predator wants. Whether it is money, status, a relationship, or anything else, the predator may choose to go after that person in hopes of getting it by association. If the person is someone powerful or influential, the predator may weasel her way into a friendship with the sole intention of pulling from that person's influence in the future. By winning what the other person perceives as a friendship, the manipulator creates an arsenal of people with a wide range of skills, abilities, and prestige that can be used when the need arises. If she wants a new job, she may be able to get a friend to pull strings and get her one, for example.

If what she desires is money, she may worm her way into a friendship or relationship with someone that has a lot of money in an attempt to attract that kind of lifestyle. If her boyfriend is wealthy, he would likely have little issue spending money on her. Further, she may feel as though associating herself with people who have what she wants will help her learn how to achieve what the other people have. Through learning what people are doing and how they are doing it, she may be able to emulate those behaviors in hopes of getting what she wants.

Caregiver-type

Some people are more prone to being caregivers than others. People who are compassionate can become easily manipulated because they seek to believe the best in others and seek to ensure that others' needs are met as thoroughly as possible. The caregiver-type person is likely to see the manipulator and all of his or her flaws, but proceed with a relationship anyway; believing that all that is needed to remedy the situation is love and patience. Unfortunately, that resilience to make sure that the manipulator is cared for and nurtured back to mental health also makes the caregiver an easy victim as well.

Because the caregiver is willing to take all of that negative behavior as signs that the manipulator needs more help, he or she will often completely overlook the warning signs and endure the manipulation, feeling as though it will stop eventually. Unfortunately, no amount of love or patience is going to change who someone is, and they are likely to be disappointed as the manipulative behaviors continue to grow, eventually beginning to drain on even the caregiver, whose personality type is prone to patience and resilience.

This is yet another common target for the manipulator because he or she can get away with far worse behavior far quicker than imagined. Because the manipulator knows that very little done will actually successfully push the caregiver away due to the caregiver's own inherent desire to fix the manipulator, the parasitic manipulator is able to continue to draw upon the caregiver's goodwill to get anything desired with few repercussions.

Empathetic

Considering that most of the manipulators you will encounter either lack empathy or know how to turn off their empathy to steel themselves from other people's emotional states, it should come as no surprise that they are naturally drawn toward the empathetic.

Empathy is the ability to sense and really understand how someone else is feeling. It is as if you have taken yourself and placed yourself in the other person's shoes, understanding exactly how they feel because you know how you would feel in their situation. This sense of putting yourself in someone else's shoes enables humans to ensure that those within their family or tribal unit are taken care of. It extends to other people as well, and those who are particularly empathetic find themselves identifying with other people. They may see the manipulator and decide that they see a person who is clearly in dire need of love and attention. They see the manipulator's flaws and want to try to fix them because they understand how lonely or down they would feel if they lacked confidence, lacked friends and family, or lacked whatever else it is that they believe the manipulator may be lacking.

The empathetic individual, like the caregiver, will take more than his or her fair share of abuse, justifying it as the manipulator being in a bad situation and that any rational person who had suffered the same way would behave similarly. The empathetic target is also far more susceptible to mind games relating to emotions and guilt trips, and the empathetic nature of the individual is eventually used as a weapon against him- or herself.

Dysfunctional Upbringing

People who have grown up in dysfunction have the disadvantage of never learning what normal, functioning, healthy relationships entail. They typically associate their own upbringing with what is normal and seek to replicate those sorts of relationships in adulthood. If a child grew up around parents who fought and argued all the time, with the mother always giving up what she wanted while the father took endlessly, the newfound adult is going to attempt to replicate that dynamic in any adult relationships.

Likewise, someone who grew up in dysfunction is not likely to understand how to set normal or healthy boundaries, or how to enforce those boundaries. They will be easily steamrolled, especially if boundaries being disrespected were a common theme growing up. This leaves the individual quite vulnerable, as he has no sense of normalcy and no sense of how to protect himself within a relationship. He does not understand that relationships are supposed to be symbiotic, and because of that, he is far more likely to deal with misbehaviors and abuse from a manipulator.

Knowing this, manipulators look for those who grew up in dysfunction. They are seen as easy targets. Their lack of boundaries make them easier to manipulate, and their lack of confidence or sense of what a healthy relationship looks like means that the target is not likely to see red flags when the manipulative behaviors begin cropping up. With red flags unseen, the manipulation is not seen as a warning sign that the relationship is unhealthy or should be ended. Particularly if abuse and manipulation were prevalent in childhood, the target may actually have a high tolerance for such behaviors, meaning the predator can escalate quickly and more effectively.

How to identify yourself as the Victim of Covert Manipulation

No one likes being manipulated. When manipulation occurs, you lose your power and your will. You must do what the other person wants. You often have no idea what the other person is really planning and you have no say in the situation. This makes life very difficult and it can cause you to do things that you don't want to do.

Now that you know the secrets to covert manipulation, you also know what to watch out for. You can reverse the techniques in this book to see when others are manipulating you. You can also flip these tactics on people and give them the manipulation that they are trying to run on you. There are various ways that you can protect yourself against manipulators.

Identify when You are a Victim

Everyone has a gut instinct that rears up when they are being used or misguided. Your gut instinct is very sound. You will know when you are a victim. The problem is, a lot of people ignore their instincts. You might ignore yours. You might think something like, "I'm just being paranoid" or "What could possibly go wrong if I hang out with this person?" You might think that the harm will be worth the benefits that you could get from knowing this person who gives you bad vibes. Maybe everyone else likes this guy, so you think that you are just being weird and you should like him too. Or maybe he is able to charm you and convince you that he is not so bad and over time you start to get over your initial bad vibes.

But vibes are not something that you should ever ignore. The minute your gut warns you about someone, listen. Your first impression of someone is never wrong. If you get a bad first impression, don't give the person a second chance. You know more about someone by just glancing at them than you would think. The human brain is amazingly powerful; you only are conscious of roughly ten percent of your brain, so there is a lot going on under the surface that you are not consciously aware of. Your brain is capable of reading people and determining the future far more than you realize.

So when you get that gut feeling, understand that your brain is working very hard and noticing things that you are not consciously aware of. The person that you get bad vibes may not be matching his body language to his words, or he may be acting oddly in ways that you can't detect easily. Listen to your gut!

If you are just not in touch with your gut at all, or if you have doubts about someone, you might want to consider looking at some other signs. You can identify a manipulator based on his actions and language choices. You can also tell by how you feel around this person. There are various clues that point out who someone really is and what his intentions are.

What Makes You Vulnerable

You may wonder why manipulators are attracted to you, especially if you have had multiple encounters with manipulative types. You may also wonder what you should change about yourself to avoid running into a manipulator in the future.

One thing that makes you vulnerable is being accepting of manipulative treatment and emotional abuse. If you were emotionally abused or repressed as a child, this type of treatment may seem normal to you. You don't know anything else. You don't how a healthy relationship is supposed to feel. So you accept the terrible treatment that others would not think of accepting. As a result, you are projecting a sense of vulnerability that draws manipulators from far away. The minute you begin to tolerate their treatment and keep them in your life, they gain power over you and choose to keep using you until they get what they want. Work on increasing your self-esteem and avoiding familiar patterns. If you get that eerie sense of déjà vu when you meet someone, you might want to avoid that person because he is probably reminding you of previous abusive patterns that you have been in.

Another thing that may make you vulnerable is neediness or weakness. If you are in a vulnerable time in life, you might be more open to manipulators. Manipulators can see that you are in need and they see it as an opportunity to offer you what you need in exchange of what they really want. They will use any opportunity to gain control over you, and when you are in a bad period of life, you basically hand them opportunities. You need to guard your heart and mind especially well when you are at a disadvantage. Be wary of extremely kind strangers or life savers. Not all heroes are good guys. Your heroes may help you, but they may have hidden intentions. Most people won't do something for free so watch out.

You may also be a target for manipulation if you have low self-esteem. Events in your life or your childhood may have stripped away your self-esteem and confidence. You may be emotionally vulnerable. So you want people who build up your ego. Manipulators can spot this and they will move in on you, working hard to please you and make you smile. They see a way into your mind through your bruised ego. Try to build your self-esteem by yourself and work on loving yourself.

Signs of a Manipulator

A manipulator is often incredibly superficial. This means that he looks good on the outside, but there is nothing to follow it up on the inside. He is shallow and lacks depth. Everything he does and says is fake, part of a façade that he erects to fool you. So beware of people who are incredibly charming and attractive when you first meet them. Get to know them before you start confiding in them or trusting them. Don't make a commitment or business deal until you are absolutely sure of yourself.

Another sign of a manipulator is that you feel compelled to confide in him or to do what he wants. You constantly find yourself saying yes when you want to say no. It's impossible to be yourself and to stand up for yourself. He has some sort of power over you that you can't resist. Unfortunately, this power is just a carefully woven web of manipulation, deception, and emotional harm. He will dump you the minute he gets all that he can from you, so don't stick around or make the mistake of thinking that this relationship will last. He does not care, no matter how well he pretends to. Get away from him before the relationship gets too harmful and he ruins your life.

You may also find yourself saying sorry all of the time. Your guilt eats you up. Every situation with this person seems like your fault. Even if he is at fault, he manages to twist things around so that you feel guilty. He will never take responsibility for anything that he does and he will always put everything on you. He can do what he wants, but he holds you to exacting standards and punishes you when you don't follow suit. He basically kills your self-esteem and causes you to hate yourself.

Finally, a manipulator is great at changing your mind. You might feel one way, but after talking with him, you feel a completely different way. He is able to change your mind and your way of thinking. Sometimes this may even be a good thing, as he makes you think more constructively or positively. But be wary of someone who has so much power over your moods and your thoughts.

What Manipulation Feels Like

Often, in the early stages of a manipulative or emotionally abusive relationship, you will feel amazing. Your manipulator will be an expert at making you feel good about yourself. He will flatter you and fuel your ego.

Some people out there will make you feel good because they genuinely love you. But it often takes times for such a relationship to build. If someone whom you barely know is suddenly super into you and trying to rush a relationship, become very wary. Don't let things move too quickly. Get to know the person first. Someone who wants you so badly right off of the bat is usually superficial and just trying to prime you into a victim. Don't fall for it. Normal people don't just jump into relationships or try to rush things. Normal people also don't start acting crazy about you in an unusually short period of time.

A manipulator will make you feel like there are butterflies in your stomach. You will strive to please him. Your biggest desire will be to make him smile. This is because he is already making you feel as if you owe him or as if you like him so much that you will work to please him. Beware of people who make you feel like a puppet. You should never want to bend over backwards for someone so urgently. You need to have a sense of dignity and personal space and value in every relationship. If you don't, something is off.

You will also feel guilty about the smallest things. You may feel inadequate or guilty for not always pleasing this person every day. A sense of guilt about living or being you may haunt you. You may feel ashamed of who you are. These feelings may seem to come out of the blue, but this is just because you are with a super covert manipulator. Trust me, he is playing some serious games with your heart to inspire your guilt. These feelings are not random or spontaneous, but rather part of your manipulator's carefully crafted plan to hurt you. So you should become suspicious and understand that these feelings are not a normal element of a healthy relationship.

Your self-esteem will certainly dive when you spend time around a manipulator. Soon, your confidence will become riddled with holes. You will be poisoned with self-doubt and angst. This is not a good thing and you should not stay around someone who does this to you.

You also will probably start to feel crazy. You will wonder if you have an undiagnosed disorder or if you are falling apart at the seams. When you argue with this person, he will deny everything that he just said. He will call you nuts for arguing with him or claim that you are just making things up. In addition, he will invent elaborate stories and blame you for things that you never did, often so convincingly that you start to believe that you did what he claims. He will also challenge your perception of reality, lie through his teeth, and make you question yourself constantly. All of these things combined will tear at your self-esteem and consciousness, making you question your sanity. Manipulators can actually rewire the neurons of your brain and do permanent damage to your mental health and personality, so you should not stick around.

One great piece of advice is that if you feel the need to record someone during arguments because he denies what he says later and makes you feel crazy, then you are in an emotionally abusive relationship and you should leave now. You are not crazy. This person is just gaslighting you.

What to Do when Someone is Manipulating You

The simplest piece of advice on how to deal with a manipulator is to just up and leave. If you can do this, great. You should immediately. There will be no good to come from this relationship, so why stay around and get hurt?

But this advice is often easier said than done. There are some situations where you cannot escape a manipulator and his traps. For instance, you might have to work with a manipulator and you can't just quit your job, or you don't want to. Or you might have a manipulative family member and you can't cut him off or you will lose all of your family. You may feel trapped and unable to leave for various reasons, such as financial reasons. Maybe you have kids with the manipulator and must speak to him or her for the rest of your life regarding the children. Co-parenting doesn't automatically end when your children turn eighteen; sometimes, you have to continue a relationship with the father or mother well into your children's' adult lives, and you must be around each other for your children's weddings, graduations, grandchildren, etc. Or maybe there is a manipulative friend in your group whom everyone else likes. There are countless reasons why you may be stuck with a manipulator in your life. Leaving is not always a viable option.

Having a Manipulative Partner and How to Avoid Manipulation

What is a Narcissistic Personality?

The word 'narcissist' comes from a story in Greek mythology, where Narcissus fell in love with his own image. The narcissistic personality is defined as a person who idealized their own self-image and attributes to the point of negatively affecting other people's lives. Many people possess narcissistic traits when it has to do with a certain section of their lives, but also possess a healthy dose of humility and self-doubt. This is not the case for a person with a narcissistic personality.

In 2004, psychiatrists Hotchkiss and James F. Masterson listed what they called the Seven Deadly Sins of Narcissism:

Lack of /bad boundaries: Boundaries simply do not exist for a person who is a full-blown narcissist. They are unaware that other people can exist not solely to suit their needs, and that other people may have different thoughts or feelings than themselves. Narcissistic supply is a term used to describe how narcissist relies on codependents in order to fill their sense of self-worth.

Exploitation: The narcissist may employ exploitation without regard for the feelings of others. This is usually done to another person who is in a position of subservience and cannot escape it, such as in a work setting or children at school.

Entitlement: Believing that they are special and deserve special treatment and begin expressing narcissistic rage they are denied it (a reaction when a threat to their self-worth is perceived).

Arrogance: A narcissist likes to raise their own self-importance by degrading others.

Envy: A narcissist may employ the feeling of contempt toward another person in order to avoid feelings of jealousy in reaction to the result of another person's achievements.

Magical Thinking: A psychological defense mechanism that allows them to see themselves as flawless and project shame onto others rather than feel it themselves.

Shamelessness: Narcissists do not express feeling shame for any behavior or belief they may possess, as the sensation of feeling shame implies that they must have done something wrong.

Narcissistic Personality Disorder (NPD)

NPD is a personality disorder that expresses a long-term pattern of behavior that is self-focused, superior, and exploitative of others and severely lacks empathy for others. The difference between NPD and the previously described traits of a person with a narcissistic personality is the consistency of the traits and to what extent they impair their lives. This difference is described as pathological; when the expression of these traits consistently disrupts the lives of the narcissist, it is when a mental health diagnosis is given. Many people possess narcissistic personality traits and are able to live a successful and stress-free life, while those with NPD may perceive themselves this way, are actually not developing and achieving success due to the crippling fear of criticism, self-doubt, and failure that lies under their inflated sense of self-worth.

The Malignant Narcissist

These kinds of narcissists are ones that are not bothered by guilt and has the ability to resemble antisocial personality disorder. APD is another personality disorder defined primarily by antisocial behavior that has no consideration for right and wrong. The malignant narcissist may take pleasure in causing pain and display forms of sadistic behavior. The key difference though between a malignant narcissist and an antisocial personality is the way the person relates to others. Narcissists share a codependent relationship with others, and deep down, require the approval of others in order to function. A person with antisocial personality disorder could not care less about the opinion of others and do not require the engagement of other people in order to feel validated.

The Narcissist and Emotional/Psychological Abuse: What Truly Lies Beneath

Abuse is the behavioral act that a narcissist applies as a defense mechanism against a variety of emotions that the narcissist is constantly attempting to suppress. Despite the outward expression of self-importance, grandiosity, lacking empathy, and cruel behavior, the narcissist is actually acting out of deeply repressed sensations of fear. They fear rejection, their own imperfections and shortcomings, of being abandoned, unwanted, and unloved.

The following section will summarize 14 behavioral expressions of a narcissist and how it connects to being abusive. A narcissist could be an authority figure, a parent, a partner, a teacher, a coach, or a caregiver. Marjalis Fjelstad writes about the behaviors to look out for if you believe someone in your life is a narcissist on Mind Body Green.

Narcissists feel the need to be the best/most at everything in their lives. Even if it means the sickest or injured, they must be at the top.

A narcissist constantly feels the need to acquire validation from a partner or important person in their lives because they subconsciously believed that they are not good enough. External validation is always required, but never enough. They will always want you to praise them because they cannot provide the confidence and assurance for themselves, despite the outward appearance of confidence and egotism.

Narcissists are perfectionists, which means that those in their lives must be perfect, they must be perfect, and everything that they have planned or envisioned for themselves must play out without a hitch. This, of course, is not how life works, which often leads to the narcissist feeling dissatisfied. Perfectionism is why it is endlessly difficult for a narcissist to receive any criticism, even if it is constructive.

Because of the perfectionism, narcissist wants to control everything around them, and this includes a partner, a child, a parent, etc. This is where control in abusive relationships comes from; because the behavior of the victim is not lining up with the exact ways the abuser wants it to.

Narcissists never take responsibility for their actions. Even if they contributed to the not so flawless way something may have been carried about, the fault is never their own. It is yours because you did do exactly as you were instructed. Nothing they ever do can be wrong.

As previously stated, a narcissist cannot comprehend what boundaries are. They cannot comprehend that you have your own thoughts, feelings, expectations, and past. They do not like when another person expresses feelings that oppose their own, because it is not perfect, which leads to more behaviors that attempt to control their entire world.

The narcissist lacks empathy, which is why they are unable to understand boundaries. They cannot correctly read body language or facial expressions because they believe that other people must feel the same way they do. However, they are also overly sensitive and aware of perceived rejection from others, and constantly believe that the source of their negative feelings is caused by the person they are closest to in their life.

Logic does not work with the narcissist. Trying to explain to a narcissist how their behavior affects you is futile because they are only aware of their own thoughts and feelings.

Splitting is a term used to describe how narcissists categorize every feeling, person, and experience into one of two categories: the good and the bad. This is due to their intense sense of perfectionism. Nothing can be a combination of a positive valence experience and a negatively perceived one. They can only cope with the single experience that is their own.

An appearance of surety and self-confidence hide the true narcissist experience of fear; fear of failure, losing money, their partner leaving them, their children being taken away, etc. No matter how close a person can get to a narcissist, they will never be able to build a trusting relationship, simply because the narcissist is in constant fear of being abandoned.

Anxiety is a looming sensation for the narcissist, who projects this sensation onto their siblings, partner, or parent. This is not an enjoyable sensation for the narcissist, so they rather throw it onto someone else.

Shamelessness may appear to be a trait of the narcissist, but it is truly an expression of the opposite. Shame means that there is something wrong about a person, and the narcissist cannot cope with this notion. Feeling shame is the enemy, so they do not allow themselves to feel it and bury it deep inside their subconscious. They hate that they possess insecurities and fear, and live with this lingering sensation that becomes projected on the closest loved one who may 'find them out.'

Since the narcissist doesn't want to accept that they feel fear or insecurities, they are unable to feel vulnerable. This makes it difficult to create and maintain close intimate relationships. The narcissist is constantly displaying this flawless sense of self-importance and perfection to the point where the true human beneath that is hidden from those that the narcissist considers the most important.

Lack of empathy means that the narcissist cannot work or communicate in a group setting, because only their wants, needs, and thoughts are what truly exists in their world.

CHAPTER 3

HOW TO USE DARK PSYCHOLOGY TO MANIPULATE OTHERS

Dark psychology is an art and a science—it seeks to manipulate others in a way that controls the other person. Through a series of behaviors such as manipulation, coercion, or persuasion, an individual seeks to get exactly what he or she wants, no matter the cost. By and large, people care about how other people feel, and endeavor to behave ethically and acceptably, but what about the minority of people who do not?

What is Dark Psychology?

Dark psychology refers to the mindset and techniques people can use to get what they want. Often aligned with the dark triad and manipulative people seeking to better themselves while harming everyone around them, dark psychology can be an effective skill to develop and master for yourself if you have to interact with other people. In fact, many people in public positions or positions of power turn to dark psychology to learn how to better get the results they want. Even salespeople frequently are taught skills that would fall within the list of dark psychology manipulation or mind control.

Keep in mind that there is manipulation, and there is an influence. Influence is normal; it involves swaying others to allow for goals to be worked toward. When influencing others, boundaries are honored and it is based on honest communication and respect for the other person, including respecting if the other person decides not to do whatever it is you would like. In contrast, manipulation is covert and coercive. The manipulator uses cunning and power to sway the other person. Rather than communicating clearly, the manipulator may lie or over-exaggerate in order to get the desired result. They may assert that they are in a position of power that they may or may not have, and they will push you to oblige them, preying on anything they can in order to get what they want. People are expendable. People's values are expendable. Anything is expendable if it means their desires are met.

Dark psychology's manipulation is primarily selfish. Every bit of manipulation is to ensure that the individual's wants come to exist. They do not care about the outcomes, or how it may impact the other person—they are only concerned with themselves.

These sorts of manipulative tactics and tendencies are encountered on a daily basis in a wide range of situations. Even television ads may inundate you with attempts to sway your perceptions of things in hopes of getting you to buy their products. In a world filled with constant attempts to manipulate you and sway your thoughts, you may be thinking, how can you possibly understand how to protect yourself from it? Or even better, how can you begin tapping into those skills to use them ethically to see the results you hope to achieve? The first step to this understands the key facets of dark psychology, from how it works to why people use it. Understanding and learning this information will prepare you understanding why.

How Dark Psychology Works

The entire construct of dark psychology and manipulation may seem difficult to understand—after all, avoiding falling for manipulation seems like an easy enough tasks to have, right? Unfortunately, manipulation can be quite covert, hiding underneath a thin veil of deniability and other pretty wrappings designed to keep the insidious nature of the manipulation undetected. There are several theories for how manipulation may go undetected, but for the purposes of this book, we will use one.

According to the psychologist, George K. Simon, there are three key aspects that make manipulation successful. These are:

Hiding the true intentions and behaviors behind something more friendly or good-natured. The truth may be hidden behind faux concern or authority.

Understanding the target's vulnerabilities so you can deliberately choose how to proceed. The manipulator takes the time to understand anything that can be exploited.

Being callous enough to not feel guilty at inflicting harm to the target if doing so becomes necessary. Even if whatever is done causes physical, mental, financial, or other harm, that is acceptable. Ultimately, the only person who matters is the manipulator, and the only goals that matter are his or her own.

Attempts at coercion and manipulation meet these three standards to be sufficiently successful to work. For example, imagine that you sell cars and you want to convince someone to buy a car that will land you a better commission. You would go through these three steps to influence your customer into buying them. First, you would likely want to disguise your interest in selling someone a specific car as concern for them. If they want to buy an older car, you may try to upsell the safety features of the newer model in hopes of convincing them to buy the more expensive car, or you may show how this newer model has some new feature that you exaggerate to make sound imperative to them. If they have children, you may try to emphasize how the trunk can be opened hands-free, or that there are a backup camera and sensors in the bumpers that will alert them in case a child were to sneak behind them.

Knowing that the parents are likely to be easily swayed by appeals to emotion, you may offhandedly mention how you had heard a story in the news about someone who accidentally ran over their child backing up, and that it was too bad that their car had not been equipped with the backup camera. You use your knowledge that parents are typically quite vulnerable when it comes to the welfare of their children and use that knowledge to your advantage.

Because you are detached from the target and motivated to sell, you do not feel any guilt about telling them the story. You want to instill fear in them that makes them feel like spending more money is necessary for the protection of their child's life. You want them to fear the consequences that could potentially follow if they do not do what you want. You want them to feel like their only option is to follow through with buying the car.

Ultimately, the three of those criteria combine, and you end up with the intended effect—the parents agree to buy a car out of their original price range out of fear of running over their child. You successfully took advantage of the situation, reading the situation and understanding exactly how best to proceed. These are the fundamentals of beginning to manipulate others.

No one enjoys being taken for a ride; no one likes being played for a fool either. Unfortunately, many people have these unpleasant experiences in almost every facet of human interaction. Worst of all, it happens to a lot of us more than once! The intriguing thing is not that we were played for fools; rather, it is that we come out of the experience with a determination to never fall for such tricks ever again only to find that we have been tricked again and again.

Perhaps, this book you are reading right now is the wakeup call you need to jar you out of your psychological slumber and do something practical about your decision to not have a repeat experience of emotional manipulation ever again.

What is Emotional Manipulation?

For the sake of clarity, let us have a working definition of what emotional manipulation is.

Emotional manipulation is the temporal takeover of your ability to think and act rationally. When someone acts or says things that distract or bypasses your rational and conscious mind, and then hijacks your emotions to the point of influencing you to feel a certain way or behave in a certain way, they are, at that moment, manipulating your emotions.

Such people who have practiced the art of emotional manipulation or who have developed the bad habit of manipulating others are capable of making you do what you would normally not do. Beyond making you behave in negative ways, shrewd influencers can completely ruin your career, destroy your love life, and cause havoc in your relationship with others. It doesn't matter how academically intelligent you are, if you do not take steps to protect yourself from emotional saboteurs by developing your emotional intelligence, you may learn the hard way why being street smart is as equally important as being book smart.

Emotional manipulation is simply a mind game. Although some people have psychopathic and sociopathic issues, while others go through some training to attain mastery in the art of mind games, everyone is born with the ability to manipulate others for positive and for negative purposes. Children do not need formal training in neuro-linguistic programming before they can push their parents' guilt buttons, neither do they have to be coached before they use flattery to warm their way into the hearts of parents and adults right before they present their requests. Passive aggression doesn't have to be taught to any child before they use it to manipulate parents and adults into submission. These things are inborn and can be used for the benefit of all involved in any interaction (a win-win situation) or strictly for the selfish benefit of the manipulator.

Usually, those who are manipulated emotionally have unknowingly surrendered a part of their self-esteem, self-worth, and self-image to the manipulator. This is why the longer a victim stays in a manipulative relationship (either personal or professional relationship), the more damage is done to their overall sense of self.

As you will discover from reading this book, self-awareness is a very important quality to develop if you must accomplish your goal of not falling again for manipulators. The more aware you are of your emotions and your tendency to react to others, the greater your chances of gaining control of your thoughts, emotions, and your behavioral response.

Look at it from this angle: since emotional manipulation is all about mind games, the person with greater control of your emotions wins the game. So, if you gain control over your thoughts, emotions, and behaviors, there is little to no chance that you will be played for a fool again and again.

Let us now give our attention to finding out who a manipulator is, their goals, and the tools with which they use in the art of manipulation.

Who is a Manipulator?

In the simplest terms, a manipulator is someone who uses people to influence the outcome of a situation usually to their benefit. In other words, when someone gets you to think and act in ways that please them, they have manipulated you. The outcome that a manipulator seeks can include:

To use their victim to gain access to power or to seize power.

To gain partial or total control in a relationship or at work.

To take the credit for another person's hard work.

To enjoy the benefits of their victim's hard work.

To make another person take the fall for their faults.

To achieve their devious goals, manipulators can use any of the following tools:

- Deceit – deliberately withholding vital information, misleading with words, actions, or inactions, being dishonest, and being generally fraudulent.

- Guilt – making you feel responsible for an unfortunate outcome.

- Lies – deliberately twisting the truth or spreading outright falsehood about their victims.

- False hope – making empty promises, using future events that may not ever occur as baits for their victims.

An emotional manipulator has a deep-seated need to be in control. Underneath that desire to always be in control of people and situations is the feeling of insecurity. To mask that insecurity, an emotional manipulator will sometimes put on the appearance of someone domineering and powerful.

A person who is in the habit of manipulating others has little to no regard about how his or her behavior affects their victims or others around them. Their desire to be in control and to feel superior is more important to them than any other thing. This is why they carefully seek out vulnerable individuals who will dance to their tune and validate them. When you succumb to a manipulator or even react in an emotional outburst, you give them power over you.

Why People are Emotionally Manipulated

From ill-famed world leaders to leaders in the workplace and other social settings, emotional manipulation has been used to rally followers around selfish causes or goals. Emotionally charged speeches, well-timed body gestures, sarcasm, intimidation, aggression, and false hope have been used to get people to stop thinking and just act blindly! The question is: why do people tend to easily fall for these types of mind control tactics?

I am not implying that only people under another person's authority can be negatively influenced. In reality, your station in life doesn't matter much when it comes to emotional manipulation. You could be a follower, subject, sibling, child, subordinate, student, or any other person and still be able to negatively influence your superior. Isn't this why kids have their way with parents? Have you not witnessed or heard of bosses who are incapable of asserting their official powers over a particular employee because that employee has them wrapped around his or her fingers?

Why then do people of all class and position fall for manipulators? Two reasons stand out from all the other possible reasons: unhealthy self-esteem and fear. A person with healthy self-esteem does not need flattery to recognize their self-worth, neither does he or she respond to covert and overt aggression. Since they recognize the inherent and inalienable worth of every person, it is difficult to get them distracted by a feeling of pity for anybody. Having healthy self-esteem ensures that you are not easily pushed into feeling guilty for someone else's actions or inactions.

However, unhealthy self-esteem can make an individual seek validation of their self-worth from external sources. When a manipulator gets wind of this fact, he preys on that weakness by temporarily soothing their emotional need. As soon as the victim becomes comfortable and lets down their emotional guard, the manipulator nudges, and sometimes, coerces them into doing things they would not have normally done.

Fear, on the other hand, drives people to succumb to a

manipulator even long after they have discovered that the person is using them. Fear is the reason why a lot of people remain in a manipulative, controlling and toxic relationship. They fear:

Loss of basic needs: for those who are in a relationship where their daily sustenance depends 100% on a manipulative partner, they may continue to endure such emotional control tactics because of the fear of losing their only means of survival.

Confrontation: many people would rather avoid arguments and conflicts that are likely to arise from being firm and courageous. Confrontation gives them the jitters.

Discomfort: this refers to doing everything possible to stay clear of the awkward feeling that being assertive can bring about. Some people prefer the seeming peace than the uneasiness that will result in their relationship if they were to take steps to protect themselves from being controlled emotionally.

Loss of friendship or partnership: some people go to great lengths to keep their relationship even when it is causing them deep hurts and subjecting them to negative influences. They simply cannot picture themselves without the other person; they are loyal to a fault. This makes them open to all sorts of manipulation as the other person takes undue advantage of their loyalty.

Loss of opportunity: this refers to remaining compliant and submissive to gain or keep an opportunity like free accommodation, gainful employment, and other benefits.

It is important to note that emotional control may not always present as someone trying to dominate and oppress you, at least, not at first. In many cases, it presents as being pleasant and nice but it later turns into manipulation and control.

If you are in a relationship that has any of the above characteristics, then you are in an emotionally controlling relationship. It is doing a lot of damage to your self-esteem. Over a long time, you will feel worthless and completely dependent on the other person.

There is a need to free yourself from such manipulation if you must regain your self-esteem.

Thankfully, this is the focus of the rest of this book.

Manipulation Techniques

Mastering the art of mental manipulation can be rewarding. Remember that a manipulator is going to try as much as they can to reach their end goal. To attain this end goal, the manipulator will apply any technique that they can to make people do what they want. The conventional techniques that manipulators like to use to fulfill their end goals include:

Blackmail

Emotional blackmail

Lying

Putting down the other person

Creating an illusion

These are going to be discussed in detail plus many different techniques not listed here.

However, if you are planning to use them, you need to be smart, practice a lot, and soon you can change the way others think and behave.

Let us dive in and discuss all the techniques in details.

Are you ready?

In the moral debate, manipulating minds of other people may appear unethical for many-and for a good reason. Basically, you are playing with other people's feelings, thoughts, and emotions for your own good. But it is up to you to decide what is right and what is not. This chapter guides you on methods that manipulators use to influence others.

You can attain a lot of emotional and financial advantage if you master how to play your cards right an how to make other people do whatever you want them to do whether men or women. The secret is to do it in such a way that they don't discover they are being manipulated. Don't forget the basic requirements that manipulators must fulfill for them to succeed.

Blackmail

Blackmail is the first method that manipulators may apply. Blackmail is described as an act that that involves threats that are unjustified to achieve a specific gain or trigger a loss to the subject unless the manipulator's demand is realized. It can also be described as an act of coercion that encompasses threats of prosecution as criminal, dangers of grabbing the target's property or money, or even risks of causing physical pain to the subject. There is a long history of blackmail. Initially, it was a phrase that referred to a payment that the settlers left to the area that was neighboring Scotland to the chieftains in charge. This payment was made to provide the settlers with security from the marauders and thieves that were moving to England. Since then, it has changed to mean something different, and in some cases, it is an offense in the US. For the sake of this section, blackmail is more than sending threats, either emotional or physical, to the subject to coerce them into performing what the manipulator requires.

In some cases, blackmail is described as a form of extortion. While there are occasions when the two are used interchangeably, there are some slight differences. For instance, extortion occurs when someone grabs the personal property of another by threatening to harm the person if the property is not given. On the flipside, blackmail happens when threats are applied to prevent the subject from taking part in lawful activities. Sometimes, these two events may work together. The individual may threaten someone and demand money to be set at bay and not harm the subject.

The manipulator is going to use this technique to achieve what they want. They are going to spend time to learn a thing of personal nature concerning their subject and then use that as a means of blackmail against them. They may blackmail their subject by threatening to send an embarrassing secret or even by destroying their opportunities of landing a new job or promotion. Or the manipulator might operate more shockingly by threatening to physically harm their subject or the family of the subject if they fail to agree with the manipulator. Whatever the blackmail may be, it is used to assist the manipulator in reaching the final goal with the help of the subject.

Emotional blackmail

It is another tactic that can be used by the manipulator. In the following technique, the manipulator will aim to inspire sympathy or guilt in their subject. These two emotions the strongest for humans to feel and they will always be sufficient to trigger the subject into the action that the manipulator requires. The manipulator is going to take advantage of this to achieve what they want. They will apply the sympathy or guilt that they motivate to coerce the subject into cooperating. The level of sympathy or guilt will always be blown out of proportion, causing the subject to likely help in the situation.

The reason for using this technique is to play around with the emotions of the subject. In the normal blackmail, the subject has to deal with a threat, mainly in terms of physical harm to themselves or a person they love. For emotional blackmail, the manipulator will attempt to activate emotions that are strong enough to incite the subject to act.

Although the subject may feel like they are helping out of their free will, the manipulator has worked to make sure that the subject is helping and will and will trigger the emotions again when it is required.

Putting down the other person

There are many alternatives manipulators have when they want to make their subject to help them attain their end goal. One successful approach is when the manipulator can put down their subject. In normal situations, if the manipulator applies verbal skills to put their subject down, they will run a high risk of causing the subject feel like a personal attack has been put on them. When the subject feels like they have been attacked, they will bristle and avoid helping the manipulator in a way that they would like. However, the subject will not like the manipulator and will distance from the manipulator as far as they can, making it difficult for the manipulator to realize their end goal.

This is the reason why the manipulator is not going to move around and put down their target. They need to be discreet about the process and look for a way to do it without making the subject feel like they are being attacked. One way that this can be accomplished is through humor. Humor can reduce the barriers that may otherwise appear because humor is funny and makes people happy. The manipulator can change their insult into a joke. While the put down has been converted into a joke, it will work effectively as if the joke was not present without creating any scars on the subject.

Usually, the manipulator will instruct their subject in

the form of a third person. This allows them to mast whatever they are saying quickly plus offering an easy means to deny causing harm if it comes back to haunt them later on.

For instance, they may begin their put down with "other people" if the subject can guess that the comments were made at them, then the manipulator would finish it with a throwaway line that may include something like "present company excepted, of course."

The concept of the put down is to make the subject feel like they are less than the manipulator. It upgrades the manipulator to a new level and leaves the subject feeling like something is needed. The subject is likely to improve things and correct any wrong that they have made. This will make the manipulator powerful, and they will easily get the subject to help them.

Lying

Regardless of the manipulator's end goal, lying is a tactic that they are an expert in and which they will exercise all the time to get what they want. A manipulator can use different forms of lies to allow them to realize their end goal. One is that they can lie entirely and in some cases, eliminate elements of truth from their subjects.

When a manipulator tells a lie, it is because they are aware that the lie is going to progress their agenda more effectively than the truth. Telling someone the fact may cause them not to want to assist the manipulator and that would go against their plans.

Instead, the manipulator will lie to get the target convinced to do something for them and by the time the subject discovers the lie, it is too late to correct the issue.

The manipulator may choose to remove part of the truth in the stories they narrate. In this approach, they are going to say parts of the truth but will hide certain things that prevent the progress made. These lies can be dangerous because it will become increasingly challenging to tell the reality of the story and what the lie is.

It is critical to note that when you are working with the manipulator, anything that they tell you could be a lie. It is not a great idea to trust anything that the manipulator is saying because they are attempting to abuse and use their subjects to reach the end goal. The manipulator is going to do and say anything possible, even lying to achieve what they want, and they aren't going to feel sorry about it. As long as they accomplish what they want, they are not too concerned about how it is changing the subject or others close to them.

Building an illusion

Apart from lying, the manipulator is going to be an expert at creating illusions that are capable of generating their final goal more effectively. They will work to build a picture that they want and then convince the target that this illusion is a reality; whether or not it doesn't matter to the manipulator. To achieve this, the manipulator is going to generate the evidence that is required to prove the point that works to their purpose.

To begin the illusion, the manipulator has to plant the ideas and evidence into the minds of the target. Once the intentions are in place, the manipulator will step back for some days and allow the manipulation to happen in the minds of the subjects over that period.

After that period, the manipulator will have an

opportunity to get the subject to follow the plan.

Manipulation is a method of mind control that is hard for the subject to avoid. Manipulation can happen in daily life, and in some cases, it can happen without the subject having enough power of it. The manipulator is going to work discreetly to attain their end goal without getting the target suspicious and affect the process. The manipulator will not worry about who they are harming or how others may feel, and most of them are not capable of mastering the needs of their subjects.

They know that they need something and that the subject they have selected is going to assist them in achieving their goal.

The strategies that are explored in this chapter are designed to help describe what happens during the manipulation process and how the brain of the manipulator operates. It is always good to distance from someone who may be a manipulator so that you can avoid this form of mind control.

The fear and relief technique

In a nutshell, the fear-and-relief method requires a person to play with the other person's emotions.

Although this technique can indeed generate a lot of stress and anxiety, it is very effective.

The method has two parts: First, make the other person fear something. It will rapidly make him vulnerable to the illogical behavior that you can apply for your advantage. Then you can provide him with a relief of the fear that he experiences. The most challenging part of this technique is to determine what to use to scare another person. Of course, you cannot continue to come up with scary things hoping that the other person will begin to be scared. You need to be creative and come up with a smart idea of what you are going to say and how you are going to say before you approach the person. Then you need to be armed with a solution that will save him from the uncomfortable feeling.

The technique is always applied in the media to catch the attention of viewers. For instance, the news channel can scare people with a dramatic headline. Then they end up with what you need to do, "keep watching for the updated information of what to do."

Probably, you know that you are not a news channel, but that doesn't imply that you cannot use fear and relief method to manipulate others. You can scare people with anything ranging from their career goals to personal relationships. Be creative, study your target and develop the best strategies of doing the method.

Once you realize that the person you want to manipulate is going to give up, that is when you assist them in relieving stress and releasing all the steam. You are attempting to give that person mood swings that will make him or her completely disarmed. When that occurs, the person in question is more likely to perform whatever you need them to, as evil as that may appear.

CHAPTER 4

MANIPULATION TECHNIQUES

Everyone in the world has likely used manipulation at some points in their lives. This could have been through telling the most straightforward lies to get out of situations or by flirting with others to get what you want. In understanding the techniques used by manipulators in their work, you need to ask yourself the following question:

Who is at threat from a manipulator? To regulate their victims, the pullers of the strings (manipulators) use several tactics, but most importantly, they do this by targeting specific kinds of personalities. You are more likely to be a victim of manipulation if you have low self- esteem, if you are inexperienced, pleased easily, if you are not confident about yourself and if you lack assertive instincts.

What are the requirements for successful manipulation? Primarily, successful manipulation encompasses a manipulator. Manipulation is also likely to be achieved through covert hostile methods. For successful persuasion, a manipulator has to:

- Cover their violent purposes, deeds, and be friendly.

- Be aware of the psychological susceptibilities of the targeted person so as to conclude which strategies are likely to be the most effective.

- Have an adequate level of callousness to have no doubts about triggering injury to the victim if necessary.

- The manipulators exploit different defenselessness habits that exist in the victim's character and such include:

- The naïveté of the targeted person - Based on naïveté, the targeted person experiences hardships to buy the notion that many human beings are always sneaky, deceitful, and hard-nosed. This means if you are the victim, you will be in denial that you are being victimized.

- If you are over-conscientiousness - This is where you find yourself ready to grant the exploiter the advantage of distrust. The manipulator ends up blaming you and supporting their side, which makes you trust them easily. If you are too honest, you end up thinking everyone else is reliable as well.

- Self-confidence - Controllers often check whether you are a self-doubting person and whether you lack self-assertiveness, and this makes you go into a defensive mode effortlessly. You end up not giving a second thought about errors.

- Over-intellectualization - This makes it hard for you to understand and therefore, you end up believing your manipulator's reasons for being hurtful.

- Your emotional reliance - If you have a submissive personality, you are more likely to be a victim of manipulation. The more you rely on your emotions, the more vulnerable you are to being manipulated.

- Loneliness - If you are a lonely person, you are likely to agree to take little proposals of social interaction. Some manipulators will propose being your companion, but at a price. This also involves being narcissistic whereby, you fall easily for any kind of unjustified flattery. Lonely people act without any consultations. Therefore, loneliness goes hand in hand with being impulsive.

- Materialistic - Having a get-rich-quick mindset makes you cheap prey for manipulators. This means you are greedy and want to get rich quickly, hence end up acting immorally for some sort of material exchange.

- The elderly are also at a higher risk of getting controlled easily because they are fatigued and not able to multitask. Likelihoods the elderly will have a thought that a manipulator might be a conman are very rare. Manipulators thus take advantage of them and commit elder abuse.

Techniques of Manipulation

Manipulators take time to explore and examine your characteristics and find out how vulnerable you are to exploitation. They tend to control their victims by playing with their psychological characters. Having read the points above, now you need to know what the tactics and techniques are manipulators use to control their victims. They include various methods, as discussed below.

Techniques of manipulation

Reinforcement: This can be either positive, negative, or intermittent forms of reinforcement.

- Positive reinforcement: This involves the case where the manipulator uses praises, charms, crocodile tears, unnecessary apologizing, public acknowledgment, cash, presents, consideration, and facial languages like forced laughter or smiles.

- Negative reinforcement: A manipulator removes you from a negative situation as a favor.

- Intermittent reinforcement: This is also known as partial reinforcement. This creates an environment full of fear and doubts. It encourages the victim of manipulation to persist.

Punishment: The manipulator acts in a nagging manner. There is yelling, silent treatment, intimidating behavior, and threatening of the victim. Manipulators cry and tend to play the victim card, thus emotionally blackmailing the victim and can go further by swearing they are the innocent one.

Lying: it entails two ways; lying by commission and lying by omission.

1. Lying by commission - You will find it hard to tell when a manipulator is lying the moment they do it, and the truth won't reveal itself until it is too late. You should understand that some people are experts at lying and thus you should not give in easily to their tactics.

2. Lying by omission - This is a subtle way used to manipulate, and it entails telling lies, and at the same time, withholding significant amounts of the facts. It is also applied in propaganda.

Denial: Manipulators rarely admit they are wrong. Even when they have done something wrong, they will refuse to believe it. They are rational and always assert that their behavior is not harmful or they are not as bad as someone else has explained. They accompany every exploitation with phrases like, 'it was only a joke'.

Attention: This includes selective inattention and attention. In this case, manipulators deliberately refuse to listen or pay attention to anything that distracts them from their agendas. They always defend themselves with phrases like, 'I do not need to listen to that'.

Deviation: Controllers never answer any questions directly and always steer the discussion to another topic. If not so, the manipulator gives irrelevant or rogue answers to the direct questions asked.

Intimidation: In this case, the manipulator applies two methods of intimidation; covert intimidation and guilt trip. In underground extortion, the manipulators throw their targets onto the self-justifying side through the use of implied threats. A guilt trip is a technique where the manipulator tries to suggest to the meticulous prey that they no longer care and this makes the victim feel bad and they start doubting themselves, hence, they find themselves in a submissive position.

Use of Sarcasm: The manipulator shames the victim by using put-downs and sarcasm that makes the victim doubt themselves. Making the victim feel unworthy gives an entry for the manipulator to defer the victim. These shaming tactics may include fierce glances, unpleasant tones, rhetorical comments or questions, and subtle sarcasm. Some of the victims end up not daring to challenge the manipulator as it fosters a sagacity of meagerness to their targets. Belittling their Target: Manipulators use this technique to put their target on the self-justifying side, while at the same time, covering the belligerent aims of the persuader. The persuader then misleadingly blames their target in response to the victim's defensive mechanisms. This also involves the case where a manipulator plays the victim role by portraying themselves as victims of circumstances to gain sympathy, thereby, getting what they want. This technique aims at the caring and compassionate victims as they cannot stand seeing someone suffer, and thus, the manipulator takes that chance to get the victim's cooperation.

Feigning: Manipulator pretends that any harm caused was unintentional or they are being accused falsely. Manipulators often wear a surprised face, hence making the victim question their own sanity. Feigning also involves the case where the manipulator plays dumb and pretends they are totally unaware of what the victim is talking about. The victim starts doubting themselves while the manipulator continues to point out the main ideas they included just in case there is any doubt. This happens only if the manipulator had used cohorts in advance that helps them in backing up their stories.

Seduction: In this case, the manipulator uses praise or any form of flattery, which involves supporting the victim to gain their conviction. Manipulators can even start helping you to increase your loyalty, and it will be hard for you to suspect their ill intents. The manipulator can as well play the servant role where their actions will be justified by phrases such as, 'I am just doing my job' or 'I am in service to a certain authority figure.' In this case, the victim will give their trust and end up being manipulated.

Brandishing anger: The manipulator shows off how angry they are in order to intensify the victim's shock to get their submission. In the real sense, the manipulator is never angry, but they act like they are, especially when denied access to what they want. A manipulator can as well control their anger to avoid any confrontations or hide their intents. Manipulators often threaten the victims by saying they are going to report the cases to the police. Anger is a way of blackmailing the victim to avoid telling the truth, as it wards off any further inquiries. This makes the victim focus more on the anger of the manipulator rather than on the manipulation technique being used.

The Bandwagon effect: This is the case where the manipulator tends to comfort the victim by claiming that, whether right or wrong, many people have already done some things, and thus, the victim should do it anyway. The manipulator uses phrases like 'Many people like you...' This kind of manipulation is mainly applied to those under peer pressure conditions. Similar cases are when a manipulator tries to lure the victim into taking drugs or abusing other substances. The techniques discussed above are the tested and proven tactics that any manipulator will strive to use to get a strong control of their victims. Before a manipulator persuades their victims, there are those steps they have to follow to make sure they fully control their victim's minds.

Whatever the reasons for manipulating someone, you should always play your cards safely. That is why you should learn how to manage and control the thoughts of people, the strategies, and steps you need to use in various situations. There are three authentic manipulating skills you can learn quickly through the steps discussed below. If you want to manipulate others in an easy way, come on! Shed a fake tear and follow the following steps.

Apply Different Persuasion and Manipulation Techniques

I. Always Start with Unreasonable Requests in order to Get More Reasonable Ones: This step is a time-tested technique for persuasion. As a manipulator, you should always start with unreasonable demands, and then wait for the victim to deny you, then follow it up with a more approachable request. It will be hard for them to reject you for the second time, as the second request will sound more appealing as compared to the first request.

II. Ask for a Rare Request before Your Real Request: This is another way of getting what you want as it entails requesting a strange thing that throws your target off guard, making them unable to deny you. Then ask for the more usual type of request, and the victim will not be able to deny it since their mind has been trained to avoid these activities.

III. Stimulate Fear, Then Liberation: For successful persuasion, tell the person what they fear, and then relieve them of it, and with no doubt, they will be happy to grant your wish. It may sound mean, but you will get your results instantly.

IV. Make your Target Feel Guilty: Making your target feel guilty is another step for a successful manipulation. You need to start by picking someone susceptible to feeling guilty. This should be followed by making them feel like they are bad for not granting your requests, no matter how absurd it is. The following can be the unchallenging victims who will fall into your persuasion technique:

- o Parents - Manipulate your parents by making them feel guilty. Mention to them how you feel your life is full of sufferings since childhood because they are not granting your wishes.

- Friends - Remind them of all the good deeds you have done for them or else tell them how they usually let you down.

- Significant partner - Conclude your quarrels by saying 'Okay- furthermore I expected this.' This will make them feel guilty about letting you down several times.

I. Bribe: In this step, blackmailing is not necessary to get your wishes granted. Bribe your victim with an unappealing present. You can as well offer something you would have done anyway. First, you should figure out what your targeted person wants or lacks at the moment, then try giving it to them. Secondly, do not make it sound like you are bribing, but portray yourself like someone who is willing to help your victim in return for something you want.

II. Playing the Victim: Making yourself the victim is always a great manipulation technique. You should use this step sparingly and effectively to pierce your victim's heart and get what you want. You have to act like you are a wonderful person, philanthropic, and that you are always the victim of every evil on earth. Play dumb as it makes your victim believe you are honestly perplexed by why evil things always befall you. Saying 'It is okay- I'm used to this' makes your victim feel like someone who cannot help you wall you a number of times and this tactic will make you get what you want. Finally, always be pathetic.

'It is okay- I'm used to this'

Apply Logic: This step works better for the rational-minded people. Logica; acts as the most excellent persuader, more so when you carry along with come-oriented whys and wherefores on how what you are after would benefit both of you. While presenting your case, do it calmly and rationally to avoid losing your control. If you want to manipulate a rational person, NEVER be emotional. In this step, act like your request is the only option you have, and your victim will judge the case your way.

III. Never Break Character: When your friend, family member, or co-worker tries to manipulate you, pretend to be more upset than them. Look more hurt and tell them you are even amazed and you did not believe they could ever think that about you. This will make the victim feel guilty and sorry for you.

CHAPTER 5

IDENTIFYING MANIPULATOR TYPES

Have you ever felt a sudden lack of self-confidence or, worse, this curious and agonizing impression of not knowing how to communicate? Have you ever been deafened by doubt about your skills or qualities? Have you ever been inhabited by that feeling of inferiority that paralyzes you, chills your blood and prevents you from reacting normally? If you have ever experienced this kind of situation, it is because you have been the victim of type III manipulation and placed in the line of sight of a manipulator.

We remember that the second type of manipulator is a selfish or egocentric person who thinks only of his interests, without worrying about the consequences. But the type III manipulator, which is also called the manipulator, has a very different characteristic intention. His only goal is to destroy. Everything he undertakes is meant to kill you, to ruin what you do, or to destroy an aspect of your personality that does not suit him.

The manipulator is characterized both by his will to harm and by a formidable ability to conceal. This is why many people do not trust him or take him for another.

The manipulator does not display distinctive signs, and his perversity does not necessarily read on his face. He is a true chameleon that hides behind deceptive appearances to better destroy. He can take the appearance of a parent who is "overprotective" and who, out of selfishness, prevents his child from becoming independent. The manipulator could be a nice grandmother who, secretly, gives money to her little girl who is in rehab to, supposedly, "help her hold on". It can also be a mistress, a lover, a boss, a neighbor, a teacher, or a long-time friend. In the cozy atmosphere of the offices, it is the collaborator willing to do anything to take your place or that colleague who seeks to devalue you because your expertise is shady.

His intention is to destroy. Sometimes it may bring him something, but in this case, it's a secondary benefit because what he's essentially aiming for is the destruction of who you are, what you do, or the other of your behaviors.

Illustration

It is through these situations and testimonies that we will examine the harmful activity of a type III manipulator.

- A man wanted his son, Jean, to succeed him by also becoming a doctor at all costs. When Jean announced his desire to leave school to become a musician, his father did everything to break that dream and bring his son back to what he thought was the right path. He tried to persuade his son that he was right in seeking to destroy this vocation. "I did it for your sake, you'll thank me later," he told him then. But what he put his son through was a terrible ordeal that almost drove Jean to suicide, as he felt rejected, devalued, ridiculed, humiliated, and disavowed deep within himself.

- A husband insidiously belittles his wife, Christelle, so that she stays at home. He has nothing against her. He simply does not want her to become independent because it's not how things are done in his family, and he earns enough to make her happy. As she does not agree, he will do everything to prove (by demeaning and humiliating her) that she is unable to do without him. From his point of view, he thinks he is acting justly and in the interest of his wife. But one can easily imagine that Christelle does not see things in the same way.

- A department head, who confronts and belittles a better-performing collaborator than himself, does not necessarily feel particular hatred toward this person. He is simply trying to break the person because he feels they are a danger to him and the only way he can defend his own mediocrity is to belittle them, to diminish them, or to put him in his place so that he does not do not encroach on the department head's work. He destroys what seems to him to be a threat that could prevent him from continuing to dominate the situation. In return, the employee can talk about bullying.

The type III manipulator is a weak man who, when he feels he is in danger, tries to diminish others. He advances masked. Where a normal person tries to surpass himself to become stronger (than whatever threatens him), the manipulator has no other resource than to weaken or treacherously destroy everything that worries him.

He destroys for the sake of destruction. He is mean and does not allow others to exist on their own. He wants to control everything. We cannot impress him. It makes you feel that you are small, weak, shabby; it turns you into a "mop", it tramples you and makes you incapable of any development.

He destroys you by giving you the impression that it is for your good, but we feel very bad in his presence. We cannot win. We are not recognized for what we would like to be. He does not listen to you, and his criticism is never constructive. When he says something, it's always negative. With him, one feels humiliated, discouraged, and degraded. He is a "mental assassin" and life with him is like slavery.

Harassment and Concealed Manipulation

Type III manipulation often goes unnoticed by those who experience it. This is called harassment or hidden manipulation. A large number of victims are thus abused and destroyed without their knowledge by the deceit and duplicity of a manipulator. After two pregnancies, Chloe cannot seem to get back to the weight she was as a young girl. She explains her fight against the pounds:

"When I discover a new diet, I hasten to try it. I am sure this time will be the right one. I do what it takes, and I feel good. I have a clear mind, I am dynamic. Sometimes I even go back to playing sports. I do everything I can without effort, and I start losing weight. And then, brutally, without my understanding why, I fall back into the fog. I have no courage, I ruminate on the same black thoughts, I do not do anything, I am exhausted, and I spend my time sleeping. Then, seeing all the tasks accumulating around the apartment, I feel guilty and without realizing it, I start eating again. I call myself names while looking at my belly and my thighs in the mirror of the bathroom. Every day, I decided that, the next day, I will put myself firmly on a diet and that this time I will get there. Today, I am completely desperate because despite all my attempts, every time I get on the scale, I can see that I still gained weight."

While a hidden manipulation is hardly perceptible from

the inside, this is not the case when we observe it from the outside. This is what a friend of Chloe tells us about her weight problems:

"I have known Chloe for many years. She was always a little concerned about her weight, but it almost became an obsession from the moment she met Guillaume, her future husband. He is a charming boy, but he attaches great importance to appearances. Since Chloe gained a little weight, having had her children, he frequently comments on it. He always comments nicely, in the tone of the joke, but I think it comes a little too often. I also see that Chloe is touched, even if she pretends to laugh with the others about her 'little bulges' as she says. But I can see that deep down she is hurt when he makes fun of her in public. Moreover, in the days that follow, she regularly buys clothes that are too small, claiming that she is going to lose weight. The other night, I was at home, and he did not stop criticizing a common friend who had grown enormously. He told multiple bad jokes about his plumpness and talked about the contempt he had for people who do not know how to control their weight. When Chloe came out of the room with tears in her eyes, he suddenly changed the subject of conversation. Everyone was embarrassed, but he did not seem to notice. The worst part was that he seemed satisfied with what he had just done as if it were a good joke. I thought about Chloe, and it was really awful to see how happy he looked."

A manipulator can be extremely pleasant and user-friendly. By appearing charming, playing on someone's guild, or using a respectable or simply authoritarian position, he creates a mirage that deceives his victims and prevents them from seeing that behind his disguise of the moment, hides a purpose that is invariably destructive and harmful. Moreover, it is very difficult to blame him for the behavior because he always has an excuse to justify himself: "I am only following the instructions. I do not have the right to disobey. I only did my duty. I acted believing it was the right thing to do. It was a joke."

To be sure, we can examine (below) the two sets of symptoms that signify the presence of a manipulator. The first contains the essentials of what one feels when one is a direct victim of a manipulator and the second enumerates what one perceives as a mere observer of a hidden manipulation.

Internal Symptoms of Concealed Manipulation

These are the main internal signals that can be seen when one is a victim of type III manipulation. These symptoms are far more indicative of the presence of a manipulator than the analysis of his words or deeds:

I alternate moments of enthusiasm and discouragement. I often feel a sense of guilt or doubt.

I find it difficult to defend myself or counterattack. I feel a sudden loss of confidence in myself.

I sometimes feel that I am "drained" of my energy. I feel physical or mental discomfort in the presence of someone.

That person belittles me one way or another. It is impossible to impress or affect her.

There is always a form of ambiguity between what she does and what she says. I am not well in my head or in my body when I am around that person.

If you have at least three symptoms, there is a good chance that you have been the victim of such manipulation. When all five symptoms are reached, manipulation is certain, and you should focus on finding out for sure who the manipulator is and how he proceeds.

Generally, someone with an outside perspective can find out much more easily because they will often notice things that one who is a victim and who lives things from within misses.

Emotional Intelligence and Manipulation

The term emotional intelligence was first invented in the 1960s and has become common over the years. However, the concept behind the term has been around for decades. In simple terms, emotional intelligence is the ability of a person to recognize and understand emotions, then using this information to make decisions. Like any other skill, emotional intelligence is a skill we can cultivate, sharpen and enhance. It is important to note that although emotional intelligence is a good skill, one can use it either for good or bad.

Once a person understands the power of emotions, he/she can use it ethically or unethically. The last thing that we want is having someone manipulating our emotions, whether it is a friend, colleague, or politician. There are some ways through which a master manipulator can use emotional intelligence against you. Please note that not everyone who has the characteristics listed below and used the said skill has selfish intentions. Some people practice them with no intended harm. Nonetheless, having an increased awareness of these behaviors will empower you to deal with manipulators strategically and sharpen your intelligence quotient in the process.

1. Manipulators play on fear.

Majority of manipulators will overemphasis specific points and exaggerate facts in an effort to make you scared and have you acting as they want. The way to identify this play is by looking out for statements that imply you are not strong or courageous enough or that if you miss out on a particular thing, you are a loser.

2. Manipulators deceive

Everybody values honesty and transparency thus will avoid deceivers. Manipulators understand this concept and are very cunning when lying. They twist the facts or try to show you only the side of the story that benefits them. For instance, a work colleague can spread some unconfirmed rumor to gain an upper hand. To avoid being deceived, do not believe everything you hear. Instead, base your choices on credible sources and ask questions if the details are not clear.

3. Manipulators take advantage of your happiness

Have you noticed that you are more likely to say yes to anything when you are happy or in a good mood? When we are happy, we tend to jump on opportunities that look good even before we think things through. Master manipulators have this knowledge thus will take advantage of the moods. To manage this emotional opportunity and avoid manipulation, work to improve awareness of your emotions, both positive and negative. strive to strike a balance between logic and emotions When making decisions.

4. Manipulators take advantage of reciprocity.

Do you know that feeling you get when you owe someone a favor especially if they helped you at one point? That feeling of debt makes one vulnerable. It is hard to say no to a manipulator if you owe them something. Most of the manipulators will attempt to butter and flatter you with small favors then ask for a big one in return. As much as giving brings more joy than receiving, it is more important to know your limits. Do not be afraid to say no when you have to even if you owe someone a favor.

5. Manipulators push for a home court advantage

It is very easy to convince a person when you are in a familiar place. As such, a manipulator will push you towards meeting you in a place he/she is familiar with while you are not. Ownership gives power and comfort thus a place like home or the office will give the manipulator some authority. you will have to make requests for meeting in a neutral place where familiarity and ownership are diluted so as to disarm the manipulator.

6. The manipulator will ask a lot of questions.

Naturally, it is easy to talk about oneself. Master manipulators know this thus they take advantage to ask some probing questions. Their agendas are hidden but basically, they seek to discover your weaknesses or other information they can hold against you. Of course, it would be unfair for you to assume that everyone has wrong motives because there are a few people who genuinely seek to know you better. However, it is okay t question people, especially those who reveal nothing about themselves.

7. The manipulator will speak quickly

In order to manipulate you through your emotions, the manipulator will speak quickly and sometimes use jargon and special vocabulary. This will give them an advantage because you will not have enough time to think. Fr you to counter this form of manipulation, do not feel afraid to ask for some time to process what the person said. Also, make a point of asking the person to repeat any unclear statements. To gain some control of a conversation, repeat the points the other person makes in your own words and let them sink.

8. The display of negative emotions

Some manipulators will use voice tones to control your emotions. The most commonly used tone and body language by manipulators are negative. For instance, basketball coaches (they use manipulation for positive purposes) are masters at raising their voices and using strong body language to manipulate the emotions of the players. To avoid such manipulation, you should practice pausing. it involves taking a break from the conversation or situation and having some time to think before reacting. In fact, you may walk away for some minutes to get a grip of your own emotions.

9. Manipulators limit your time to act

Basically, every manipulator wants to win. They may do this by ensuring that you do not have enough time to think. For instance, an individual may force you to make a serious decision in an unreasonably limited amount of time. He/she will try to steer your thoughts to their advantage. You will not have enough time to weigh the consequences. To avoid a situation where you give in without thought, do not be in a rush to submit. Ensure that the demand is reasonable. Take the pause, ask for some time, and if the person does not allow you to think, walk away. You will be happier looking for whatever you need elsewhere.

10. The silent treatment.

According to Preston Ni, a manipulator will presume

power in a relationship by making you wait. For instance, when a person deliberately fails to respond to your reasonable messages, calls, emails, or other inquiries, he/she makes you wait and at the same time, places uncertainty and doubt in your mind. Some manipulators use silence as leverage. To avoid being a victim of manipulation through silent treatment, give people deadlines and do not allow them to intimidate you. For instance, after attempting to communicate to a reasonable degree, let go of the mater and let the other person reach out.

Manipulators will work to increase their emotional awareness so as to have an upper hand on others. In fact, a large number of people are learning how to be emotionally intelligent. You too should seek to sharpen your emotional intelligence levels, for your own protection.

CHAPTER 6

THE MOST POWERFUL MIND-POWER TOOL

Humans spend countless hours seeking new ways to work just about anything. Through endless hours of research, they pour over books and journals looking for the message that will tell them the secret to harnessing mind power. Many never realize that the most powerful mind power tool is already on board and just aching to be used. It is the human brain, the mind itself.

Every time a person practices a new habit or thinks a new thought, they make a new pathway in the brain. Every time the habit is used, or the idea is thought, the nerve pathway becomes even stronger. The human brain is wired at birth to be an efficient machine and it is ready, from birth, to make an ever increasing amount of nerve pathways and to strengthen the pathways that are used the most.

Sometimes thoughts and habits need to be changed

for the improvement of the person. When people decide that they would like to make a change in their lives, there will be a period of adjustment. This is true whether the change is mental, emotional, or physical. During this period of adjustment, there will be some level of discomfort. When a habit or a thought is already formed, it has made its own path in the brain. When a stimulus is seen or heard, the message travels along the preset nerve pathway to the spot in the brain that controls that thought or habit. In order to change a thought or a habit, it is necessary for the nerve path to be changed. Until the nerve path is changed, the old nerve path will remain in the brain. The discomfort comes from the brain trying to automatically access the old pathway and the new pathway at the same time. This is painful for the brain to do.

It is easy to become frustrated when the brain goes back to its old patterns of thought and habit. Never fall into the habit of placing blame on a lack of willpower. Willpower has nothing to do with it. It is a very difficult thing to override preset pathways in the brain. The brain is a very powerful tool. When will power fails and mistakes happen, remember to use kindness and compassion in dealing with the failure. The brain is very efficient at doing what it does. The only way to change the pathways in the brain is to keep working on new pathways that will eventually obliterate the old, undesirable ones.

The brain needs a clear understanding that changes are about to take place and new pathways are about to be laid down. Remind the brain that new habits and new thoughts will be replacing the old ones. Blaming failure on a lack of will power is a self-defeating statement. The process of making new nerve paths in the brain takes hard work and time. It will help to keep reminding oneself of the impending change. By doing this over and over, it makes the process no longer about possible character flaws. The focus is now put on the habit of thought that is being built.

Is it possible to build new nerve pathways in the brain? Yes, it is possible, and it can be done. If more proof is needed, just compare the adult brain to the baby's brain. Every current habit and thought a person has is the direct result of having spent time practicing them over and over until they created a pathway in the brain. New pathways can be created. Think of it this way: they already have. The baby's brain has no idea of anything. It has no thoughts or habits. Every nerve path currently in the brain was practiced until it became a part of the brain. Think of the baby. The baby lies around day after day and does baby things. Then one day the baby notices the shiny rattle that mommy is waving in front of its little face. The baby wants the rattle. As the baby is waving its tiny arms around, the mommy puts the rattle close enough so the baby can touch it with its wavering hand. After a few of these sessions, the baby gets the idea that if the arm is in the air it can touch the rattle. A nerve pathway is beginning to grow. So the baby decides to lift its arm to actively reach for the rattle. The baby will be unsuccessful at first because the arms will wave wildly and will not connect with the rattle. One day, the baby will actually grab the rattle, and the nerve pathway is then complete.

While this may seem like a very simple example, it is exactly how nerve pathways are created in the brain. Every action, thought, or habit has its own nerve pathway. All pathways must be created. No one was born knowing to sit in front of the television and mindlessly eat dip with chips. No one was born lamenting the excess pounds they carry in strange places. No one was born hating their body. All behaviors are learned, good and bad. And the bad ones can be replaced with good ones.

So if the ability to program negative thoughts into the brain exists, then the ability to disrupt those negative thoughts with positive thoughts also exists. The brain can be reprogrammed. It is a powerful tool, and its main function is to turn thoughts into reality. The brain is always working, so why not use the power of the brain to benefit rather than harm? Just because a particular habit or thought has been around all forever does not mean it needs to stay. Use the power of the brain to choose new habits and thoughts to focus on and replace the old, negative thought pathways in the brain.

The new thought needs to be believable; the new habit needs to be doable. It does not real good to try to stick to a habit that is impossible to accomplish or to try to believe a thought that is unbelievable. After years of seeing the reality of an obese body, it would be nearly impossible to suddenly believe that the image in the mirror is that of a skinny person. But the brain will likely accept something that mentions learning to take care of the body or learning to accept the body in order to correct its flaws. The brain will turn a belief in reality. Believing a positive thought will lead to quite a different result than the ending where only negative thoughts are present.

Be prepared to repeat and repeat some more. The primary key to being able to make a new habit stay is repeating it constantly. The more a new, desirable habit is practiced, the more the brain begins to accept it. The nerve path becomes stronger every day. With constant practice, this new nerve path will become the path the brain will prefer to use, and the old one will cease to exist.

In any case, be sure to allow enough time to effectively create a change. Accept the starting point and constantly visualize the ending point. Accept the fact that the path to the goal of a new habit or thought will not be easy or perfect. The path will almost never travel in a straight line. Sometimes people fall completely off the path, and that is okay too. Just get back up and get back on. Do not get sidetracked by the idea that this journey will be easy and carefree because it will not be. Just keep thinking of the new nerve pathway that will be created by the new thought or habit and it will eventually become a reality.

Most of the pathways in the brain are stored in the subconscious mind. This is the part of the mind that is always working without always being thought of. Think of learned skills like tying shoes, zipping a coat, and pouring milk into a glass. These were all learned behavior whose nerve pathways are firmly set in the subconscious part of the mind. This part of the brain is the bank of data for all life functions.

The communication between the conscious mind and the unconscious mind works in both directions. Whenever a person has a memory, and emotion, or an idea, it is rooted in the subconscious mind and translated to the conscious mind through mind power. The subconscious has the power to control just about anything a human does regularly.

For example, during meditation steady, deep breathing is usually practiced. The control of the breath is brought from the subconscious mind and given to the conscious mind to tell it to control the breathing. Once a pattern of deep steady breathing is begun by the conscious mind, the subconscious mind takes over and keeps the set rhythm going until it is told to stop. This is done by a conscious end to the deep breathing or an encounter with an outside stimulus like stress. The subconscious mind also processes the great wealth of information received daily and only passes along to the conscious mind those things that are necessary for the brain to remember.

When sending thoughts from the conscious mind to the subconscious mind, the brain will only send those thoughts that are attached to great emotion. The only thoughts that remain in the subconscious are those that are kept there with strong emotions. Unfortunately, the brain does not know the difference between positive emotions and negative emotions. Any strong emotion will work. Both negative emotions and positive emotions can be quite strong. Also, unfortunately, negative emotions tend to be stronger than positive emotions.

Step one in learning to use the power of the subconscious part of the mind will be to eliminate any thoughts that come with negative emotions. Also, negative mental comments will also need to cease.

Fears will usually come true, specifically because they are drowning in negative emotion. This is why negative ideas need to be eliminated because they can be very harmful roadblocks on the road to harnessing brain power.

One best practice to use to get rid of negative thoughts is to counter them with positive thoughts. This will take time and practice, but it is a very powerful and useful technique. Whenever a negative thought pops in the conscious mind, immediately counter it with a positive thought that is dripping with strong emotion. The actual truth will come out somewhere in between the two thoughts.

Another way to counter negative emotions is to delete them, just like using a remote control. When a negative thought comes into the conscious mind, imagine destroying it. Imagine writing that thought on paper and burning it. Imagine pointing a remote control at the thought and pressing a huge delete button. Whatever form used to imagine deleting the thought, the important thing is to get rid of it before it can take hold in the subconscious mind.

Find something energizing and use it to reach a goal.

Those things that are found to be energizing bring boundless energy to positive thoughts. It is often necessary to invent motivation, at least in the beginning, to learn to create new habits and thoughts. But with a bit of practice and a lot of positive thought, new positive habits will soon be burned into the subconscious mind and the old negative thoughts and habit will fade away.

CHAPTER 6

MASTERING YOUR EMOTIONS

Master manipulators are not at the mercy of their emotions. Instead, they have learned how to master their emotions and be in control, thus allowing themselves to think rationally while utilizing their mind instead of their feelings. If you are not in control of your emotions, you'll find yourself getting angry, sad and even frustrated in the course of your relationships. Such loss of control will be detrimental to your objective of having the upper hand. Learning how to control your emotions is a process that requires time and practice. You will not wake up one day and be a happy, confident person that never gets angry or sad. It is not an overnight process.

To control your emotions, you will need a period of time to go through the motions of recognizing your emotions and reigning in on them. Train yourself not to react immediately and irrationally to every emotion that presents itself in your life. Instead, step back and process this emotion by identifying what triggered it and what solutions you can apply to alleviate this trigger. For instance, if you get angry whenever someone makes a particular comment about you, you might want to go back and understand why this comment upsets you so much. Once you work on the root cause, you can thereafter start the process of being unbothered by such a comment.

In certain other instances, you might want to think of your relationships as business transactions where nothing should be taken personally. Detaching yourself from people will mean having fewer emotions to deal with as you will no longer be affected by their opinions about you. Instead, you will look at them from a benefits point of view where you take what you need and then go on your merry way. If you come across as the emotionally stable guy who can control himself in any situation, people will begin to trust you a little bit better. This is a handy advantage to have over others when you are trying to manipulate them subtly.

Timing and opportunity

No matter how good of a manipulator you are, you will never be successful if you do not get your timing right. There are instances where your tactics will not work, and not because they are not good enough, but because your timing is off. It is important to know when your target is more susceptible to manipulation, and when they just do not have the time to deal with you. Identifying the right opportunities will guarantee you far more success as opposed to going about the process haphazardly. Why do you think retail stores have sales at particular times of the month? They know that at this time their customers have the money and are ready to be manipulated aka indulge in some shopping.

Choosing a time that is most convenient for your target will yield better results for you. Consider this: you are trying to relax on the beach when this salesperson comes to you trying to sell you something. What are you likely to say? If you are a normal human being that likes their alone time and does not take well to vacation intruders, you will send the salesperson on their merry way--complete with a cuss word or two. What this salesperson does not know (besides proper etiquette) is that they chose the very worst of times--a time that was not convenient for you. As such, you will be looking to get rid of them and whatever they have to sell as swiftly as possible.

There are times in the day when you are likely to hear "yes" more often than "no". It is important to identify these times and then work them to your advantage. Sometimes, the issue of convenience is ignored, and it becomes a matter of vulnerability. A person who is tired is less likely to put up a fight. A boss who is rushing to catch a flight might be more inclined to say yes to your question so that they can be done with you and head for the airport. When it comes to timing and opportunity, you must balance the facts with your own assessment of every individual situation.

Physical contact

Physical contact is one of the most powerful tools at the disposal of a human being. A hug from a loved one, a pat on the back by a family member and even a cuddle with someone you are close to can do wonders for the human spirit. Soft, gentle, safe touch is healing to the human soul. It reassures the other party and creates an emotional connection. The firm touch of a masseuse kneading away at your tense muscles if rejuvenating. An innocent brush of the fingers with a stranger or a date might be all you need to know whether they are the one or not. When touched correctly, your body's stress hormone (cortisol) levels reduce while the happy hormones go up. You might not be aware of these fluctuating hormones, but you will instantly feel happier and lighter when properly touched. It is no wonder that merely hugging a loved one can take away all your worries instantly. In this state of happiness--and less cortisol cruising around their body--a person is not in flight or fight mode anymore and will likely comply with your requests.

If you are trying to make someone feel safe and secure around you, to the point where they can trust you, make use of the power of touch. There are different types of touch. The type of touch you choose will depend on the type of relationship you have with the other party. Seeing that touch is so powerful, it is important to acknowledge the double-edged sword that it is. Your touch can either make someone feel particularly comfortable around you or the exact opposite. The last thing you want to do is creep someone out when all you are trying to do is get them to agree to work your shift for you.

Here's the proper way to use physical contact to your benefit:

Watch their body language for signs that your touch will be well-received. Such signs include an upright posture coupled with a happy or neutral facial expression. If the person has a negative facial expression and seems to be hunched over, walk away. Such a person will not take kindly to your touching.

There is a safe zone for touching someone that is not well-known to you. This safe zone is the region between the elbow and shoulder. Any touch within this area is likely to be well-received, especially if you already determined that their body language is open to it. Consider touching this safe zone while shaking the other person's hand, as it would be awkward to just walk up to someone and touch their upper arm.

To properly touch someone, it must seem as if your action was entirely unplanned and spontaneous. The last thing you need is someone noticing that you planned to touch them because this would come across as creepy and awkward. Make your technique so swift and smooth that your touch comes and goes like a whisper in the wind. Do not touch and linger; touch and let go, in the most seamless execution that you can master. This is the difference between being a charming and affectionate guy and being the creep that everyone avoids.

Be confident when touching a person. People can tell if you are insecure about what you are doing, and this not only puts them off, but it also makes them incredibly uncomfortable. If you want to touch someone in order to make them compliant with your request, go for it without hesitation. Make it seem as if you have been touching people all your life. Remember that lack of confidence can show itself in your body language, so make sure you have taken care of this as well. Stand tall and exude confidence--then touch your target.

Smile as you touch your target. By touching this person, you are showing yourself to be open to them and willing them to be open to you. The rest of your body must communicate this. Do not touch someone while wearing a sour face, as this will come off as aggressive. Smiling makes you look more warm, welcoming and open, and your target will think that you are just a happy person who likes to be affectionate.

Fear and Manipulation

Why is fear such an effective tool in manipulation? Why do companies like to threaten you into compliance by asking you to buy something before stocks run out when they know full well that they have an entire warehouse of products? Why do manipulators like to instill fear in their victims? Fear is a negative emotion whose presence in the body inhibits rational decision making. Here's why:

When you are scared, there are only two thoughts on your mind: fight or flight. Nothing else. You really do not have the mind to start engaging in critical thinking or anything of the sort. Being scared or anxious sends your body into survival mode, and when you are in survival mode, you will choose one of two options that make the most sense to you. The neuroscience behind this is critical to understanding what makes fear such a favorite tool for manipulators. When your entire bodily systems are in that flight-or-flight response mode, your critical thinking circuitry is bypassed. In short, your brain does not have the intention to start processing the tiny details at the moment. So, instead of utilizing the more analytical neocortex to think, you rely on the primitive limbic system. Later on, when you are in a more relaxed state, your critical thinking capability is activated, and you start to wonder why you made that particular decision when in fact there were other options to explore.

At all times, be careful of anyone who cries wolf. They might be trying to distract you from the other options that are available to be explored in your decision-making. At the same time, you must take advantage of the opportunity presented by fear to influence other people. There are various ways of taking advantage of fear in situations. For a start, you can exaggerate a situation and make it seem far worse than it is. Let's say you are a manager and you catch this one employee skipping work without official leave. It's a slow day anyway, and there's not much work to be done--but they know they should not be skipping work, and you intend to take full advantage of this situation.

What to do? For a start, you need to make this seem like the biggest deal of the century. How dare they hide from work and expect to receive a paycheck at the end of the month? Do they know what would happen if this got to the other bosses? You might even want to mention that they have put you in a really awkward position by engaging in such a foolish act. Now that you have got your employee shaking in their boots (assuming that they really need the job and the paycheck) ask them whether they would be willing to work the weekend shift to make up for this lost time, in exchange for a slap on the wrist. The employee will most likely say yes. They have not had time to even come up with a good lie because their minds are in flight or fight mode. You'll then go on about your day happily knowing full well that you do not have to work the weekend shift and can instead spend the day doing what you truly enjoy.

Aside from exaggerating the truth, you can instill fear by spreading blatant lies. This approach has worked since time immemorial and continues to be effective to date. Using the same example of a manager, let's assume you have noticed that the employees are slacking in their duties, including coming in late for work and generally being lazy. You have tried all means to motivate them, and nothing seems to be working. What can you do? Consider this: find the one employee with the loosest mouth and let it slip that there will be an impromptu performance review by management sometime soon. This loose-lipped employee will do the legwork for you and ensure that the entire rumor mill knows what's about to happen. You will begin to notice that your employees are working harder and coming to work earlier because they are fearful of the consequences of facing management.

Fear in manipulation works best where the party that is being manipulated stands to lose or miss out on something. You must determine that whatever carrot you are dangling in front of your victim is worth their attention. Otherwise there will be no interest and consequently, no success in your manipulation efforts. If you know what makes someone tick, you will always know what buttons to push to make them fearful.

Raising Your Emotional Cleverness

Emotional intelligence is definitely something you have to work on throughout life. There are professions, or lifestyles, where high emotional intelligence might not be that necessary, however, the majority of us could do with better people skills, both in and outside function.

There are many ways of enhancing or developing your emotional intelligence. However, whichever method you choose to use, your time and efforts should concentrate on the seven simple routines which will help increase your EQ and indirectly make it easier to reach your goals, whatever they might be.

7 ways to increase your emotional intelligence:

Develop self-awareness

Self-awareness is about self-knowledge, about getting mindful of what is happening in your life, and about having an idea how you see your daily life or career developing. To be self-aware you need a certain degree of maturity and at least a vague idea of what you'd like to do with your existence. When you know what you want, it becomes easier to find a method of getting it. If you don't, you are left drifting aimlessly, with neither a goal nor a plan.

So, how can you develop self-awareness? Begin by increasing your sensitivity to your very own gut and emotions emotions, as they are generally the most trusted close friends you'll ever have. Make an effort to set aside a while for self-reflection, and think about your behavior, thoughts, emotions, frustrations, goals, etc.

Those who are used to self-analysis will find this easy probably, but if you're not used to this type or sort of thinking, this may be hard, even unsettling. In that full case, start by setting aside 30 minutes each night, once you're finished with the work for the day and may relax a bit, and think about the day or week behind you. If you had a difficult day/week particularly, ask yourself everything you can find out from the experience.

The purpose of this exercise is to truly get you used to considering how you feel and why.

Or, you may start journaling, and this is not about keeping a diary and covering your day-to-day thoughts and activities. Journaling is about recording any unusual or frustrating experiences, thoughts or emotions you might have had. Some things are not easy to go over with others, and anyway, not really everything is for posting, so why not get it off your chest by authoring it. The great thing about journaling is normally that to write something down, you need to believe about what to write, in fact it is often this technique of thinking about a problem that helps you see what's at the root of it. Therefore, if feeling upset, angry or disappointed, write it out and move on.

Understand your emotions and what triggers them

To comprehend your emotions you have to be willing to experience them. It's sad just how many people are afraid of their own emotions, especially negative ones, eg sadness, anger, bitterness, etc and the moment they feel these feelings taking over, they perform something that may interrupt their train of thought, eg they could active themselves with something in order to distract themselves from these unpleasant emotions.

In the event that you recognize yourself in this, you should know that all you will achieve this way is postpone (perhaps indefinitely) facing your own demons and dealing with whatever it is that's troubling you. Feelings need to be experienced and dealt with, not buried.

Intelligent folks are not scared of their emotions emotionally. Whatever it really is they feel, they keep at it for so long as it requires for the emotion to end up being identified. There is a reason you feel how you do, and instead of ignoring them, you should try to "decipher" your emotions because they are trying to let you know something.

To become proficient at understanding others, you first have to be able to understand yourself. So, even the emotions you don't actually want to feel should be addressed, processed, and let go.

Listen without judging

Good listeners are uncommon, mainly because this involves a whole lot of empathy, willingness to give up your time and effort for others, and mental energy to be present when you are listening.

The primary trait of a good listener is to pay attention with empathy, and which means without judging. This is not easy always, and may in a few full cases be difficult, so if you understand you are biased towards someone, it's perhaps better not to talk to them in the event that you know you have already made up your mind about how you are feeling about what they are going to say.

So, to become a great listener you should attempt to be present during the conversation, and stay focused. This can be hard, as some social people don't stop talking, or have a problem stating what they mean so you may be looking at a few hours. However, if you are not interested in this person really, or you are in a rush, or are not feeling well, try to postpone the conversation for another time. The tell-tale indications of disinterest or boredom, eg glancing at your watch, or checking your cell emails or phone, can be extremely insulting and discouraging for the person you are having a conversation with.

Emotionally intelligent people show interest in others by encouraging them to speak even more (even if indeed they don't agree with what they are saying), and by creating a host where it's safe to start and say everything you really mean.

So, the next time you speak to a person who requirements your opinion, advice or simply a shoulder to cry on, try to be patient (some people have a long time to come to the point), focused (reserve this time limited to them and switch off your phone), and non-judgemental (provide them with the benefit of a doubt). By not becoming and judging open-minded, you might not only help the person by giving them an opportunity to obtain something off their upper body, nevertheless, you may also gain insight into what's going on in your team, or a family.

Also, focus on body language, both yours' and theirs', eg the modulation of voice, facial expression, body posture, etc. To a casual observer, these would be clear symptoms how you both feel about the conversation.

Active listening takes a complete lot of practice, but it

is among those skills that you can practice every full day, of where you are regardless, and what it really is you are listening to.

Mind-Body Connection

This is about listening to the body and understanding what it's trying to tell you. According to the mind-body connection doctrine, irritation in a part of your body is definitely a sure indication something is not right. For instance, lower back discomfort is linked to financial problems, upper back discomfort to being overwhelmed with life, a knot in the tummy with nervousness or fear, etc.

Understanding how to notice these signals and interpret them, can help you save considerable time and difficulty with regards to understanding why you feel a certain way.

But, what frequently happens is that while your body is informing you that you are anxious, anxious, angry, or harm, you ignore these symptoms simply, hoping they would eventually go away.

Unfortunately, Western culture pays an excessive

amount of importance to feeling happy and high at all times, so folks are not encouraged to deal with their negative feelings, but are advised to ignore them, eg by repeating positive affirmations, or repair them, by taking something that will make them experience better. Do you really believe that if you ignore your adverse feelings, do it again a mantra or take something to make you feel high, you will eventually become happy, confident, and fearless???

Sometimes, when you're overwhelmed with emotions, it may be OK to calm yourself straight down, in unhealthy ways even, until you may clearly think. But, this only gives temporary respite and is not a solution to your problem.

Emotional intelligence will help you get to underneath of your emotions by showing you how exactly to work out what the triggers are, and how exactly to interpret and release these emotions in the least harmful way.

Engage

How involved are you with your community? Do you volunteer? Is there someone you are helping with by moral support frequently, financially or otherwise? Are you there for others if they need you even though you know it'll ruin your weekend which you had planned to invest with your family?

Empathy is the primary trait of intelligent people emotionally, and it could easily be developed by anyone if they follow a couple of simple tips on how to develop or improve these abilities. But, the simplest way to develop empathy can be through practicing it. Put simply, whenever you engage with others, you are doing what emotionally smart people do: you listen, you try to understand, you listen in.

Nevertheless, many people fake empathy due to the fact they'd like to be observed simply because emotionally intelligent. They say the right matter, are politically correct always, appear to be filled with deep empathy, listen thoroughly, offer help, etc. However, if caught off-safeguard or if for a few good reason not feeling in the feeling for putting up an act, their true character quickly comes out. Today, to advance professionally, if you see yourself as a head especially, you have to prove that you have high psychological intelligence, so those that fake it do that for self-promotion usually.

The easiest way to improve your empathy is to start

taking interest in others, eg how they live, what's troubling them, how they cope, etc. Improve your listening skills and try to possess at least one deep conversation per month. By engaging with others, you automatically increase your emotional intelligence.

Develop self-management

Self-management is about controlling your emotions, not in the feeling that you suppress them or ignore them, but figure out how to deal with them, and only release them after you have processed and understood them. Self-management is also about being accurate to yourself. Some of the real ways you can improve your self-administration are through developing your integrity, eg:

- Practice what you preach

- Be prepared to speak up, even though you risk being made fun of

- Don't make promises you are unlikely to keep

- Continually be polite and respectful with co-workers, it doesn't matter how close you might be

- Be self-disciplined, especially if you anticipate that of others

Learn to cope with criticism

Negative feedback is usually often undeserved and a result of the person presenting it is not fully aware of your performance, or using the opportunity to sabotage your self-confidence perhaps, or undermine your job openly.

However, if truth be told, atlanta divorce attorneys negative feedback there is usually a grain of truth. Although there might have been very good reasons why you underperformed or experienced a score of people complain about you, the truth is you failed. However, when you come to a stage when you're able to accept negative opinions, or open criticism, without taking it you demonstrate which you have both self-confidence and psychological intelligence personally.

So, how to become more open to negative feedback? Of all first, not all criticism is important equally, nor should you react to it in the same way. A colleague's remark about your brand-new hairstyle is actually a sign she's making fun of you, nonetheless it may be a subtle suggestion that the design doesn't suit you.

Besides, in the event that you receive less than

satisfactory feedback on your own performance repeatedly, or behavior, instead of sulking or throwing a tantrum, try to look in yourself through other people's eye. Imagine if you ARE lazy actually, or short-tempered, or unreliable?

The key thing is to consider why you are feeling bad about the feedback. Is it because it's really undeserved and due to the person giving it devoid of a complete picture, or are you angry with yourself for not having masked your underperformance better? Or simply jealous others do better?

Admitting you were wrong isn't easy, but surviving in denial is even worse. So, than experience upset about the opinions rather, try to find out something from it. Especially if it's not the very first time the same thing have been brought to your attention.

But, regardless of how you feel, be aware that negative feedback, if given without malice, can perform more for your personal development, than can false praise.

Besides, there is something noble about admitting you had been wrong. It could not be a pleasant thing to do, but it teaches you are mature more than enough to take both the credit for your successes and blame for your errors. This may encourage others to do the same.

The effects of emotional manipulation

Manipulation is a mechanism that the affective manipulator uses to assert itself due to a lack of self-confidence even though it seems resolved and decided.

He needs to have many individuals around him to continually confront and humiliate them to feel successful. The needs of those around him are not taken into consideration.

He is a true self-centered whose only goal is to admit that he is the best, denigrating the other. To humiliate one's victim has the aim of affirming her presumed superiority through direct criticism, irony, and indifference.

The manipulation produces devastating effects on those who suffer it, generates feelings of guilt, aggression, anxiety, fear, and sadness.

On the physical plane, migraines, digestive disorders,

lack of appetite or bulimia, knots in the stomach or throat and sleep disorders emerge.

If exposure to a manipulator is prolonged, these symptoms can turn into disease, which can also be followed by depression that can sometimes culminate in suicide.

Emotional counter-manipulation the fogging technique

No manipulator will ever admit to being the cause of these disorders, indeed. He will advise those affected to seek treatment without ever questioning themselves. The only way to defend yourself from an affectionate vampire's attacks is to not approach or manipulate them.

According to the therapist I. Nazare Aga, the manipulation of the "fog" consists of using vague and imprecise communication, not engaging in the verbal exchange.

The purpose of a superficial communication is to respond as if you were indifferent to the contents expressed by the manipulator, which consequently will no longer feel important. Communicating without aggression and vehemence will make the manipulator understand that the interlocutor is putting in place a passive resistance and this will lead him to spontaneously move away from the victim.

The most common verbal methods to counter manipulate are

- Not telling the details of one's own life, using a vague communication.

- Not answering uncleared questions.

- Not believing those who give compliments without knowing you.

- Communicating clearly when you don't agree.

- To express oneself firmly.

- Recognize the responsibility for one's actions and delimit it rationally. Whoever becomes the prey of an affective vampire does not recognize the danger and is in need of receiving the approval of others for their own choices.

Raising your Self-Esteem Levels

All of the aforementioned reasons a manipulator chooses a victim are related to self-esteem levels of the victim. It's very easy to fall into a pattern of nitpicking at everything we do wrong. I'll give you a personal example.

A few months ago I missed a deadline with a client at work and I felt terrible about it. Meanwhile, I had been doing awesome with other projects and excelling in areas that I never thought I would excel in, but that one missed deadline seemed to drag me down. The rest of my projects suffered and I ended up missing more due to my lack of motivation and ultimately, the low self-esteem I was beginning to suffer from due to stress. It doesn't take much to drag a person down in today's rough and tumble economy where we're constantly competing for jobs, love, and respect.

That's why it's extremely important to follow some of these steps to keep your self-esteem boosted that you are in a better position to defend yourself against the ruthless manipulators out there who want to drag you down.

Thirteen Ways to Boost Your Self-Esteem

These thirteen ways will help you boost your self-esteem levels so that you can handle the people who are attempting to manipulate you. If these do not help, I strongly suggest you see a therapist to get some more tips and discuss why you're feeling so low about yourself.

Start with Something Small

You're not going to change your outlook in just one day, so start with something small and easily obtained in order to give yourself a gentle boost in the right direction. It's like trying to clean an entire house that is stacked full of junk. You have to start somewhere, so start in the hall closet and celebrate your success. Then move on to the kitchen and keep going to each different room. Before you know it, the entire house is clean and your self-esteem has elevated.

Use Visualization and Make it Compelling

Your imagination is a very powerful tool and you should utilize it is often as possible when it comes to your self-esteem. When you imagine an outcome, make it positive and reinforcing, not doom and gloom. Take ten minutes every morning and find a quiet place in your home. Visualize how you want to be as a confident person and then write down all of those attributes you saw in yourself. By doing this, you are training your subconscious to behave the way you want to be.

Don't Underestimate the Power of Socializing

Find people who will support you no matter what and hang out with them more often. They will give you an opportunity to practice your interpersonal skills and help you see that there are other people out there who care about you. You don't need to rely on one person for your happiness.

Do Something that Frightens You

If you're afraid of going out to parties, go out to one alone and experience it to its fullest. Don't rely on someone else to hold your hand through the situation, and if you need to, practice some breathing exercises to get through it.

Do Something You're Good At

It doesn't matter what it is. It could be painting model airplanes or even crunching numbers for a budget. Do something that you know you're good at and that you will excel at so that you feel accomplished. This will boost your confidence sky high.

Have Goals

Without goals, you have no idea where you're going in life and whether or not you've accomplished something. You should always have something you're working toward and always reward yourself when you're finished with a goal. It doesn't matter if your first goal is to clean the bathroom, do it and reward yourself for taking the actionable steps to clean the bathroom. By accomplishing things and feeling good about them, we're boosting our self-esteem levels.

Helps Others Feel Good

Give others compliments when they're feeling low or teach them something they've always wanted to learn. By helping others, you're helping yourself feel wanted and productive. Just be sure that the people you're helping are not manipulators. Do not allow them to have control over the situation and always be aware of those who are trying to take advantage of you.

Get Clarity

You need to have a clear idea of where you are at your lowest on a self-esteem scale and which category you need to work on first. There are three main categories: health, relationships, and finances. Rate yourself on a scale of one to ten through those categories, and work on the one that is at its lowest point. By doing this, you will boost your self-esteem in all the other areas, too.

Have a Plan

Treat your life as if you're baking a cake. You need actionable steps in order to accomplish your goals, so make a list of small goals beneath your large one and then make a list of tasks underneath those goals. Take everything a step at a time so you don't become overwhelmed and quit prematurely. This will only hurt your self-esteem, so you have to be ready with a plan when you have a goal.

Become Motivated

It can be as simple as setting rewards for each milestone you complete underneath a goal, or it could be reading an inspirational book. We find inspiration and strengthen in others' ability to overcome hardships, so find something that really makes you want to get started.

Get External Compliments

It may seem awkward and a little odd, but go to a family member or a friend and ask them to be honest with you about your strengths and what they love about you. Sometimes we need to hear someone else tell us what we're good at, but don't rely on this too much. Take those strengths and expand on them with the knowledge you have about yourself.

Use Affirmations

Affirmations have to be used in the correct way in order to be productive and helpful. You cannot be sitting on your couch and tell yourself that you are highly motivated and productive. Instead, ask yourself why you're sitting on the couch and is this your best self? Is this what you want to be doing right now in order to be ideal? Your affirmations must be the truth, and not something that you want to be true. You have to be honest with yourself and take the first step toward doing something of value.

It would be empty words with no meaning if you sat down in front of a mirror and told yourself you were beautiful every morning without believing those words. You have to dig deep and find the belief that you are beautiful inside and mentally repeat it in order to make it stick.

Stop Comparing Yourself to Others

All too often we're stuck in this vicious cycle of comparing ourselves to others. We need to know what the latest fashion models are wearing so that we can emulate them. If our coworker has something that's better than what we have, well then, we must not be worthy of love or companionship. Stop looking to others for how you should feel about yourself. Just accept that you have to move at your own pace and travel your own path to becoming the person you want to be.

The Art of Subliminal Messages

Subliminal and dark psychology

Subliminal impact and subliminal informing are terms used to depict when messages are disguised out of sight of clamor (for example music, radio communicates, business jingles, and so forth.) or potentially pictures to embed specific data in your subliminal musings.

Reason

The thought is that your conscious personality can't recognize these messages, and in this manner, the subliminal mandate is ingested unchallenged into your intuitive where it can impact your contemplations and conduct. If you can deliberately recognize the message, at that point, it wasn't subliminal

One of the most well-known instances of subliminal informing are messages played during rest. ... In any case, in spite of it being made up, individuals weren't excessively content with the idea of this subliminal advertising.

Subliminal messages are boosts that lie beneath the edge of conscious mindfulness. ... Any change you need to make that can't be framed by mindfulness MUST be made on the intuitive personality level. The subliminal Affirmations in the sound is short explanations that rehash again and again.

A concealed message is data that isn't quickly recognizable, and that must be found or revealed and deciphered before it very well may be known. Shrouded messages incorporate in reverse sound messages, concealed visual messages, and symbolic or secretive codes, for example, a crossword or figure.

Laws. The United States does not have a particular government or state law tending to the utilization of subliminal messages in promoting. Instead, it is the nation's publicizing and broadcasting administrative organizations that manage the point and its effect on general society.

Anything a body can normally do you can summon with entrancing or subliminal messages. If it's outside of the body's capacity, you can't. So you can move digestion. However, you can't develop wings.

Dark psychology

Dark Psychology is the workmanship and study of manipulation and mind control. While Psychology is the investigation of human behavior and is integral to the considerations, activities, and connections, the term Dark Psychology is the marvel by which people use tactics of inspiration, persuasion, manipulation, and intimidation to get what they need.

While dealing with the doctorate and examining irregular psychology, a term called "The Dark Triad" that alludes to what numerous criminologist and analyst pinpoint as a simple indicator of criminal behavior, just as problematic, broken connections. The Dark Triad incorporates the qualities of ...

Dark Psychology Triad

Narcissism – Egotism, pomposity, and absence of compassion.

Machiavellianism – Uses manipulation to trick and endeavor people and has no sense of ethical quality.

Psychopathy – Often enchanting and well disposed at this point is described by impulsivity, selfishness, absence of compassion, and callousness.

None of us need to be a casualty of manipulation, yet it happens frequently. We may not be liable to someone specifically in the Dark Triad, however ordinary, everyday people like you face dark psychology tactics once a day.

These tactics are frequently found in plugs, web promotions, deals systems, and even the supervisor's behaviors. If you have children (particularly young people), you will, without a doubt, experience these tactics as your youngsters explore different avenues regarding behaviors to get what they need and look for independence. Clandestine manipulation and dark persuasion are regularly used by people you trust and love. Here is a portion of the tactics periodically used by typical, everyday people.

Love Flooding – Compliments, fondness or adulating someone to make a solicitation

Lying – Exaggeration, falsehoods, fractional realities, false stories

Love Denial – Withhold consideration and warmth.

Withdrawal – Avoiding the individual or quiet treatment

Decision confinement – Giving specific decision alternatives that divert from the decision you don't need someone to make

Turn around Psychology – Tell an individual a specific something or to accomplish something to inspire them to do the contrary, which is genuinely what you want.

Semantic Manipulation – Using words that are expected to have a typical or common definition.

Who uses Dark Psychology and manipulation tactics? Here's a rundown of people who appear to use these tactics the most.

Narcissists – People who are genuinely narcissistic (meeting clinical diagnosis) have an expanded sense of self-worth. They need others to approve their conviction of being predominant. They have dreams of being venerated and revered. They use dark psychology tactics, manipulation, and untrustworthy persuasion to keep up.

Sociopaths – People who are genuinely sociopathic

(meeting clinical diagnosis), are regularly beguiling, smart, yet incautious. Because of an absence of emotionality and capacity to feel regret, they use dark tactics to assemble a shallow relationship and after that exploit people.

Lawyers – Some lawyers center so eagerly around winning their case that they resort to utilizing dark persuasion tactics to get the result they need.

Lawmakers – Some government officials use dark psychological tactics and dark persuasion tactics to persuade people they are correct and to get cast a ballot.

Sales reps – Many salespeople become so focused on accomplishing a deal that they use dark tactics to inspire and convince someone to purchase their item.

Leaders – Some leaders use dark tactics to get consistency, more noteworthy exertion, or higher execution from their subordinates.

Open Speakers – Some speakers use dark tactics to increase the enthusiastic condition of the group of spectators, realizing it prompts selling more items at the back of the room.

Selfish People – This can be any individual who has a motivation of self before others. They will use tactics to address their very own issues first, even at someone else's cost. They don't mind win-lose results.

People attempt a wide range of things to recover their ex yet some of the time they come up short. Dark psychological strategies may assist you with getting your ex back powerless to resist you in a short time. There are a few procedures to recover your ex; however, they ought to be connected methodically to get excellent outcomes.

We as a whole, on occasion face some agitated minutes and the most horrifying thing in life is when your cherished one leaves you. There are various approaches to recover your ex throughout time; however, some tolerance is vital. Do whatever it takes not to surrender all expectations regarding sparing your relationship and give your total endeavors to recover your ex.

The Dark Psychological Strategies

Claim to their sense of interest. Interest is an incredible driving variable in the majority of the makeups. People will go along to what you wish to fulfill their curiosity.

Stir their self-interest. Self-interest is a unique spark in each one of us. Many will go to unimaginable lengths to gratify their selfishness.

Try not to attempt to surge indiscriminately to recover your ex. Set up an idiot-proof intend to approach your ex. The precise approach will assist you with getting accomplish your closures. As a matter of first importance be arranged sincerely and rationally and afterward proceed considering the arrangement you have. Adopt time to strategy your ex as hustling won't take care of your problem.

Be sure on the means you take to recover your ex. Energy the correct way will assist you with getting out from the condition you are in. Approach your ex in an efficient mode with your readied arrangement. Taking assistance from your companions will likewise assist you with solving your problem as they can consistently and bolster you.

Attempt to talk about the things with your ex transparently and furthermore do whatever it takes not to conceal items. Point to point talk will assist you in solving the problem. Attempt to gift the things which your ex loves in your meeting as it will please and the odds of taking care of the problem will likewise increment. Be agreeable when you are chatting with your ex. In this way, these are a portion of the things to remember as you continue to your subsequent stage.

CONCLUSION

Throughout this book, we have discussed all of the things that are important to remember to avoid being manipulated, and to include positive persuasion in the way that you interact with others. It isn't something that is going to be achieved overnight, but with more and more practice, you can remember that you have what it takes to get the things that you desire most.

The biggest mistake that some will make after learning of these methods is to use them to only their advantage and take from others rather than spreading the happiness and satisfaction received through influence. It is a lot easier to negatively manipulate someone than to positively persuade them. Sometimes, persuasion means building trust.

Manipulation can simply mean instilling fear. While manipulation might be easier, it is going to cause a lot more difficult things in the end that you will have to clean up afterwards!

Remember that this process starts with really

understanding someone's personality. There are common types of manipulators out there and you might be able to sense this personality trait in another person right away. Similarly, you will also recognize that there are hidden qualities that won't always emerge at first.

Remember to recognize that not all manipulative behaviors presented by an individual indicates that she is a malicious person. Having manipulative parents or long-term partners can rub off on our behavior, so we might sometimes say and do things that aren't meant to be manipulative but can come off that way. Always look at intention when determining if someone is really being manipulative or not.

Also, don't forget that body language can play a huge role in how someone will be perceived. You can start to see persuasive body language in others more often than you did before as soon as you become aware of what this kind of body language looks like. Ensure you are aware of your own body language as well so as not to be manipulated by others.

At the end of the day, manipulation is generally a way for a person to get the things that they desire most.

We all have basic human needs and instincts that drive our behavior. If we are not careful with how we go about getting these things, we can hurt others. The more equipped we are with the skills needed for positive influence, the easier it will be to achieve our deepest desires in a healthy way that benefits many.

To continue to grow your level of influence, remember that it starts with small moments of persuasion. Don't tell people what to do, encourage them from personal experience and stories learned from others. Don't try and trick someone into doing the things they don't want to do. Be honest with reward and consequence so that they can properly make the decision for themselves.

Always ensure that you are reflecting on your own behavior to make sure that you aren't going about things in the wrong way. With becoming influential, there is a certain level of confidence that comes along as well. If you are not careful, that confidence will drive you too far ahead of others, and you can get lost in what you perceive to be best for everyone. The better you can reflect and ensure you have the right intention, the easier it will be for others to be legitimately inspired by you.

While it might be hard to do the right thing in times where what is easiest will also benefit you the most, remember to be empathetic towards others. Though it might be challenging, you will still ultimately get the things you desire most when you are doing so in a fair and rewarding way.

DARK PSYCHOLOGY

The Art and Science of Manipulation and Mind Control. The Secrets and Tactics That People Use for Motivation, Persuasion, Manipulation and
Coercion to Get What They Want.

© Text Copyright 2019 – Jason Halpa

The content contained within this book may not be reproduced, duplicated or transmitted without direct written permission from the author or the publisher.

Under no circumstances will any blame or legal responsibility be held against the publisher, or author, for any damages, reparation, or monetary loss due to the information contained within this book. Either directly or indirectly.

Legal Notice:

This book is copyright protected. This book is only for personal use. You cannot amend, distribute, sell, use, quote or paraphrase any part, or the content within this book, without the consent of the author or publisher.

Disclaimer Notice:

Please note the information contained within this document is for educational and entertainment purposes only. All effort has been executed to present accurate, up to date, and reliable, complete information. No warranties of any kind are declared or

implied. Readers acknowledge that the author is not engaging in the rendering of legal, financial, medical or professional advice. The content within this book has been derived from various sources. Please consult a licensed professional before attempting any techniques outlined in this book.

By reading this document, the reader agrees that under no circumstances is the author responsible for any losses, direct or indirect, which are incurred as a result of the use of information contained within this document, including, but not limited to, — errors, omissions, or inaccuracies.

INTRODUCTION

The knowledge of dark psychology presented in this book is not intended to be used to cause harm to others. Rather, the main objective is to help you recognize manipulation in its various forms for what it is and if need be, to turn the tables to protect yourself. If you can manipulate a manipulator before they get the best of you, then that is a win for you and the rest of humanity.

You are probably confused by this one because you have always believed that smarter people are harder to outwit, right? Here's the thing though: intelligent people like to use logic to aid their decision-making process. Logic is easier to manipulate. Hence, intelligent people are more likely to manipulated when you corner them with logical arguments. Less intelligent people are harder to convince with logic and tend to be more stubborn in the face of facts and scientific arguments. It is no wonder that a whole lot of people who have been scammed by con artists and Ponzi schemes happen to be people who are relatively smart and who you'd not expect to be easily fooled.

The reason why this is often the case is because scammers know to appeal to this kind of people with facts and statistics. People who are less smart will be easily dismissive of anything that sounds like hullabaloo because they do not understand it.

You are trusting and like to believe the best about everyone

Believe it or not, there are bad people in this world. There are people who leave their homes every morning with the intention of harming others. There are people who have no qualms about inflicting heartache and turmoil upon others. While you may be seated in your house worrying about mega rich corporations who steal from the poor, there is a boardroom full of corporate big shots who are about to steal from the very poor that you are worried about. Simply put, not everybody shares in your conscience and your empathy. People are wired differently. People on the dark triad are wired even more different than you could ever imagine. When you meet a new person, it is noble to want to believe the best of them, but it is wise to expect to be surprised in a not-so-great way. Keeping your expectations of people to a minimum is a great way to protect yourself against everyone that is trying to get a piece of you.

WHAT IS DARK PSYCHOLOGY?

Most psychological techniques have a dual purpose – they can be used for both dark psychology and white psychology. What differs is the intent of the person employing the techniques.

In this chapter, we will concern ourselves with psychological techniques employed to achieve nefarious intents.

Dark persuasion

Persuasion is by far the most employed psychological technique. Most of the time, it is used for White psychology. As a tool for White psychology, almost all of us have used it in one way or another. However, very few of us have employed persuasion as a dark psychology tool.

Before we venture into the depth of Dark persuasion, let's look at the crucial components of persuasion as a whole.

What is persuasion?

Persuasion is a psychological technique of presenting arguments in such a way that motivates, influences, or changes a person's attitude, or behavior in order to achieve the desired outcome.

Persuasion tips

The following are important tips you need to master in order to become successfully persuasive:

- Do your research – to gain knowledgeable authoritative
- Be a thought leader – to guide people in your thoughts
- Be confident
- Appeal to emotions

Use rhetoric statements and assertions

- Keep sarcasm to the minimum
- Sound reasonable
- Watch reactions

- Be subtle in responses
- Actively listen
- Suggest, don't demand
- Be actively observant
- Be emotionally intelligent

Persuasion tactics

The following are basic yet important persuasion tactics:

- Use the name of the person you are engaging with
- Make a personal connection
- Build rapport
- Create an opportunity for reciprocity
- Use motivating words
- Be dynamic and adaptive – like a chameleon, change to suit your target's uniqueness (no blanket approach). Use NLP's mirroring and matching technique.

- Take advantage of the Bandwagon effect

- Create some scarcity in the mind of the person you are persuading

- Inspire curiosity through deliberate information gap (suspense)

- Use a foot in the door tactic – make a small request that opens the door wider for an eventual big request

- Clearly, point out the benefit of your proposition to the person you are persuading. Remember everyone subconsciously asks "what is in it for me?"

The Bandwagon effect

Bandwagon effect refers to that effect a crowd or group of people has on its constituent member.

The following are some characteristic attributes of the bandwagon effect:

- The herd mentality – people are persuaded to follow each other

- Social proof - people tend to follow the most

popular cause of action. For example, decrying negative social proof (such as littering, logging, bad sexual behavior, bingeing, smoking, etc) may actually promote it. For example, in case of 20% absenteeism, instead of the manager decrying that there is an increase of absenteeism from the previous 15% to now 20%, the manager should also reinforce positive social proof by pointing out to the majority who have remained not absent (i.e. 80%) and talk of the 20% as few spoilt apples that should be minimized.

Deception

Deception refers consciously and deliberately promoting that which is not true with the aim of covering-up, misleading, or promoting a belief, concept or idea with the aim of manipulating the recipient to act or respond in a certain predetermined way.

In other words, deception is manipulation of appearances such that they convey a false reality.

The core essence of deception is to disguise. Some of

the common deception methods include:

- Propaganda – propagating false information and packaging it as truth or facts

- Camouflage – disguising the true nature of things. For example, a spy using philanthropy to penetrate a community.

- Pretension – taking a form that is false from the true form. For example pretending to be innocent while guilty, pretending to be sick while well, pretending to grief while inside you are celebrating, etc.

- Mystification – creating a supernatural sense by hoarding truth and acting in a way that appears supernormal. This makes you attractive to those who are prone to beliefs.

- Paltering – speak or act in such a manner that bamboozles people and as such draw their attention away from themselves and towards you. Eventually, you manipulate their attention towards achieving your own set goals. Conjurers, magicians, and actors employ this tactic.

Types of deception

Deception occurs in two primary forms:

- Lie by commission (dissimulation) – this is the active part of the deception. In lie by the commission, a person deceives or lies directly by deliberately altering material facts.

- Lie by omission(simulation) – lie by omission is indirect. In this regard, a person engaged in deception does not deliberately alter material facts. Rather, the person knowingly and deliberately conceals material facts which he or she knows that would have altered the decision of the person being deceived.

Dupery

Dupery is an act of deception. However, dupery goes further to selfishly gain from the victim. In dupery, the manipulator sets traps or baits into which the victim falls in and then gets exploited for selfish or nefarious gains.

Indoctrination

Indoctrination is the act of imparting someone with a

set of beliefs without offering that person an opportunity for critical inquiry.

Indoctrination strategies:

Rote training – this is an act of enforcing information into people's memory through repetitive action. For example, uttering certain mantra during prayers, or counting mala beads while praying.

Affirmation–making people say words that positively approve certain statements. This way, they are programmed to hold those statements as true.

Obstruction of truth and facts–this is a deliberate action aimed at making those being indoctrinated not to access sources of truth or facts. For example, they can be barred from reading certain books that are deemed "satanic". Fear psychology is often employed, like telling people that they will have nightmares or be visited by vampire spirits in their sleep if they read such a book.

Confession–everyone one of us has a "sinful" past. We all have skeletons in our past... things that we did and feel guilty about. One indoctrination strategy is to force people to confess. Once they confess, they lose the moral authority to stand upright before the indoctrinators. As such, they become more submissive toward indoctrination.

Isolation – the main aim of isolation is to cut out someone from the influence that may make indoctrination impossible or difficult to achieve. Thus, the victims are cut off from the rest of the family, society or normal relationships. Isolation is one form of obstruction of truth and facts since the victims cannot get a second opinion about assertions being made by the indoctrinators.

Guilt imposition – guilt imposition is closely related to forced confession. However, in guilt imposition, a sense of guilt is postulated into the victim's mind. The victim may be unknowingly ensnared to commit a wrong and then indoctrinator finds ways to discover it. Later on, the indoctrinator uses that act to impose guilt on the victim. The primary objective, just as forced confession, is to lower the victim's moral standing and hence cower the victim into psychological submission.

Phobia imposition – phobia is psychological fear.

Indoctrinators induce phobia into their victims such that they find it hard to exist outside the indoctrinator's domain. For example, the victim can be told of how the 'devil' wants to kill him and the only way to salvation is to leave that devil-infested home and come to live with the indoctrinator who has the powers to chase away the devil. There are many forms of phobia imposition. For example, insurance companies impose phobia on their potential clients by exaggerating the potential risks that may happen should the potential client not insure the life of loved ones or property. Governments also prey on their citizens by instilling phobia, especially when they want their agenda to prevail.

Rituals – rituals have a strong effect on one's psychology. This is why most traditions, religions, cults, political organizations, and even some civil organizations have rituals. For example, it is common for rituals to be performed prior to prayers, prior to burials, prior to the war, etc. Rituals enhance a person susceptibility to a certain proposition being advanced by the indoctrinator.

Induced dependency – induced dependency is commonly applied by manipulators in a relationship where they want to gain an upper hand over their victims. For example, imperialist or colonialist entities can perpetuate poverty in their target society and then pretend to be saviors of that society. They may dish out conditional aid, conditional grant, etc... with the conditions carefully crafted to increase dependency and make the victims more susceptible to exploitation. Since, without this deliberate impoverishment, that particular society would not have become susceptibly poor or would not have welcomed the conditional aid and grant, this becomes and induced dependency. In marriage partners, it is common for an insecure partner to create a condition that makes the other partner dependent. For example, an insecure husband can push or trigger his wife to lose employment. Once the wife loses employment, then, the insecure husband feels comfortably in control of the unemployed wife since he is the main breadwinner. The wife's lack of financial independence makes her become more susceptible to the dictates of the husband.

Punishment – by having a system of tests and exams and offering incentives for those who pass the indoctrination program

Characteristics of indoctrination

Unsurprisingly indoctrination takes place in most domains of our lives. It takes place in our homes (by parents), in schools (by teachers), in public life (by politicians and governments), etc.

The following are some of the key characteristics of tools used for indoctrination:

- Fear
- Dogmatism
- Fundamentalism
- Cognitive closure
- Feeling of inadequacy
- Perceived deprivation

Sources of indoctrination

While there are some covert sources of indoctrination, the following are some of the common overt sources of indoctrination:

- Religious institutions
- Schools and educational establishments
- Media – mainstream, alternative media, social media

- Parents
- Politicians
- Marriage partners

Brainwashing

Brainwashing refers to erasing from one's belief system the existing set of old beliefs and in its place supplanting a new set of beliefs. Brainwashing happens without someone's will.

While sometimes brainwashing is subtle and involuntary, a lot of time it is violent. For example, we've had forced conversions during the crusade period and also during the jihad. In the forced conversion, the victims are fully aware that they are being brainwashed but accept it as a coping mechanism to avoid greater harm such as death.

Violent brainwashing happens most in the militant cultic or criminal organizations where victims are trapped and have no exit option.

Potential victims of violent brainwashing include:

- Prisoners (especially prisoners of war)

- Slaves under captivity

- Kidnapped victims

- Illegal aliens

In the subtle brainwashing, often the victim voluntarily and unknowingly accepts brainwashing. In this case, the perpetrator looks out for susceptible victims who are more malleable. The victims are often in a desperate situation and thus have a psychological void that desires fulfillment.

- The following are some of the potential victims of unknowing brainwashing:

- Those suffering from unknown chronic illness

- Minors who have left their home to live alone and often faraway

- Those who have lost their jobs and are in deep despair

- Those who have lost their loved ones, especially through divorce or death

Common steps in brainwashing

The following are some of the common steps taken by brainwashers to brainwash their victims:

- Isolation
- Attack on self-esteem
- subjugation
- Testing
- Love bombing

Isolation

The brainwasher knows that a person's family or close circle can easily notice what is happening and thus rescue the victim. As such, the first step they take is to isolate the victim from close family and friends.

Some, like cultic leaders, can instill negativities about close family and friends. This brings division between the victim and loved ones and thus breeds psychological isolation. For example, a cultic leader can claim that your closest friend is a psychic vampire that drains your energy thus making you chronically ill and as such you ought to keep off from that friend.

Since you are sick and desperate, you are likely to follow this brainwashing tactic and thus find yourself isolated from the very person who could have saved you from brainwashing.

Attack on self-esteem

It is only a victim who has self-doubt, low self-confidence, and on the overall suffers from low self-esteem that can easily be brainwashed. As such, the brainwasher seeks to achieve this state in the victim by attacking the victim's self-esteem.

Some of the ways by which the brainwasher attacks the victim's self-esteem include:

- Verbal and physical abuse – this often applied in violent brainwashing where the brainwasher uses abuse as a means of demeaning the victim so that the victim loses self-worth.

- Sleep deprivation – a sleep-deprived person is more likely to submit to psychological pressure since there is lack of full consciousness. It is much easier for a sleep-deprived person to submit to brainwashing instructions just to have an opportunity to be left alone and sleep.

- Intimidation–Intimidation is one of the tactics employed by brainwashers to push someone into involuntary submission. For example, the threat of punishment is a form of intimidation.

- Embarrassment – this is used especially if the victim has some dark secret that he or she wouldn't like to be revealed. For example, a brainwasher may resort to using tricks to obtain nude photos of a potential victim or trick such a victim into marital infidelity. Once the brainwasher acquires these materials, he/she starts subtly embarrassing the victim. In this subtle embarrassment, the brainwasher doesn't reveal the materials to the public but uses generalized terms that insinuate immorality on the part of the victim. The victim knows where the cues are leading to and thus does everything possible to dissuade the brainwasher from revealing these embarrassing contents. Thus, the brainwasher attains an upper hand which he/she uses to brainwash the victim. For example, the victim could be forced into performing rituals that wear the victim's self-worth and self-esteem thus becoming deeply captive to the brainwasher. Eventually, the victim may be infected by the Stockholm syndrome, where, instead of acting against the brainwasher, acts to protect the brainwasher – an act, which, subconsciously is more about protecting the "secrets" (embarrassing content).

- Scarcity creation such as rationing of basic necessities and only released upon the victim's obedient performance.

Subjugation

Brainwashers seek to bring the victim under their absolute control so that the victims become absolutely obedient.

The following are some of the tactics used to achieve subjugation:

- Extreme abuse
- Us -vs- Them
- Love bombing

Extreme abuse

The victim is passed through extreme abuse. Almost often emotional and psychological abuses are employed. Physical abuse is only employed in violent brainwashing. Physical abuse is not employed in the subtle brainwashing.

Us -vs- Them

The victim is coerced to make a choice between the brainwasher and the rest of the world. However, the victim is not granted an exit option.

The victim is introduced to those who are already brainwashed and thus praise the brainwasher. In case the victim still thinks of "them" (the outside world) as an option, the victim continues to be subjected to extreme abuse until he or she comes the ultimate choice of belonging to "us", that is, joining the rest of the brainwashed subjects.

Testing

Testing happens to establish whether the victim has ultimately made the "us' choice and no longer desires to join "them". It is also done to test the victim's level of obedience.

Sometimes, under secret control, the victim may be released to "them" (the rest of the world) on the condition that he or she should return on a certain date. The victim is then secretly monitored to see whether he/she desires to return to "us" (the brainwashed group).

If the victim doesn't desire to return to "us", then, the victim is kidnapped and returned to the fold upon which the vicious cycle begins.

On the other hand, if the victim voluntarily returns to us, then, the victim is taken to the next stage, that is, love bombing.

More often than not, due to isolation and induced dependency, even if the victim desires to rejoin "them", the victim finds it such a long journey to recovery and hence prefers getting back to "us" rather than starting all over again to rebuild the lost life.

Love bombing

Once tests are done and prove that the victim has been effectively brainwashed, love bombing is applied to galvanize the victim into the fold.

Love bombing could be in the form of praising, promotion in the order of subjects, receiving gifts, etc.

Dark Seduction

Dark seduction refers to the use of dark psychological tools to entice someone into engaging in a relationship that satisfies seducer's self-interest with no apparent benefit to the seducee.

A dark seducer orchestrates the victim's longings to suit his/her selfish desires.

While seduction is traditionally related to the opposite sex, it can also be of the same gender and asexual.

Dark seduction is not necessarily about sex but taking advantage of sexual arousal to achieve certain objectives.

When a victim is sexually aroused, the victim becomes less logical and less rational and thus more susceptible to manipulation.

The following are some of the dark seduction techniques:

- Love bombing

- erotic expressions
- platitudes
- gifting
- sexual innuendos

The primary objective of dark seduction is to appeal to the primitive Id within every individual and reduce the effect of anti-cathexis. This makes the victim break away from super-ego and hence lowers to the primitive level of Id where hedonism is prevalent.

Erotic actions and rewards are applied to the victim to reinforce this state of Id and completely wear off the super-ego and anti-cathexis.

More often than not, indoctrination and brainwashing can be applied to facilitate the wearing off of the super-ego.

Hypnotization

Hypnotization is the act of drawing a person's mind to a receptively vulnerable state that is irresistibly open to your suggestions.

A hypnotized person is like a sleep-walker whose

consciousness is deeply focused on the act of walking and completely isolated to signals emanating from the rest of the environment.

While in that state of hypnotism, the hypnotized person cannot consciously draw references from external sources but only from the suggestions. The person either largely or completely loses peripheral awareness. Thus, the person's mind is trapped into some sort of a conscious bubble that is impermeable to intrusive signals from the rest of awareness.

Hypnotic induction

Hypnotic induction refers to employing a series of preliminary instructions and suggestions to draw someone into hypnosis.

Key features of hypnosis:

Concentrated attention to a single object or idea

Isolation from peripheral awareness

Increased reception to suggestions

Dark vs white hypnosis

The difference between white and dark hypnosis rests in the intent of the hypnotist. Dark hypnosis is intended to exploit the hypnotic person for selfish gains by the hypnotist.

White hypnosis is intended to improve the condition of the hypnotic by helping the hypnotic snap out from a traumatic or harmful state of consciousness.

Hypnotherapy is the most common type of white hypnosis. White hypnosis is often referred to as therapeutic hypnosis.

Hypnotherapy

Hypnotherapy is a form of white hypnotic induction practiced by medical practitioners for therapeutic purposes. The main aim is to help a patient heal from psychological, emotional, emotional, and even physical trauma.

Hypnotherapy can be used in pain relief in such a manner that enables the patient to dissociate himself from the source of the pain thus lessening sensitivity to that pain.

Facts about hypnosis:

- It is voluntary
- It is willful
- Children are more susceptible to hypnotism than adults
- 15% of people are highly susceptible to hypnotism
- 10% of people can hardly be hypnotized
- Those people who are easily absorbed in fantasies are more susceptible to hypnotism

Negative effects of Dark hypnotic induction

There are many victims of dark hypnotic induction. The following are some of the common causes of dark hypnotic induction:

- Being hypnotized to such an extent that you willfully give your possession to the hypnotist
- Being hypnotized such that you willfully open your door to robbers
- Being hypnotized such that you voluntarily follow kidnappers to their den

Psychological manipulation

Psychological manipulation is the act of employing deceptive, abusive or underhanded tactics to change a person's perception or behavior.

THE FOUR DARK PERSONALITY CLASSIFICATIONS

After a thorough rundown of what Dark Psychology is and how it affects society as a whole, let's delve into the specific classifications with the dark psyche. There are hundreds of terms to describe dark psyche actions. We listed the nine major traits related to dark psyches in recent chapters. These traits are sometimes obvious, and other times very difficult to pinpoint, especially when you are faced with them head-on. It is important, that you understand these traits in order to understand why there are four major classifications in Dark Psychology.

These traits are often the initial tell-tale signs when psychologists begin to treat a patient. They are looking for specific qualities that an individual exhibits on a regular basis. Once these traits are listed and quantified, the diagnosis then can move forward. These types of diagnosis can be difficult since many of the classifications of dark personalities have interwoven characteristics. On top of that, not all of the traits are equally brandished by the patient. Therefore, a deeper look into the behaviors of that patient needs to be taken into account.

Despite the complexity of diagnosis by a licensed professional, on a personal level, you will be able to understand the specific characteristics that dark personalities often carry. This will help you to spot the dangerous red flags that we can often miss when interacting with a person.

Spitefulness

Spitefulness dates back to even before human beings existed. In fact, spite has been studied within organisms in order to further understand the relevance in the human species. In the land of ash and fire, when the Earth was transitioning into a greener and more livable space, organisms were forming deep in the watery depths of the oceans. Some of these organisms had a reactionary defense that released toxins that killed the other organisms. In doing so, however, those same toxins often killed the releaser. Ever heard the saying, "cut off your nose to spite your face?"

S.A. West, A.S. Griffin, and A. Gardner, the authors of

the study entitled, Social Semantics: Altruism, Cooperation, Mutualism, Strong Reciprocity, and Group Selection from the Institute of Evolutionary Biology defined Spite as, "a behavior in which is beneficial to the actor and costly to the recipient." But what this definition does not include is the fact that spite quite often backfires in the "actor's" face.

Self-Interest

Self-interest is pretty simple to explain in normal terms. It is simply putting yourself before all others despite the cost to the other party. In psychology, there are two subsets of self-interest, egoism and narcissism which will be explained below. Within the philosophical realm of self-interest, there are several concepts behind self-interest.

- Enlightened Self-Interest- This concept states that if you do for others, ultimately you will be serving your own self-interest as well.

- Ethical Egoism- This concept is the thought that people should do what is best for themselves.

- Rational Egoism- This belief centers around the

idea that any rational action that you take should always be done in your own self-interest.

- Hedonism- Hedonism makes the assertion that the only type of good is pleasure. Hedonism also includes the pre-Socratic Cyrenaics and the philosophical system known as Epicureanism.

- Individualism- This is a philosophy that teaches people to have a very strong sense of self-worth.

Psychopathy

The term psychopath is a commonly used word in society and doesn't often fully encompass the reality of the mental disorder. Psychopaths are too often written off as patients that do not hold the capability to be treated. However, this is not true in a majority of the cases. Like so many other mental illnesses through the years, they are often tossed into a mental institution and forgotten about. The psychological world is beginning to change that trend. This will be discussed further below.

Psychological Entitlement

Psychological Entitlement is a term that has become

more and more well known in today's society. It is the belief that some people deserve more than others. Through history, we have seen entitlement between financial classes, races, sexes, and even religious institutions. A sense of entitlement can come from your background, your surroundings, the teachings you had growing up, and just an innate inner belief that you should have more because you are better than others. Psychological entitlement can also be seen within the workplace. When someone is more educated, has had a longer time on the job, or even has a higher title than others, they can develop a sense of self-worth that makes them believe they are more important than others and therefore, more deserving of things like better pay and easier tasks. Psychological Entitlement is a trait that is usually burrowed deep into someone's psyche. It can be hard to break but it is possible through regular treatment programs. However, many people overlook entitlement on a deep seeded psychological level because they assume it is simply a product of the environment, not a mental illness that needs to be treated.

Narcissism

Narcissism is a trait that, though healthy in small children, can become dangerous if it is developed after puberty. Narcissists are incredibly selfish and always have some sort of sense of entitlement. Narcissists always lack empathy, and crave attention and admiration from everyone around them. They are usually very good at getting their way, and often talk circles around arguments in order to confuse the other person and remove blame from themselves. Narcissists can be found in all walks of life, from high political offices to the neighbor down the street. Narcissistic behavior is not only dangerous to the people it is aimed at but can be dangerous to the aggressor as well. Narcissism will be discussed in greater depth later in this chapter.

Moral Disengagement

Moral Disengagement is a term related to social psychology. It is the act of convincing your own mind that ethical and moral standards don't apply to you. A person suffering from moral disengagement is able to disconnect the part of the brain that tells them what they are doing is wrong. They often are part of inhumane activities to which they justify through verbally recited morals, comparison to others, removing responsibility from themselves, shrugging of serious injuries to others as if they weren't as bad as they seemed, and one of the worst, they immediately begin to dehumanize the person in which they have acted against.

One not so talked about form of moral disengagement is used in military tactic on a daily basis. The military morally justifies the killing of "enemies" for the greater good of society. They go so far as to convince the soldiers that their actions made them heroes. And this does not just happen to the members of the military, but to society as well when we shake the hand of a soldier and justify the actions they took because we've been told that there is some sort of moral caveat when it comes to enemy lives.

Machiavellianism

Machiavellianism is a personality type that encompasses manipulation. Those that fall under this type are often master manipulators without ever even knowing it. Their temperament exposes them to be deceptive, conniving, and for all intents and purposes, amoral. Machiavellianism will be discussed more in length below.

Egoism

Psychological egoism within a personality creates a belief that every motive you have is for the betterment of yourself. Egoists are often considered nonmoral and do not all operate in the same fashion. There is no specific, verifiable course or personality that an egoist takes but the base of their person cares for themselves first over all others.

Now that we understand some of the major traits within Dark Psychology, we will be able to better pinpoint why the following four are more often diagnosed on a clinical level. They can arguably also be some of the worst Dark Personality traits you could have.

Psychopaths

Psychopaths are those that suffer, ultimately, from psychopathy. They have a tendency to have multiple diagnoses and can exhibit strange, and often violent behavior. When you hear or read the word psychopath, almost everyone has some sort of image pop into their mind. Whether it is Michael Myers inhumanly walking at a glacial pace always catching up to the screaming girl, or the face of Norman Bates as he flaunts his mother's most beautiful dress while slaughtering people, the word brings a connotation of fear and horror.

TECHNIQUES OF DARK PSYCHOLOGY

Persuasion

The first thing that we need to take a look at here is what a dark persuader is all about. If you look through the dictionary, it is going to talk about how persuasion is to prevail on someone to do or to believe something using a number of methods, often with reasoning and advising. This may seem pretty much the same things as regular persuasion, but the difference is that intention that comes with the persuasion. Basically, persuasion is when you are going to use reason and other techniques in order to get someone to do what you want, whether that is for the good of the other person or not. Let's take a closer look at what persuasion is all about, and how we are able to use this for our own needs.

There are six main elements that come with persuasion and understanding how these do work is how the manipulator is able to use persuasion for their needs. These are also kind of like the techniques that you are able to use for persuasion, and you are able to bring these out in order to help you see some success with what you can do with the other person. Some of the different techniques that can be used when it comes to persuasion and making it work for you include:

Reciprocity

The first tactic to use will be an idea that is known as reciprocity. This is going to be a principle that works on the idea that when someone does a favor for us, or provides us with something of value, no matter how big or small that item or action may be, we are going to try and repay them, and pay off our "debt" to them in some manner. Oftentimes, the item or favor that the persuader offer is going to be smaller than the thing they want from us. But because they offered us something, often without us asking for it, and they helped us out with a task of some sort, and then asked for their turn right after, we are the target are more likely to agree to help, even if we really don't want to.

When a dark persuader brings out the ideas that come with reciprocation, the point is that they want to create some sort of obligation in the target to agree, which is going to be a very powerful and effective tool to use with persuasion. The reciprocity rule is going to be this effective because it can be really overbearing to us, and we don't want to seem ungrateful for the help or like we are shrugging off our duties. And so we end up agreeing to help out, without a ton of push from the persuader in the first place.

If you are using this technique, you will find that the item or the favor that you offer to the other person is going to be pretty small. You may run to the office in order to make some copies for them or grab them a coffee when you are already going up. But once you are done with this small thing, and you have helped them out, it is the perfect time for you to ask them to help you with something that you want. Keep in mind that the sooner you ask for your favor after you are done helping, the more likely it is that you will be able to get the target to agree to do what you want, even if your request is much larger than the thing you helped them out with.

Commitment and Consistency

Once you have worked with the idea of reciprocity for a bit, it is time to move on to commitment and consistency. Consistency is an important part of society and relationships, and it can be important when it comes to persuasion because:

- It is something that society is going to value quite a bit.

- It is going to provide us with a beneficial approach to our daily life.

- It is able to provide us with a valuable shortcut through some of the complicated parts of our modern way of life.

Consistency works because it is going to allow us to become more effective at making our decisions and processing the information that we receive. The concept of consistency is going to state that when someone commits to doing something, whether they commit through writing or by speaking. They are more likely to honor the commitment that they made.

This is going to be especially true when something is written down because this ensures that the evidence is more concrete and this gives the person the hard proof that they need to really fix the issues that they need. Someone who commits to a stance tends to behave according to the commitment that they agree to.

You will find that this commitment is going to be a really effective technique to use with persuasion because once you are able to get the other person to commit, then they are more likely to engage in the form of self-persuasion providing themselves and others with the justifications and the reasons to support their commitment in order to avoid some of the other issues that can come up with not following the commitment. If you are able to get the other person to make this commitment in front of a group or at least one other person, then you will find that you will be able to persuade them to do something even more readily.

Social Proof

The third technique that we are going to take a look at is known as social proof. As humans, we find that the people around us are really going to influence us in many aspects. Even if we want to be unique and do things on our own terms, there is always going to be someone who will influence you in some way. We want those in our lives to like us, we want to be seen as acceptable in our group, and we want to do and have what other people do. It may surprise us to find out how much our beliefs and our actions are based on what others are doing in our own social groups.

This idea is going to be like following the power of the crowd, and a persuader is going to find that it can be a nice tactic to use. We all want to know what those near us and around us are doing. This is often going to be the most effective when the other person is uncertain about the area around them, such as when they are in a new location they have never been. When the situation is uncertain, or when the situation presents someone with more than one choice to make, it is likely that we are going to conform to what others are doing around us to help us make our decisions.

What this means is that if you are interested in influencing those around you, then you need to be able to show the target that others around them, the other people they want to be like and admire, are doing the same course that you are suggesting. Convince them that everyone is doing it, that this is what they need to do to be seen as cool and to fit in with society, and more, and you will be able to convince the target to do what you would like.

Likeness

We can also work a bit with the persuasion element of likeness. This is a principle that is pretty concise and simple to work with, but it still brings in a lot of power to your tactics and techniques with the target. People are often going to say yes more often when they are talking to someone they like. But if they don't find the other person likable that they just met, or they don't like someone they have known for a while, it is much easier to tell that person no when they ask for some help.

When it comes to the likeability of someone, there are a few factors that we can consider with this one to determine if a target is going to instantly like you or not. We will just limit our focus here to the two major factors that you can concentrate on. The first factor to consider is whether or not the target is going to find you physically attractive. This sounds shallow and may seem a bit silly, but it is definitely something that is going to be true with your target, and because of this, you can use this idea to your advantage any time you want to use persuasion on your target.

When the target finds that you are physically

attractive, they will automatically agree with you, and you will find that you are more persuasive with them. Those who have better looks physically, no matter how shallow it sounds, are going to be able to get what they want from others, without even really needing to try. Physical attractiveness is able to send a message to your target and can even make the target think you have other good traits including talent, intelligence, and kindness, even if you haven't taken the time to show any of these characteristics, and even if you don't even have them.

The second factor that we need to consider with likeness is the idea of similarity. It is true that your target is so much easier to persuade to do what you want when they feel that you and they are similar to one another in some manner. If you pay attention to their body language and actually listen to what they are trying to tell you when they speak, you will find that it is so much easier to match up your personality and cues to theirs. And this helps make it so that your target sees the two of you as similar, and decides to listen to you.

Authority

Authority is a very effective method that you are able to use in order to get the other person to listen to you and to do what you would like. We all are going to have some kind of tendency to believe an expert if they say something. We think that if they tell us some facts or some information then it needs to be true and we should believe what they are saying. People like to find a quick way to make decisions, and they like listening to those who are trustworthy and knowledgeable about the topic at hand. If you are able to bring out both of those and show it off to the target, then you will be able to get others to believe and listen to you.

You need to make sure that you are able to convince the other person that you are the authority figure. If you are able to do this, they are going to come to you for advice, and they will believe that the advice that you give them is going to be in their best interest and that they need to listen to you. Whether or not it is actually going to be in their best interests is not going to matter to the persuader, but it does help them to get the results that they want.

Scarcity

This is going to be considered one of the best and most effective methods of persuasion that you are able to use against one of your targets when you want to get your goals. When something appears to have a limited amount of availability, and won't be around for long, it seems like people are going to give it more value than it is worth. The reason for this higher value is because people want to get more of what they are not able to have. When you can manipulate the system so that you can make scarcity a real issue, then the target is going to want to rush right towards that item or the path that you are suggesting and get it for themselves.

What this is going to mean for you as the persuader is that, within the right context, scarcity is going to help you reach your goals. In order to get people to believe that an item or a chosen path is scarce, they need to get their hands on it right now, for example, the marketer is going to explain what the product does and why it is so much better at it than anything else on the market. Another approach is telling the customer what they are likely to lose out on if they choose not to go with that item, rather than talking just about the benefits. So, you may avoid saying something like, "You will save $5 by using it," and instead you would go with something like, "You will lose $5." The second option is going to bring up the idea of scarcity a bit more and can make the target run to get that item.

Now, you will find that the persuasion tactic of scarcity is going to be effective and powerful, and there are a number of reasons for this one. Some of the biggest reasons that the scarcity tactic works so well include:

When it is hard to get something that people are going to see it as more valuable. This makes it seem like that item is going to be higher in quality even though that doesn't have to be true.

When things start to have a limited amount of availability, this means that we are going to lose the chance in the future to get them, and we don't want to miss out.

The idea that we get with this one is that we want to get anything that we think it out of our reach, or will be gone soon because it is rare. We want to stand out, or we don't want to miss out on something. If we notice that there is a path we can come back to later, or that there is a deal that is always around, then we won't put as much value on it. But when something seems like it is rare and going to be gone soon, then we give it more value, and we want it more. This is how the idea of scarcity is going to work with your target.

This is going to be helpful when we are looking at persuasion. If we are able to convince the other person that what we are offering or what we have to say and want them to do, is rare or only available for a short amount of time, then they are more likely to agree to it. This doesn't work all of the time, but it has a higher level of success and will ensure that you are more likely to get what you want out of that other person.

These six techniques of persuasion are going to be some of the best that you can use to get the results that we want from our target. These persuasion techniques take some time to learn, and we have to be able to use them in the proper manner to ensure that we convince the target to do what we want, rather than choosing their own course of action. But you will find that, while these techniques are going to seem pretty simple, and the ideas that come with them are not that hard to learn, they are going to be effective and can be modified and pulled out no matter who your target is, or what situation you are dealing with, which makes them some of the best dark psychology techniques to use to get what you want from others.

Manipulation

Manipulation is the act of utilizing backhanded strategies to control conduct, feelings, and connections.

What Is Manipulation?

The vast majority participates in occasional control. For instance, telling a colleague you feel "fine" when you are really discouraged is, in fact, a type of control since it controls your associate's view of and responses to you.

Control can likewise have progressively guileful outcomes, notwithstanding, and it is frequently connected with psychological mistreatment, especially in private connections. The vast majority see control contrarily, particularly when it hurts the physical, enthusiastic, or psychological wellness of the individual being controlled.

While individuals who control others regularly do as such in light of the fact that they want to control their condition and environment, an urge that frequently originates from profound situated dread or uneasiness, it is anything but solid conduct. Participating in control may keep the controller from associating with their credible self, and being controlled can make an individual encounter a wide scope of sick impacts.

Psychological Well-Being Effects of Manipulation

In the event that unaddressed, control can prompt poor emotional wellness results for the individuals who are controlled. Incessant control in cozy connections may likewise be a sign psychological mistreatment is occurring, which at times, can have a comparable impact to injury—especially when the casualty of control is made to feel regretful or embarrassed.

Casualties of incessant control may:

- Feel discouraged
- Develop nervousness

- Develop undesirable adapting designs
- Constantly attempt to satisfy the manipulative individual
- Lie about their emotions
- Put someone else's needs before their own
- Find it hard to confide in others

Now and again, control can be inescapable to such an extent that it makes an injured individual inquiry their view of the real world. The exemplary motion picture Gaslight outlined one such story, in which a lady's significant other quietly controlled her until she never again confided in her very own discernment. For instance, the spouse clandestinely turned down the gaslights and persuaded his better half the diminishing light was all in her mind.

Control and Mental Health

While the vast majority take part in control now and again, an unending example of control can demonstrate a fundamental psychological wellness concern.

Control is especially basic with character issue analyses, for example, marginal character (BPD) and narcissistic character (NPD). For some with BPD, control might be methods for gathering their passionate needs or acquiring approval, and it frequently happens when the individual with BPD feels shaky or surrendered. The same number of individuals with BPD have seen or experienced maltreatment, control may have created as a method for dealing with stress to get necessities met by implication.

People with narcissistic character (NPD) may have various explanations behind taking part in manipulative conduct. As those with NPD may experience issues framing cozy connections, they may depend on control so as to "keep" their accomplice in the relationship. Qualities of narcissistic control may incorporate disgracing, accusing, playing the "person in question," control issues, and gaslighting.

Munchausen disorder as a substitute, during which a parental figure makes someone else sick to pick up consideration or fondness, is another condition that is described by manipulative practices.

Control in Relationships

Long haul control can have genuine impacts in cozy connections, including those between companions, relatives, and sentimental accomplices. Control can decay the strength of a relationship and lead to the poor psychological well-being of those in the relationship or even the disintegration of the relationship.

In a marriage or association, control can make one accomplice feel harassed, segregated, or useless. Indeed, even in solid connections, one accomplice may coincidentally control the other so as to evade showdown or even trying to shield their accomplice from inclination loaded. Numerous individuals may even realize they are being controlled in their relationship and neglect or make light of it. Control in personal connections can take numerous structures, including embellishment, blame, blessing giving or specifically indicating warmth, mystery keeping, and latent hostility.

Guardians who control their kids may set their kids up for blame, wretchedness, uneasiness, eating issues, and other emotional wellness conditions. One investigation likewise uncovered that guardians who normally use control strategies on their kids may improve the probability their youngsters will likewise utilize manipulative conduct. Indications of control in the parent-youngster relationship may incorporate making the tyke feel regretful, absence of responsibility from a parent, minimizing a tyke's accomplishments, and a should be associated with numerous parts of the kid's life.

Individuals may likewise feel controlled in the event that they are a piece of a kinship that has turned out to be harmful. In manipulative fellowships, one individual might utilize the other to address their very own issues to the detriment of their friend's. A manipulative companion may utilize blame or intimidation to concentrate favors, for example, crediting cash, or they may possibly contact that companion when they need their very own passionate needs met and may discover pardons when their companion has needs in the relationship.

Instances of Manipulative Behavior

Here and there, individuals may control others unknowingly, without being completely mindful of what they are doing, while others may effectively chip away at reinforcing their control strategies. A few indications of control include:

- Passive-forceful conduct
- Implicit dangers
- Dishonesty
- Withholding data
- Isolating an individual from friends and family
- Gaslighting
- Verbal misuse
- Use of sex to accomplish objectives

As the thought processes behind control can change from oblivious to pernicious, it is imperative to distinguish the conditions of the control that is occurring. While severing things might be basic in circumstances of maltreatment, an advisor may help other people figure out how to manage or face manipulative conduct from others.

Instructions to Deal with Manipulative People

At the point when control ends up lethal, managing the conduct from others can be debilitating. Control in the working environment has been appeared to diminish execution and manipulative conduct from friends and family can cause reality to appear to be faulty. On the off chance that you believe you are being controlled in any sort of a relationship, it might be useful to:

- Disengage. In the event that somebody is attempting to get a specific enthusiastic reaction from you, decide not to offer it to them. For instance, if a manipulative companion is known to compliment you before requesting overextending support, don't play along—rather, answer courteously and move the discussion along.

- Be certain. Some of the time, control may incorporate one individual's endeavors to make someone else question their capacities, instinct, or even reality. In the event that this occurs, it might adhere to your story; in any case, if this happens regularly in a cozy relationship, it could be an ideal opportunity to leave.

- Address the circumstance. Get out the manipulative conduct as it is going on. Maintaining the attention on how the other individual's activities are influencing you as opposed to beginning with an accusatory proclamation may likewise enable you to arrive at a goal while underlining that their manipulative strategies will not take a shot at you.

- Stay on-point. When you call attention to conduct that makes you feel controlled, the other individual may attempt to limit the circumstance or jumble the circumstance by raising different issues as a diversion. Keep in mind your primary concern and adhere to that.

Types of Manipulation

There are several types of manipulation because it can often depend on where the manipulator is or who they are manipulating. For example, there are some manipulators who focus on workplace tactics while others will manipulate their significant other. Of course, there are manipulators who will use their tactics no matter where they are or who they are with.

Covert Emotional Manipulation

Covert emotional manipulation is a part of any form of manipulation. However, it is stronger in people who are known as "master manipulators" or people who will manipulate anyone in order to get anything they want. It is not as strong in manipulation tactics people use when they tell someone they are fine, even though something is wrong.

At the base of manipulation is working to change the way people feel and think, which is covert emotional manipulation. They focus on your conscious awareness in order to control you. Because of this, people don't often realize that they are being manipulated.

First, the manipulator will get you to trust them. Then, they will start to control the way you feel, think, and perceive situations. This will happen slowly as they don't want you to catch on to the manipulation. Once they feel that your emotions and thoughts are in their hands, they will start to tear apart your confidence. A master manipulator knows they have to lower your self-esteem in order to control you the way they want to. They will also work to take away your identity, which allows you to fully become theirs.

While they are trying to break you down emotionally and mentally, they will also try to keep you away from your family and friends. One of the biggest reasons for this is people who knew you before they came into your life are a threat to them. Your family and friends will notice a change in you, and they won't like it. They will try to find out why you are changing and, typically very quickly, they point their fingers at the manipulator. When this happens, your friends and family will do what they can to try to see what this person is doing to you and how you are being treated. This is one of the most common signs of manipulation in relationships.

Of course, you will start to notice a change within yourself. Unfortunately, it is usually after the manipulator has had control over you. You start to notice yourself change when you begin to feel different. You might notice you have anxiety, you are depressed, having trouble sleeping, you struggle trusting people you once trusted, and you have become increasingly isolated ("About Covert Emotional Manipulation", n.d.).

For most people, it is hard to spot the signs of manipulators. This is especially true for people who suffer from manipulation from their significant other.

In general, it is hard to spot certain signs of manipulation. Furthermore, it is often harder to spot these behaviors from people who you love and believe love you back. In relationships, people often turn a "blind eye" to their significant other's manipulative ways because they see them as faults. We work to understand the faults of each other in relationships.

While you will want to notice the personality traits of a manipulator discussed previously, there are a lot of other signs when it comes to manipulation in relationships. This is because manipulators often let down their guard a bit when they are at home. They are in their comfort zone and believe they can do anything, and you won't protect yourself or try to change it because you are too weak.

1. They will start a fight with you over something minor.

Manipulators need to win, and this is frequently displayed in their relationships, especially their romantic ones. Therefore, you may notice that if you are having a minor disagreement with your significant other, they will turn it into a fight so that you allow them to win. They want you to give up and do whatever they want to do.

2. They are great secret keepers.

While they don't like it when you keep any secret from them, they can keep anything they want from you. Furthermore, they don't have to tell you anything they are doing or where they are going. This simply doesn't matter to you. In other words, what they do is their business and you need to mind your own.

However, if you treat them the same way, they will start a fight, tell you that you don't love them, or become angry. This is because if they don't know everything about you, they are losing their control. They are also able to keep control away from you by not letting you know their secrets.

3. Their actions and words don't match.

Manipulators realize that in order to keep you in their control, they need to sometimes give you what you want. While this can come in the form of gifts, they will usually focus on telling you what you want to hear. However, they will not follow through with their words. For example, if you are feeling lonely and don't want your significant other to go out with their friends again, you will ask them to stay with you. You will ask for time alone or to go with them. They will give you an excuse for why tonight won't work, but then make a promise to spend more time with you or both of you will do something another night. Unfortunately, they will rarely follow through with their promise.

4. They will act like the victim.

There is always a time that you are going to argue with your significant other or try to stand up for yourself. This not only happens in the beginning but throughout the relationship. When it does, the manipulator is going to play the role of the victim. They will twist your words to make it seem like you are the one who is doing something wrong. While you might not agree with this perception at first, they will continue to use their emotions to persuade you to believe them.

Manipulation in the Workplace

Many people deal with workplace manipulation at some point in their career. Sometimes it is because one of their co-workers is a manipulator while other times it is everyday forms of manipulation. For example, a co-worker manipulates you into helping them with their task or gets you to do their task. They only do this because they don't like this specific responsibility.

Sometimes you will start to notice your supervisor is a manipulator. Unfortunately, this is highly common in the workplace as many supervisors have used manipulation to get their position, especially if they worked themselves up the ladder. However, you should never assume your supervisor is manipulative. If they are, they will typically demonstrate signs of being a manipulator, such as bullying, blaming others, guilting their staff, giving staff the silent treatment, and distorting facts.

One way you know if you work with a manipulator is by the way you are treated. Manipulators need to make sure you know your place, meaning you are beneath them. Therefore, they will often make sarcastic comments that make you feel inferior. For example, you come to work one day in professional attire that is more casual than your company usually wears. Instead of a white shirt and a suit, you are wearing a white shirt with slacks. When your co-worker notices your attire, they start to belittle your clothes, making fun of your lower-paying income and that you can't afford nicer clothes.

When Can Manipulation Be Positive?

Manipulation is a valuable tool, just like a hammer and nails can be. You can either use the hammer, or the manipulation, to destroy something or you can use these tools to create something new and useful. The act of having all this control over a situation or other people can be a compelling position. That power can be used for bad, but it can also be used for good.

For example, let's say that you see a piece of paper laying around that has the username and password for the boss's computer. You could choose to throw the paper away and not use it, or you can log in to the computer and look up the information that is on there. If you find that someone left their wallet behind in the bathroom, you could take the cash and throw the wallet away without anyone knowing, or you can turn it into the front desk.

Those examples are sometimes a little more clear cut. We know what the right thing is and what the wrong thing is. And most of us are going to pick the right one and stick with what is good. But a manipulator would do the option that benefited them the most. They would use manipulation to find the weaknesses of someone else and then exploit these things. But you could also use these weaknesses as a way to improve the life of the victim and encourage these individuals any time that they feel weak.

No matter who you are, most people are going to choose to use manipulation to their advantage, and in the wrong hands, this can be a dangerous behavior it is important to note that not everyone who exhibits some of the qualities of a manipulative person is using it negatively. Some people may see that this is a tactic for their survival. Others may use it because they think that they know what is best for the other person, rather than just trying to trick them.

An excellent example of positive manipulation, or at least manipulation that isn't meant to be evil or bad, is that of children. All children use some level of manipulation, but this doesn't mean the children are evil. This is merely because they are learning how they should interact with other people. They will learn how to make changes based on the responses that they get from others in their little world.

Positive social influence

Now, let's take a look at some of the ways that manipulation can be turned into a positive thing. First, we will look at social influence. This is how our society, as well as the people that are around us, have developed ideas that will influence the individuals in those institutions. Things like ethics, morality, religion, and social norms are going to be in this group, and they can affect how we interact and shape our personal views.

There are going to be three varieties of social influence. The first one is going to be compliance, which means that you would keep your opinions to yourself, even if they happen to be different than what others have. The second one is going to be identification. This is going to be the influence of someone that is respected and admired. And then there is the third one that is known as internalization. This is when a belief, behavior, or an idea is accepted, and everyone in that society or group agrees to it privately and publicly.

Social influence can be a good thing, but there are times when it can be harmful to the victim and others as well. When it is good, it could be a doctor who is using some persuasion to help ensure their patient does the right treatment to get healthy. They will believe that there is a specific medication that is best to treat a certain disease. Because of this, they will work on manipulation to convince their patient to take that medication; without any other motives or personal gain, outside of the patient getting better.

Another example of good social influence is when there are some campaigns done to help educate users on certain things that need to be changed in society. Think about those commercials that try to get people to stop smoking. They can be manipulative sometimes, and they often exaggerate the truth a bit to get the person to stop. There is usually some fear tactics as well. The manipulation isn't there to help the advertiser benefit. It is there to try and get the individual to stop smoking and to improve their health.

Not all manipulators you encounter are going to be evil.

Just because someone you know is labeled as a manipulator, this doesn't mean that they are already an evil person and you should never have anything to do with them. Everyone has a different motive for trying to manipulate others around them. There are always better ways that you can confront issues rather than using the tactics of manipulation, but for some people, these tactics are the only way they know how to handle the problems.

Many manipulators are not aware of the proper means to express their emotions. So instead of trying to work with the situation at hand in a more constructive manner, they are going to use the tactics of manipulation to get what they want.

Let's take a look at this differently. There is a girl who sees that her sister is struggling through many aspects of her life. Maybe the sister is having trouble with her classes in college, is addicted to drugs or alcohol, and is having trouble paying her bills. The girl could decide to use some of the tactics to work on getting her sister to change these behaviors.

Does this make the first girl evil? She may be using the manipulation techniques that we talked about before, but the result is that she wants what is best for her sister. And maybe in the process, she believes that tricking her sister into doing something would end up with both of them getting better results in the process.

Manipulation is usually a form of avoiding a bigger truth. Maybe a wife would use some humor to joke about the way that your husband's hair looks, but she needs to be more honest and come out and tell him he needs a haircut. It is possible that the husband is not going to agree with this, but at least if the wife is honest, the husband isn't going to be made to feel like less by the cruel humor.

There are many times when manipulation can be used as a way to improve a person or improve society. It has gained a very negative connotation over the years because of how most manipulators use it. But overall, it is a great option that can be used to make things better, and even benefit other people that you know. You need to learn how to use it properly to get these results.

Mind Control

Mind control is at its heart the notion that certain psychological methods can alter or regulate the human mind. This practice is said to decrease the capacity of its subject to believe critically or independently, to allow the entry into the mind of the subject of fresh, unwanted thoughts and ideas, and to alter its attitudes, values, and beliefs.

To manipulate, reforming thought, brainwashing, coercive persuasion and control and abuses in group dynamics, are also considered versions of mind control. The fact that so many names exist shows a lack of consensus that makes confusion and distortion possible.

Forensic psychologist Dick Anthony, 2003

In 2016, Van Leer Jerusalem Institute member Adam Klin-Oron, who is also an Israeli religion anthropologist said of the "anti-proposed" And ultimately, judges dismissed expert witnesses, including in Israel, who claimed there was "brainwashing." Cults usually execute all or some of these techniques to recruit and gain followers.

Once a follower is gained, these tools are also use to control them. Cults may use these following techniques:

- Chanting and singing
- Isolation
- Dependency and fear
- Activity and pedagogy

- Sleep deprivation and fatigue

- Self-criticism and finger pointing

- Love bombing

- Mystical manipulation

- Thought termination

The first technique is chanting and singing. Singing mantras is an significant component in many religions, especially Buddhism and Hinduism, as well as other types of mass singing in every organization. As band employees, the phrases are sung or mantras in unison, with all of their voices becoming one, a robust sense of belonging and company distinctiveness builds. When the technique is used, a state of lowered heart rate and relaxation occurs. This occurrence may help cast the worshipping group practice in a constructive light. But the ongoing succession of brief phrasings in a cult is planned to become head-numbing, eradicate rational thought, and establish a state of mood.

Psychologists Linda Dubrow-Marshall and Steve Eichel

Group control using singing and chanting is

manipulated by cult leaders to break the individuality, and critical thinking abilities of a person instead of meditative purposes.

Isolation is the second technique. Physical isolation give cults the farther advantage of mind control by moving people away from external influences, such as relatives and loved ones. Public events, such as group meetings and social events with other members can be beneficial and effective for the cult's message to be conveyed. Forced solitary confinement, both as punishment and a conditioning tool is used to strengthen control though isolation. A slower way of building a relationship and persuading to isolate the individual away from outside forces is by establishing a one on one relationship. As long as there are not any dissuading messages are seen or heard, emotional isolation will soon follow physical isolation.

Without the outside influences of friends and families, a cult can use this as proof that the individual is unwanted.

Hearst was abducted in 1974. during her captivity, she was subjected to abuse, both physical and psychological. Through this conditioning using dependency and fear, she quickly ended up becoming an associate of her captors, who may of taken advantage of her age and reputation (she came from a rather influential family), even participating in an armed back robbery. Her continual refusal of her being brainwashed when asked during her arrest hindered her defense. She was sentenced to prison for seven years, but her sentence was reduced.

Activity and pedagogy are also techniques. Several cults use this, in which they assign or encourage members to perform endless series of activities, such as physical labor or exercise to make the individual tired and exhausted both mentally and physically in order to lower their mental defenses and resolve, which will make them more susceptible. The activities are performed in a group setting, where the individual is never left alone or given any private time. Usually the activity is performed over and over again in repetition. The activity may also be of an academic nature, such as attending a long lecture or study. The leader or a trusted follower may be the "instructor".

What makes physical pedagogy different from regular sports is that the cult will take advantage of the group mentality to showcase certain ideological beliefs, which might be met with skepticism if the prospect were awake and alert.

As an example, Russia hosted mass sporting events for their citizens where they had to participate in physical activity.

In the 1970s, the followers of Jim Jones would work constantly on various duties for the church, It was usually for several days straight. If followers quit or stopped, they would be shamed or threatened.

The next technique is sleep deprivation. Sleep deprivation explains itself. Individuals are not allowed to sleep or rest, which in turn, harms the ability to make good decisions and be more susceptible. Activities such as weekend long events or functions, such as lectures which go on through the night which may include loud music or flashing lights to keep followers awake. Keepings followers on a strict diet containing low protein and other nutrients can also lead members to have low blood sugar, continuing their fatigue. Limiting sleep or rest can contribute to this too.

A former follower of the Aum Shinrikyo described that while campaigning to get their leader elected to parliament, they consumed one meal each day and slept only one to two hours every night.

Self-criticism and shaming is a technique where the group of followers denounce each other, talk about their own faults, leading to feelings of inadequacy and self-doubts, which in turn can lead to a dependency to the cult or group in an effort to "be fixed".

An example of this would be the experience of POWs during the Korean War. The Chinese forced them to participate in sessions where they would talk about their own faults and insecurity about capitalism and the US. These ongoing "discussions" began to work a little and the POWs began to question their own patriotism and their own self-worth. In the end, these sessions were unsuccessful, since only 23 POWs refused repatriotism and the Chinese abandoned their brainwashing program.

Love bombing is an effective technique in which the cult will make them appear welcoming and inviting by using the principle influence of recipocracy by showering potential recruits with affection and attention, since we are more inclined to feel like we must reciprocate the same affection and love. Love bombing is meant to create a sense of debt and obligation. When the generosity is not returned, the individual is supposed to feel guilty and it may reinforce devotion.

Not all attempts at love bombing are negative. Members of the Unification church use this technique as an expression of friendship, interest, concern or interest in a welcoming way. Other churches and organizations such as twelve step programs in which combat addictions practice love bombing as a way to welcome already vulnerable individuals in a genuine and real way as to build a welcoming atmosphere.

Mystical manipulation is a technique where the cult leader controls the information and circumstances in the group as to where it can be conveyed that the leader themselves can get their followers to believe that that they have supernatural or magical powers or divine favor by giving the false impression they give. The leaders claim that their word is indisputable and to question their words is to question the divine.

The final technique is thought terminating clichés.

These are the uses and phrases, usually with rhetoric, that when used intensely, can help replace individual thoughts. The words and phrases, noted by Psychologist Robert Jay Lifton, were "all-encompassing jargon". The Soviet Union and China used this technique frequently.

Lifton considered their jargon to be:

"abstract, highly categorical, relentlessly judging"

and was, "the language of non-thought".

An interesting example of this technique was during the trial of Nazi official Adolf Eichman. When questioned, Eichman would constantly reply in stock phrases and clichés which pertained to National Socialism. The Soviet Union and China used this technique frequently. Eichman was so entrenched in the Nazi ideals, that it may have been virtually impossible for him to really understand the magnitude of his crimes, which is what mind control is all about: the complete and utter control of another living being.

Mind control, when used in the ways discussed are still used today. Sex traffickers use some of these techniques to gain a level of trust through feigning affection and generosity before beginning to monitor and control their actions and movements. They can prey on their prospective victims through promises of a great paying jobs, then instill dependency and fear using threats of deportation, involvement of law enforcement and deportation. Some victims may achieve a form of traumatic bonding or "Stockholm syndrome" with their captor or captors through prolonged imprisonment, which could lead to the victim's inability to seek assistance.

Mind control techniques, when used in the ways discussed, can be abused to take advance of the vulnerability of the individual to make them more susceptible to the group's/leader/ other individual's needs or gains. Some of us may have wanted or may have been tempted to use these techniques in our daily lives (to make a boyfriend/spouse/ children more compliant, make it so our boss would give us a raise), what mind control takes away is the free will and independence of the person. That individuality at its core builds the character of that person.

BRAINWASHING TO STOP BEING MANIPULATED

Brainwashing tends to be a little more "personal" and subtle. Brainwashing often requires the victim to be isolated, and more dependent on the individual or group of individuals who are brainwashing them. This is a favorite tactic of cults, religious groups, and yes, even your favorite sports teams.

Let's focus on national, televised sports, the most seemingly innocent form of cult worship. Billions of people all over the world tune into to watch football, baseball, swimming, car racing, cricket, volleyball, curling... the list goes on. Those same billions spend even more billions of dollars on tickets and travel to live games, merchandise, and the access to watch their favorite teams on their favorite channel in the comfort of their own home. What would happen if the Super Bowl didn't air in February? An honest, logical guess might be: "The world would end as we know it." Championship games of all kinds draw larger audiences than political rallies, religious observations and even the release of the latest iPhone.

But let's see what happens: Does it really affect a fan's life if the Patriots win or lose the Super Bowl again? Not really, yet millions of television screens turn to the game every February regardless of their team affiliation. What kind of power is this?

A dangerous one, that's it. Just how the politician or businessman has a wide reach in order to emotionally manipulate an audience, large groups of brainwashers can wipe your conscious down to the bare essentials. Then it replaces that person's "personhood" with an identity, set of ideals, beliefs, likes and dislikes that aren't their own.

How is the NFL or NHL capable of Advertising and affiliations? The NFL is one of the largest and most prominent sponsors and advertisers of the United States military. Commercials for different branches play during breaks, certain games or national anthems are dedicated to veterans, POWs, or current individuals serving. Players even don camouflage, military-inspired gear as part of this relationship.

Then there was the debate over the national anthem

when Colin Kaepernick knelt in solidarity for all of his fellow people of color brutalized by police violence. The NFL immediately launched a vociferous media campaign, that was picked up by NFL fans everywhere. Soon, stickers, hats and t-shirts could be found everywhere saying "I stand for the anthem."

The NFL took this opportunity to use their fan base's interests, as well as the hold on they already had on loyal fans. As television ratings were dropping, the NFL created a problem that didn't exist, turned it into a media tornado, and unleashed their rhetoric on millions of viewers nationwide. It had a discernible effect by creating a reason for people to watch other than for the game itself.

The Fundamentals of Brainwashing

Many people tend to get hypnosis, CEM, NLP and brainwashing confused. But brainwashing isn't just a dark psychological technique, but one identified by psychologists all over the world as well. It's not only a tool of sports teams, in fact, but it's also been the go-to method of acquiring members for cults for decades, if not centuries.

Brainwashing from here on out means the process of forcing an individual into accepting belief systems completely and utterly different than their own, often under duress.

The simplest example to illustrate brainwashing are cults, or small groups of individuals who practice either a form of religion or other belief that from the outside looks a bit sketchy, questionable, and perhaps even evil. Some examples of famous cults and their leaders include:

Jim Jones, leader of the People's Temple Cult. Jones was a zealous religious leader who convinced hundreds of his followers to participate in a mass murder/suicide by drinking poisoned Kool-Aid.

Children of God/Family International, founded by David "Moses" Berg. Founded in California in 1968, members were encouraged to have sex with children to achieve "divinity." This cult still exists today on multiple continents and over 70 countries. This cult, in particular, was perpetuated by founder David Berg's master of propaganda writing and publishing, which drew new members to his group and kept older members close by.

Branch Davidians – This was a splintered extremist group of Seventh Day Adventists that had been in existence since the 1950s. It wasn't until leader David Koresh took over as leader that he began to claim that he was the Messiah and claimed all women and female children for his own. The group did believe that the end of the world was nigh, but many never got to see it. The cult was disbanded in1993 after a standoff with FBI agents that resulted in more than 80 deaths.

Raëlism. Followers of this cult, founded in 1974, believe that all life on Earth is scientifically created, thus, not organic, and challenging all prevalent scientific theories of evolution. The Raël creator is named "Elohim" and that leaders within the movement are former aliens that will teach the earth how to carry on Raël traditions, including peace and mindfulness

Now that we have a few examples of cults, let's dissect what makes up a cult. Usually, this small, strange group will have one or two leaders with strong personalities that lead their followers and often make decisions on their behalf.

Cults also usually seem very accepting at first, but that's because they're looking to increase their numbers. Don't mistake friendliness for desperation on their part.

Cults also make followers feel safe. The boisterous and charming leader is also a comforter – those who end up lost or confused by traditional religion are comforted and brought into the fold. Existential questions like "Why am I here?" and "What is my purpose in life?" are easily answered by the cult's lore (usually a cult will have a few strong oral storytellers, too).

Acceptance. Purpose. Belonging. The things people crave most of all are the things cults are most willing to dish out.

Cults and Brainwashing

Cults and brainwashing go together like peanut butter and jelly. The latter enables the former. In this book and in this context, brainwashing is a type of total "reboot" of thought and framing of the mind. Again, unless the victim is perceptive, this technique will likely go unnoticed.

Before we return to cults, it's important to establish that this is not the only way brainwashing is used. For example, a dress code at your job could be brainwashing if you work there long enough for the brainwashing to work its way in. After working there long enough, you might believe that a certain length of the skirt is more appropriate than another or a style of shoes more "business casual" than just "casual." This can be harmful in the long run because the victim has internalized the self-reproach the dress-code encourages.

UNDETECTED MIND CONTROL

The term mind control has many definitions and interpretations, but the crucial thing to note is that it doesn't involve any sort of magic or supernatural ability; it just requires a rudimentary understanding of human emotions and behavior. Mind control can involve brainwashing a person, reeducating them, reforming their thoughts, using coercive techniques to persuade them of certain things, or brain-sweeping. There are many forms of mind control, and we could fill an entire book discussing all those forms, but for our purposes, we will look at the concept in general terms. Mind control means a person is trying to get others to feel, think, or behave in a certain way, or to react and make decisions following a certain pattern. It could vary from a girl trying to get her boyfriend to develop certain habits, to a cult leader trying to convince his followers that he is God.

Mind control is based on one thing: information. We have the thoughts and beliefs that we do because we learned them. When we are subjected to new information on a deliberate and consistent basis, it's possible to alter our beliefs, thoughts, or even memories. The brain is hardwired to survive, and towards that end, it's very good at learning information that is crucial for our survival. When you receive certain information consistently, your brain will start to believe it even if you know it's not true. For example, even if you are the most rational person out there, if you go online and watch 100 videos about a certain conspiracy theory, you will start to believe it to some extent. That explains why people who seem smart can end up getting indoctrinated into cults or even terrorist groups.

Mind control also works more effectively when one is dependent on the person who is trying to control his/her mind. Even in relationships that are involuntary, the victim can start buying the perpetrator's world view if they have been dependent on the perpetrator for a long time. That explains phenomena such as Stockholm syndrome (where people who are kidnapped or held hostage start being affectionate towards their captors and empathizing with their causes). The worst thing you can do is assume that you are too smart for mind control to work on you. Under the right circumstances, anyone can be persuaded to abandon their world view and adopt someone else's. Mind games are covert tricks that are deliberately crafted in order to manipulate someone. Think of them as "handcrafted" psychological manipulation techniques. While other techniques are applied broadly, mind games are created to target very specific people. They work best when the victim trusts the perpetrator, and the perpetrator understands the victim's personality and behavior. Most of the psychological manipulation techniques we have discussed thus far can be used when crafting mind games. A person who understands you will tell you certain things or behave in certain ways around you because they are deliberately trying to get you to react in a certain way. It almost always involves feigning certain emotions.

People who play mind games use innocent sounding communication to elicit calculated reactions from you. Psychologists refer to such mind games as "conscious one-upmanship," and they have observed that they occur in all areas of life. Mind games occur in office politics, personal relationships, and even in international diplomacy. At work, someone could try to make you feel like you are not up to the task so that they can steal an opportunity from you. In a marriage, your partner could make certain seemingly innocent slights against you so that you feel like you have something to prove, and you take a certain course of action as a result. In dating, there are "pickup artists" who use different kinds of tricks to get you to lower your guard and let them in. Mind control is not the whole of the vague information you hear in gossip, accompanied by conspiracy theories. It is the product of secret experiments with systematic studies dating back to World War II, perhaps older. Of course, the 20th-century totalitarian regimes, who wanted to robotize their subjects, also played a major role in this. Therefore, the first thing to note is that developing technology facilitates the mind-control efforts of the oppressors every year. Like Telegram scourge that happens today… But mind control; it is something that can be done without technology with the support of psychology and orator. The most striking example of this in history; this is the work carried out by Goebbels, the Minister of Propaganda of the Nazis. Goebbels succeeded in engraving his name in gold letters in this lane, which was the disgrace of humanity.

Mind control; It is the name given to all the unethical activities of some power centers to manage people in line with their goals, to shape their ideas and control their lifestyles. While technological opportunities can be utilized in mind control, human psychology, propaganda knowledge, and social engineering are essential. Also, mind control; it is applied in a highly systematic, insidious way by people who have done as much research as required by a master or doctor. In other words, it is essential that people don't realize the engineering applied to them, so to be hypnotized. Therefore, it is challenging to recognize and resist.

Effects of Mind Control on human

The effects of using mind control on human beings are seen in different ways. Some of them are as follows;

- "Memory loss and behavior disorders
- Change in direction, intensity and content of sound heard
- Speech deterioration by checking eyelids
- Severe heart palpitations
- Forcing accidents on the shoulders and arms

during laborious work

- Jogging of the elbows and preventing work while doing something
- Pain and unnecessary movement of the legs, right and left swing and excessive stiffness
- Itching and blushing in hard-to-reach areas
- Contractions of large muscles in the back
- Checking hand gestures
- Reading thoughts or transmitting thoughts from outside
- Seeing moving imaginary images
- Keeping eyelids constantly open
- Continuous tinnitus
- Jaw and teeth shivering for no reason

THE POWER OF PERSUASION

At this point, you have had some time to analyze the target and figure out what makes them tick. You know whether they are driven more by logic or by emotions, and you know a lot more about what will work as a technique of manipulation for them. Once you are done with that, it is time to move into planting some of the seeds of how you would like the target to behave. These are hopefully going to get the target to agree to your course of action, but they are planted in a manner that makes it so the target feels they got to make the decision, rather than them feeling like they are forced to make the decision by someone else.

When all of that is done, it is time to move on to the third part of influence the process of persuading people. This is going to be the part that will require you to bring in some physical actions, rather than just using your words. These physical actions are so important because they will really push things over the edge and will get your target to agree with you, or get them to comply, with the thing you are asking for.

The trick to this one is that you need to use persuasion in a way that is going to work on your target. This is where the other two parts come in. if you were successful with all of this, and you really worked towards making the target understood then you will find that the persuading part of all of this was pretty easy. You will be well equipped to deal with the target because you will know the perfect tactic of persuasion that you can use each and every time.

Persuasion is such an important part of this. And we are going to take some time to explore how to make this work and some of the different techniques that come with persuasion later on. But right now, remember that persuasion is going to be a big part of the manipulation, and it is the step that will help to seal the deal. If you are able to put all three of these parts together, you will be amazed at the results that you are able to get from the target, and how easy it is to get them to do what you want.

This guidebook is going to spend some time working on the different techniques that you are able to use when it comes to the art of persuasion. This can sometimes be something that we see as a good thing.

And often persuasion doesn't have the same evil or bad connotation that manipulation may, even though it is possible that it is going to be used for evil purposes along the way as well.

There is a lot of persuasions that we kind find in the world around us, and it is often going to depend again on the intention that is behind it, and how much choice the other person has. If they are able to see it working and then walk away without feeling any guilt or anything else in the process, then this is seen as a good form of persuasion that still lets you have some kind of choice. But if the manipulator, or the person behind the persuasion, is able to get you to behave in a certain way because it is really hard to walk away and say no, then this is often seen as a bad thing.

Think of some times when you have seen persuasion at work, and it didn't seem like such a bad thing to work with at all. You may have seen countless advertisements out there telling us to purchase this one product, and not another one. We may have had a parent or another family member try to convince us to do something because they needed help or because they thought that it was in our best interests.

We are able to see these kinds of manipulation and find that they are not so bad. We are able to walk away from the advertisements on TV because we have seen a lot of them in our lives, and they all say the same thing over and over again. We know that when a family member, for the most part, tells us about a plan and how they want us to try something, we recognize that it is usually for something that is good for us and we are willing to consider doing something.

But then there are times when the manipulation may not be the best thing for us at all. We find that this persuasion is going to be used against us and that the answer and the reaction to it are not going to be able to benefit us really at all in the process. This is the type of persuasion that we need to be really careful about, the kind that can sometimes sneak up on us without us even knowing. And then we are going to end up losing our control and giving it to the person who is trying to manipulate us.

Staying secret when you manipulate

While we just talked a bit about the three steps or stages to influence, we also need to take a look at what can be known as the final part of this process. It is not really a step like the others but it is important to consider when you do manipulation. When you are working with this process, it is important for you to remember that your intentions need to be kept hidden as much as possible in order to see the results.

Think of it this way. How would you feel if you found out someone was trying to manipulate you against your will? It's likely that you would not feel the best, and would want to stay as far away from them as possible. If someone else finds out that you were working to manipulate them, there are going to be two different things that could show up.

First, it is likely that your target is going to stop trusting you. They will wonder how many other things you have lied about over time and will try to distance themselves from you as much as possible. This is basically going to take away any kind of chance you have to manipulate them now or in the future.

The second issue that you are going to have is when the target sees that you are manipulating, it is going to shed some more light on what you were trying to do. This means that even if you were to try a new kind of tactic for persuasion or manipulation in the future, it is likely they are going to notice it. This is because they no longer trust you, and they are going to start putting all the actions that you do under a microscope to see what adds up and what doesn't.

This means that if you want to be as successful as possible with the process of manipulation, you have to be good at staying secretive about your intentions throughout the whole process. To do this, you need to take things slowly and make sure that you are picking out the right kind of target to work on for all of your needs.

Manipulation is a practice that you can technically use on anyone. There is not going to be any kind of limitation or restriction on who is able to use these techniques, or even when they are able to use them. Of course, most people will also make sure that they are not using the techniques of manipulation when it is seen as something illegal or when it is considered morally wrong. For example, most of the time it is frowned upon to manipulate another person into a relationship with you when it is against their will.

However, these strategies are going to be great to use

in situations like negotiations with business because it helps you to make sure that you are getting what you want, helps you to change up the perception that the other person has of you, and other similar manners. There are some people who will use these techniques in the wrong manner and will use the techniques to get what they want, whether it is seen as illegal and unethical or not.

It is so important that if we want to be able to see some success with persuasion or manipulation or anything else that we are doing, that we are able to remain secretive, at least a little bit. We may be able to get away with the analysis and not being as tricky and sneaky as the others because people are always analyzing each other in our modern world. But if you don't be careful with the way that you are using the techniques that come with manipulation and persuasion, then the other person is going to catch on, and you are going to end up in a world of trouble then.

If you are worried about giving yourself away, or if you have had a few close calls that could have derailed the whole thing, this means that you are going through the process too fast. It is much better to take things slow and work through them, forming a good connection with the other person and really getting them to feel like they know you and trust you, rather than just jumping in and hoping that it is all going to work out.

The moment that the other person, the moment that your target, realizes what you are doing against them, and they find out that you are going to use persuasion and manipulation against them for your own benefit, then they are going to want to have nothing to do with you, they may tell others, and you are going to be exposed for all that you are trying to do against them.

It is much better to take your time, do a good analysis, and then pick the technique that you want to use and get them on your side ahead of time. it may take a bit longer, but you will find that this method is much more effective in the long run.

Subconscious Techniques for Persuasion

Persuasiveness is an effective aptitude everybody ought to learn. It is helpful in incalculable circumstances. For both your business and your personal life, being inspiring and influential to others will be the foundation for accomplishing objectives and being successful.

Learning about the traps of persuasion will give you new awareness for when they appear in sales messaging you read. The greatest advantage? Your cash stays in your pocket. It literally pays for you to understand exactly how sales representatives and marketers offer you items that you don't really require. The following are some persuasive techniques that work on a subconscious level.

Outlining Impacts Thought

Let's say you're thirsty, and someone hands you a glass of water not-quite full. "The glass is half full." An optimist would "outline" the reality of your glass of water in that way. Outlining is used as an approach to modify how we classify, connect, and attach meaning to every aspect of our lives.

The headline "FBI Operators Surround Cult Leader's Compound" creates a mental picture strikingly different from another version of the headline for the same story: "FBI Specialists Raid Small Christian Gathering of Women and Children." Both headlines may convey what happened, however, the selected words affect the readers' mental and emotional responses, and therefore direct the impact the target events have on the article's readers.

Outlining is employed by apt government representatives. For example, representatives on both sides of the abortion debate refer to their positions as "pro-choice" or "pro-life." This is intentional, as "pro" has a more positive association to build arguments on. Outlining an event, product, or service this way unobtrusively utilizes emotional words strategically to persuade individuals to see or accept your perspective.

Creating a convincing message is as easy as selecting words that summon strategic pictures in the minds of your audience. Indeed, even with neutral words surrounding it, a solitary stimulating word can be powerful.

Reflecting as Persuasive Strategy

Reflecting, often called "the chameleon effect," is the act of replicating the movements and non-verbal communication of the individual you want to persuade. By mirroring the actions of the individual listening, you create an appearance of empathy.

Hand and arm motions, inclining forward or reclining away, or different head and shoulder movements are types of non-verbal communication you can reflect. We, as a whole, do this without much thought, and now that you're becoming aware of that, you'll notice not only yourself but others doing it, as well.

It is important to be graceful, thoughtful about it and allow just a couple seconds to pass between their movements and you reflecting them.

Highlight Scarcity of a Product or Service

The concept of scarcity is often employed by marketers to make products, services, or associated events and deals appear to be all the more engaging on the grounds that there will be restricted accessibility. The belief is that there is a huge amount of interest for it if availability is scarce. For example, an ad for a new product might say: Get one now! They're selling out quickly!

Again, it literally pays to know that this is a persuasion strategy that you will see everywhere. Consider this concept the next time you settle on your buying choice. This principle triggers a feeling of urgency in most individuals, so it is best used when applied in your marketing and sales copy.

Reciprocity Helps Make a Future Commitment

When somebody helps us out, we feel responsible to provide a proportional payback. All in all, the next time you need someone to accomplish something beneficial for you, consider doing something unexpectedly pleasant for them first.

At work, you could pass a colleague a lead. At home, you could offer to loan some landscaping tools to a neighbor.

The details, where or when you do it, won't make a difference; the key is to supplement the relationship without being sought out first. Lead with value and give it freely, without overtly expecting anything in return, and their response will come.

Timing Can Bolster Your Good Fortune

Individuals will be more pleasant and accommodating when they're mentally exhausted. Before you approach somebody for something they may not otherwise participate in, consider holding back until they've recently accomplished something mentally challenging. Consider making your offer toward the end of the work day, for example, when you can get a colleague or collaborator on the way out of the office. Whatever you may ask, a reasonable reaction could be, "I'll deal with it tomorrow."

Enhance Compliance to Acquire a Needed Result

To avoid cognitive dissonance, we all try to be true to how we've acted in the past. A reliable technique business people use is to shake your hand as they are consulting with you. We have been taught that a handshake equals a "sealed deal," and by doing this before the arrangement is really sealed, the business person has taken a step to persuade you into believing the deal is already done.

One approach to employing this yourself is influencing individuals to act before their minds are made up. Let's say that you are roaming downtown with a companion, and you decide you want to go see a movie at the local theater; yet, your companion is undecided.

Compliance can come into play if you begin strolling toward the theater while they are still thinking about it. Your companion will probably consent to go once they realize you are strolling in the theater's direction.

Attempt Fluid Discourse

In the natural flow of our speech, interjections and reluctant expressions act as fillers when we need a moment to think or select the "right" word, for example, "um" or "I mean," and obviously the newly pervasive "like." These fillers have the unintended impact of making us appear to be unsure and doubtful and, in this way, less convincing. When you're certain about your message, others will be more effectively persuaded.

If you have trouble finding the right words at the right time, practice some free-flow association every day in front of the mirror for 60 seconds. You can add it to your morning ritual, or you can do it while having a shower, like I usually do. Basically, your goal in these 60 seconds is to jump from one topic to another very quickly, by associating words; do your best to avoid "um," "like," or other fillers.

Example: The water on my back right now is so hot, it reminds me of the hot weather in California. I love Cali; I like the food there. Mexican food is so spicy and hot, like Mexican women. I remember Marcella, that one Mexican girl I met last time I was there; she was probably the only blonde girl from Mexico. She was blonde like a Swedish model. I've never been to Sweden, but I've heard it's cold out there...

And so on, until you get to 60 seconds without pauses or interjections. Once you reach that point after some practice, you can aim for 120 seconds. Once you've done that, the next step is to practice this game with other people. You don't need to go on for a full two minutes straight, but while you're talking to someone, you can go on a tangent for 20 seconds and practice the free-flow association skill. You'll practice and improve tremendously, while they'll be wondering "This guy is interesting. I really want to know what he's going to say next..."

Group Affinity Can Affect Decisions

We always seek the people around us to help us make decisions; people have an inherent need for belonging and acknowledgment, as previously discussed. We have a much higher tendency to imitate or be persuaded by somebody we like or by somebody we see as an influential leader.

A compelling approach to make this work for you, bolstering your good fortune, is to be viewed as a leader by your target audience—regardless of whether you officially have the title. It helps to be enchanting and sure, so individuals will have more confidence in your message. Keep improving yourself, and you'll soon become more magnetic than everyone else.

If you're interacting with an individual who doesn't consider you to be a powerful person (for example, a rival at work or your irritating in-laws), you can, in any case, exploit group affinity. For example, if you praise a leader that individual respects, that praise then activates the positive associations in that individual's brain about that admired leader, which creates a mental space where they can relate those qualities with you.

Create a Photo Opportunity with Man's Best Friend

Give your target audience the idea that you're trustworthy, and motivate them to be loyal to you, by taking a photo of yourself with a pooch (it doesn't need to be your own puppy). This can make you appear kind and cooperative, but keep these kinds of photo-ops to a minimum; setting up an excessive number of pictures looks amateurish. On a side note, it pays to know your audience; if you know they share a lot of cat pictures, maybe try a picture or two with a feline friend, too.

Offer a Drink

This might seem too easy, but giving the individual you want to persuade a warm drink to hold while you're conversing with them can be persuasive in itself. The warm vibe you've offered their hands (and their body) can intuitively make them see you as candidly warm, affable, and inviting. Offering a chilly drink can do the opposite! As a rule, individuals tend to feel "frosty" and seek out warm beverages when they're feeling stressed or overwhelmed, so take care of that need keeping in mind the end goal to make them more open.

Start with a Simple "Yes" Question

Start the discussion with an inquiry that creates a "Yes" reaction. "Nice weather we're having, isn't it?" or "You're searching for a great price on a car, right?"

When you get somebody saying yes, it's anything but difficult to motivate them to proceed, up to and including "Yes, I'll get it." You can counter this in your daily life by giving cautious answers to even the simplest questions.

Gently Break the Contact Boundary

You could be sealing a deal or asking somebody out for coffee, and touching them (in a modest and suitable way) can enhance your odds of hearing "Yes," because you have intuitively triggered the human yearning to connect.

In a professional setting, it is normally best to "touch" verbally by giving consolation or acclaim, as a physical touch could be seen as lewd behavior.

In sentimental circumstances, any delicate touch from a lady will more often than not be taken well. Men will need to proceed here with extreme caution—keeping in mind the end goal is to abstain from making a lady feel uncomfortable.

UNDERSTANDING DECEPTION

Once manipulation is identified, the next step is to get through it. Overcoming manipulation can be very challenging. In some cases, a 60 year-old-man might realize just now that his 85 year-old-mother is manipulative. They might never get through their issues, but they should still be confronted. Manipulation takes a part of both the abuser and the victim. It can ruin people's lives, altering the direction they take and affecting the rest of their years. Manipulation can be hard to identify and even harder to overcome.

It can be done, and it should be attempted to get through. In a relationship based around manipulation, there might not be any coming back. Sometimes, people might just have to break up. You might have to get a divorce or stop calling your mom. It takes two people to partake in a manipulative scenario. Not both people will end up identifying it as a manipulative situation, however. In that case, the person that realizes what's actually going on might just have to move on, the manipulator never realizing the damage they caused.

This can be a challenging part of overcoming manipulation. Usually, some instance of codependency formed, making it even harder to break away. There are ways to overcome this, and we will cover that in the next few sections.

Know Your Worth

The first step in overcoming manipulation is for the victim to identify that they still have value. A manipulator likely took everything from their victim. They belittled them, ridiculed them, and made them feel as though what they thought didn't matter. In some situations, they might have even used gaslighting tactics to make their victims feel as though they're insane. It can be hard for a victim to then recognize just how much value they still have once they become aware of the manipulation.

It's important for everyone to know, no matter who is reading this, that you have worth. Everyone has value. No one deserves to be manipulated. No one deserves to feel as though they don't have any purpose, reason, or value. You have the right to be treated justly, and with respect from other people. You are allowed to express your emotions, feelings, wants, and opinions. No one else has the right to tell you how to feel. You set your own boundaries, and no one else gets to decide for you.

If you feel sad about something, that is completely valid. No one gets to decide if what they say hurts you or not. Not everyone might intentionally mean to hurt you, but that doesn't mean you're not allowed to still feel bad. You have the right to feel the way you do, and you have the same right to express those beliefs.

If you feel like you need to protect yourself, you are just in doing so. If you feel like your safety is being threatened, or someone is taking advantage of you, you have the right to remove yourself from that situation without guilt. No one gets to treat you badly, and though that can be hard for many of us to hear, it's the truth.

Manipulators aim to take these thoughts away. They want to deprive their victims of their rights in order to work towards getting what they want. This can't happen anymore. It's up to the manipulator's victims to now recognize their worth and stop the cycle of manipulation.

Don't Be Afraid to Keep Your Distance

Many people that feel as though they're being manipulated end up being too afraid to do anything about it. They have been stripped of their own thoughts and opinions, their own feelings invalidated and instead focus on how other people feel. Those that have been continually manipulated might be afraid to leave those that have hurt them. They've depended on those that abused them for so long they don't know where else to go.

You're allowed to keep your distance. You don't have to feel guilty about protecting yourself. It can be hard to separate yourself from a manipulator, especially in a romantic relationship. You might see the very weaknesses that cause their manipulative behavior. Maybe in a relationship, a boyfriend's dad was an abusive alcoholic, and it greatly hurt him. It also caused his violent manipulative behavior that led him to hitting his girlfriend on a few occasions. It's true that he has his own pain, but that doesn't mean he's allowed to inflict it on others. The girlfriend has every right to leave her boyfriend and find her own peace and protection.

Ask what is really lost by leaving the person that's manipulating you. More often than not, value in a relationship is placed on codependent tendencies. A person is afraid to leave not because they love their manipulator, but because they are afraid to be alone. It can be scary to be on your own, but mostly because manipulators put that idea in their victims in the first place. Manipulators will trick their victims into staying with them because deep down, they know that the victim will be just fine without them.

It's Not Your Job to Change Them

Once manipulation is recognized, the next step is to try to talk to the person about the manipulation. It's time to get down to the root issues of the relationship and figure out what can be done to help both partners get what they need, instead of just the manipulator. There has been an imbalance of power for far too long, and it's time to rebalance.

Unfortunately, not many manipulators are willing to

admit their faults and later change their behavior. Instead, they'll do whatever they can to distract others from their faults, placing the blame on their victims instead. When this happens, the victim has to accept that their manipulator isn't going to change, and they must find the strength to leave.

There will likely be a desire to change the other person and help them improve their life as well. Not everyone will always be on the same page of their journey towards self-discovery. It can be hard to accept for some victims, but they have to realize that it's not their job to change their manipulator.

You can only help a person so much, and if they're not willing to change or improve themselves, it's not going to happen. Many people wait around for the other to change in their relationship, hoping their manipulation will get better. If a person isn't aware of their behavior and aren't actively trying to change it, nothing is going to happen in the end.

Hypnosis

If mind control is the best set of manipulation strategies for beginners to pick up and be able to learn quickly, then hypnosis is the next natural step in the process towards becoming a master of manipulation. In general, hypnosis lasts longer and is far more powerful than mind control is, although it also requires more skill to successfully pull off. While hypnosis has some concepts that overlap with mind control and brainwashing, it also has completely unique components, which can make it more challenging to learn. Hypnosis has a long a rich history, and today it is used in a wide variety of fields and industries, including in medicine, sports, psychotherapy, self-improvement, meditation and relaxation, forensics and criminal justice, art and literature, and the military. Of course, all instances of hypnosis share common characteristics no matter what context it is used in, and these same characteristics can come in handy when attempting to manipulate someone else. Having a good understanding of the principles and concepts of hypnosis can turn you from a mediocre manipulator into a highly skilled one.

The Hypnotic Trance

At its core, hypnosis is all about planting ideas into somebody else's subconsciousness in order to influence their consciousness. If you manage to infiltrate a person's subconsciousness with enough skill, they will not be aware of what you are doing, and will never know that you ever influenced them at all. The best way to access someone's subconsciousness is to coax them into a relaxed, meditative state known as a hypnotic trance. Getting your target into a trance is the most difficult part of the process of hypnosis, but once you finally manage to pull it off, you will have a much easier time successfully manipulating them. Putting your target into a trance allows for you to have direct access to their subconsciousness, as their consciousness will no longer be an active part of their mind for the duration of the trance. The trace is what separates hypnosis from mind control, and the ability to induce it in somebody else is what separates a beginner of manipulation from a budding expert.

The best way to think of a hypnotic trance is a form of deep relaxation. You are likely already familiar with the overall concept of the trace, due to portrayals of hypnosis in book, movies, and popular culture in general. Of course, in real life, you cannot put somebody else into a hypnotic trance simply by waving a watch in front of their face or by using a magical code phrase that will put them to sleep. Instead, putting someone into a hypnotic trance takes lots of time and skill, and it may not always work on every single person that you try it out on, especially when you are first starting to attempt to use it. In fact, for the best introduction to the hypnotic trance, you may want to find a friend who is willing to allow you to put them into a trance in order to practice doing it, or if you cannot find someone who is a willing participant, you can always put yourself into a hypnotic trance using this same method. If you fail at putting somebody into a trance, you are likely to face a negative reaction from that person, as they are likely to recognize suspicious behavior when they see it if they still have full awareness of their surroundings. This is why it is important that you practice this technique several times before attempting it on any outsiders, as you are far more likely to succeed in putting somebody into a hypnotic trance if you have some familiarity with how it already works.

The first step in putting your target into a hypnotic trance is to make sure that they are in a sitting position, or even better, lying down. After all, once your target is in the trance and their consciousness has temporarily faded away, they will no longer physically be able to stand up or support the weight of their own body. An action as forceful and abrupt as falling on the floor will be enough to wake them up from the hypnotic trance, and once they have regained their awareness, they will likely want an explanation as to what happened. Obviously, this is not a situation that you want to be caught in, so it is important to make sure that your target's body is in a secure position that will not fall over or cause them to wake up once you have put them in the trance. This also means that you should not attempt to hypnotize anybody unless there is a couch, chairs, a bed, or another piece of comfortable furniture for your target to use. Convincing your target to sit or lay down sounds more difficult than it actually is. Remember that your target will be more likely to sit or lay down if a piece of furniture is offered to them to do so on and that you should be prepared to sit or lay down first, as your target will be more likely to do the same if they are following your lead. If all else fails, you can always mind control them and influence them to sit or lay down where you want them to. Do not worry too much about how you make your target get into the best position and instead focus your attention on what comes after you have already convinced them to do so.

The next step in the process of putting someone into a hypnotic trance is to get your target to listen to the sound of your voice. In hypnotic techniques, your voice can be a powerful tool as long as you know how to use it correctly. Take special note of the fact that this step does not instruct you to start a conversation with your target, but rather to get them to listen to you. This is because when attempting to put another person into a hypnotic trance, your voice is not being used to express any meaning or to describe any information, but rather as a way to create a sort of white noise, which will allow your target to slip further and further into a deeply relaxed state. If your target is engaged by what you are saying and tries to respond, then they are not letting go of their awareness, and their consciousness is still very much active. When attempting to put your target in a hypnotic trance, when you are first beginning to speak to them, the content of what you are saying matters a tremendous amount. You need to choose a topic that is interesting enough for them to want to stick around and listen to, but not so interesting that they are completely engrossed in what you are saying and are trying to speak back to you. The topic that you choose is likely to vary from target to target, as everyone has different tastes as to what kind of subject they are willing to pay attention to or not. This is where skills learned under controlling the narrative can come in handy; if you are able to tell a long, meandering story instead of a short and sweet one, especially about something that your target does not particularly care about, then they should begin falling into a hypnotic trance relatively easily. When you are speaking, be sure to use a calm, soothing voice, and choose words and phrases to use that are generally simple and easy to understand. This allows your target to focus on the overall sound of your voice, rather than what exactly you are saying. However, if you make your voice sound too calm and soothing, your target may think that something is wrong with you or may grow suspicious of your intentions. Therefore, try not to sound too much like a guided meditation instructor and instead attempt to model your voice in the style of the narrator of a nature documentary. Keep in mind that your goal is to relax your target, but not to put them to sleep. If you make yourself sound too soothing, you will run the risk of having your target be too relaxed. If your target is asleep, after all, they will not be open to any suggestions that you make, as they will be unconscious. Once you see that your target has fallen into a more and more relaxed state, the content of what you are saying to them will not matter as much, and as long as you keep your voice in a steady, soothing tone, you will not have to worry about what topic you are speaking about any longer.

Advanced Techniques and Suggestibility Testing

At this point we have learned about various methods of manipulation through neuro-linguistic programming and hypnosis. By now you are armed with a plethora of weapons to use on any given subject, and you are prepared defensively if someone attempts to use any of these tactics against you. In this chapter, we will go over a couple of new topics that aren't manipulation tactics in and of themselves – they are nonetheless crucial for knowing upon whom to deploy these tactics on and for the defense of the manipulator.

Suggestibility Testing

Many hypnotists will tell you that suggestibility testing is best left to the street performers and entertainment hypnotists. This may be true as it has limited viability in hypnotherapy but what many hypnotists don't think about is everyday manipulation. Suggestibility testing is vastly utilizable in the realm of conversational hypnosis and everyday hypnosis towards the ends of manipulation. So what it is?

Suggestibility testing can refer to any number of verbal or physical "feelers" that help the hypnotist determine whether or not their subject is a good target for hypnosis and manipulation. They can serve as a guide for one to determine how likely a subject will bend to their will. Some hypnotists use suggestibility training to determine how deep into a hypnotic trance their subjects are but our purposes will be a little different.

For our intents and purposes we will use suggestibility testing to find our subjects in the first place. The reason anyone would want to use suggestibility testing is to find the right subject for manipulation. The caveat with hypnotism, even conversational hypnosis, is that some people are more suggestible to others. In other words, some people are less likely to be inducted into hypnosis than others. For this reason Dark NLP practitioners often use suggestibility testing to have a better idea of who they can manipulate and who they might not be able to.

The reason you will want to learn these tests is essentially for efficiency. For example, you wouldn't want to use a lot of your time and effort trying to manipulate someone whom you've tested to have low suggestibility. It would just take too long and besides, there are tons of easily suggestible targets to choose from. In fact, it is estimated that as much as 80% of the population is in the average range of hypnotic suggestibility – meaning that up to 80% of the population can be successfully hypnotized with moderate effort.

That is why suggestibility testing is so useful for the Dark NLP practitioner. It gives a good guideline on who a prime subject might be and helps the practitioner avoid difficult subjects.

Suggestibility tests can be deployed fairly easily. In most cases you should try at least one of these tests before you try using any of the tactics we have discussed so far. Let's take a look at some of the best methods for testing suggestibility.

The Light/Heavy Hands Technique

This method of suggestibility testing depends heavily on the concentration and that imagination of the subject. How keenly a person can bring their concentration and imagination into alignment is a very important factor. It will determine how susceptible they will be to actual hypnotic suggestion.

In this test you will be able to see a physical manifestation of their level of suggestion. It is sometimes called the book and balloon test as well and you will see why in just a moment. The idea behind this test is to see just how deeply one can delve into their own minds. The belief is that the body will react physically if someone is concentrating on something that they believe is true. If you see that your subject reacts bodily to the light/heavy hands technique then they are more than likely a prime target for Dark NLP and hypnosis. So here is what you are going to want to do:

Ask someone, or multiple people, to close their eyes and hold their arms straight out in front of them. Tell them to have one hand turned palm-up to the sky and one hand palm-down to the ground. Now tell them to imagine that in the hand that is facing toward the sky, they are carrying a watermelon. In the hand they have facing the ground, tell them that there are a bunch of helium balloons tied to their wrist.

Go into detail about the watermelon. They can smell it, feel its rind and most importantly, feel how heavy it is. With each passing moment their arms are getting more and more fatigued from the weight of the heavy watermelon. Meanwhile the arm with the balloons tied to it is getting lighter as the balloons are slowly and gently ascending towards the sky. What you should be doing while their eyes are closed is seeing if their arms are actually moving. If they are, then you've most likely found your subject.

The Amnesia Technique

The amnesia technique is a verbal test. In it you will ask the potential subject to forget about something for a period of time (it shouldn't be more than a few minutes). For example, you can ask your subject to forget the letter P. Tell them to pretend that the letter P never existed and to forget that you even told them to forget about it. Then ask them to recite the alphabet. People who are moderately or highly suggestible will skip over the letter P (or whatever letter you tell them to forget) and not even realize it. Once again, if the person you tried this test on skips over the letter you told them to forget, they may be a good subject to zone in on.

The Locked Hand Technique

The locked hand technique (also known as the hand clasp technique) is another physical test that the subject will have to be willing to participate in. Like the light/heavy hand technique, it will test just how deeply a person can concentrate on the words you are saying to them and what you are telling them to imagine. Ask your subject to clap their hands together and keep them together, palm to palm. Then tell them to interlace their fingers. Make sure that you maintain fixed eye-contact with them throughout this test and tell them to push their hands together as tightly as they can. Tell them to imagine their hands merging into one piece of solid flesh and bone. After a minute or two, tell them to stop pushing and try pulling their hands apart. Again, a potential manipulation subject will find it hard to pull their hands away from each other.

SPEED READING PEOPLE

What Is Speeding People?

Ignite the Art of Reading People through Your Super Senses

If you want to read people, you have to don the garment of a psychiatrist who has the power to interpret cues which are verbal and nonverbal. You need to observe beyond people's masks into their real self. You may not get the entire picture about anybody through logic alone. You have to surrender to their critical forms of information to interpret the essential nonverbal perceptive cues that individuals exude. For you to achieve this feat, you need to be eager to surrender emotional baggage like ego clashes or old resentments and also any preconceptions which can prevent you from making out the person. It is crucial, as well, for you to obtain information without bias and continue to be impartial without twisting it.

In the process of reading a colleague, your boss, or partner for you to understand them accurately, some walls need to come down, and you need to surrender biases. You need to be ready to let go of limiting, old ideas as far as intellect is concerned. Those who read other people well are taught to comprehend the hidden. They have discovered how they will draw on what is called 'super-sense' so they can take a profound observation beyond where you usually steer your focus when you attempt to hack into transformative awareness.

Examine cues of body language

When you are reading the cues of body language, you have to surrender the focus by releasing your struggle to understand the hidden signals of body language. Never get analytical or overtly intense. Stay fluid and relaxed. Observe by sitting back comfortably.

Focus on appearance

When you are reading other people, take note of what they are wearing. Are they putting on well-shined shoes and power suit? The indication for success is when someone deck out decently. For someone wearing a T-shirt and jeans may be an indicator of that person being comfortable with casual. It may be a signal of a seductive choice when someone wears a tight top with cleavage. A pendant like Buddha or cross may indicate spiritual values.

Notice posture

Postures are an essential aspect of reading people. It's a sign of confident when people's head is held high. Or you can get an indication of low self-esteem when they cower, or they walk irresolutely. You can also get a sign of a big ego when they have puffed-out chest and swagger.

Pay attention to physical movements

When you read others, look out for their distance and learning. In general, people bend forward at those they like and keep a distance from others they don't. Also, when people cross their arms and legs, you can see signs of anger, self-protection, or defensiveness. It is an indication that people are hiding something when they hide their hands by placing them in their pockets, laps, or place them behind them. With cuticle picking or lip biting, you will get a sign of people attempting to calm themselves in a difficult circumstance or under pressure.

Read facial expression

Our faces provide the outline for our emotions. Profound frown lines indicate over-thinking or worry. The smile lines of delight are crow's feet; pursed lips is a signal of contempt, anger, or bitterness. While teeth grinding and clenched jaw are indicators of tension.

Take note to your intuition

It is possible to tune into someone ahead of their words and body language. Though not what your head says, what your gut feels is intuition. Instead of logic, intuition is your perception of nonverbal information through images. If you are in the process of understanding a person, their outer trappings are insignificant, and it is only who the person is what counts. To reveal a richer story, intuition gives the power to distinguish beyond the obvious to tell a richer story.

You need to watch out for these checklists cues of intuition:

Respect your gut feelings

Pay attention to voices of your gut, in particular when

connecting with someone for the first time, an automatic rejoinder that happens out of impulse. Gut feelings are as a result of if you are tensed up or at ease. As a cardinal response, gut feelings occur in an instant. They are meters of your inner truth that relay to you if you should trust someone.

Goosebumps feelings

Pleasant, intuitive shivers are goosebumps, and they happen when something strikes a chord in us in connection with our resonance to individuals that inspire or move us. Also, goosebumps occur in the course of going through déjà-vu and when you have never met someone before but still recognize them.

Listen to sparkles of insight

During a conversation with people, you may be impressed by those who come quickly. Watch out and stay alert. Or else, you might fail to spot it. For most of us, this crucial awareness is lost because of the inclination to move onto the next idea.

Look for insightful empathy

This cue happens when you have a passionate type of

empathy through the feelings of someone's real emotions and symptoms within your body. So, while reading people, take note whether you had pain on your back when it wasn't there before, or if you are upset or depressed following a mind-numbing conference. To determine if empathy is at play, get feedback.

Discern emotional power

The vibe we radiate and the remarkable demonstration of our energy are emotions. It is with an intuition that we procure these emotions. For some people, you will be happy to be around them because they enhance your vitality and mood. Others tend to be draining; get away from them is what you want. Though it is undetectable, you can feel this 'subtle energy' feet or inches from the body. It's called **chi** in Chinese medicine, an essential healthy vitality.

Be aware of the presence of people

Though not substantially similar to our behavior or words, the accustomed energy we discharge is when we sense the presence of the people. It is typical of a rain cloud or the sun that borders around our emotional atmosphere. In the process of reading people, take note of if you get attraction with their presence or retreating due to the willies you are getting.

Watch people's eyes

Humans' eyes convey compelling forces. As the eyes cast off an electromagnetic signal, according to studies, the brain does the same. When you watch people's eyes, you will know if they are tranquil, sexy, mean, angry, or caring. Also, you will have the ability to determine if a person wants intimacy in their eyes or their eyes can give signs that they are comfortable. Even in their eyes, you will know whether they appear to be hiding or guarded.

Observe the feel of a hug, handshake, or touch

Most of us shake emotional energy, similar to an electrical flow during physical contact. You can ask yourself if a hug or handshake feel comfortable, warm, or confident. Or if it is repulsive so much that you wish to withdraw. You can know the sign of anxiety with someone's hand clammy or limp to suggest being timid or non-committal.

Listen to the tone of laugh and voice

Our voice's volume and tone are capable of telling a lot about our emotions. Vibration is as a result of sound frequencies. Notice how people's pitch of voice affects you in the course of reading them. Envisage if the tone is snippy, abrasive, and whiny or if their tone feels soothing.

To read people can be hard sometimes. It takes practice and courage. However, once you are past that, you will gain a significant advantage. Not only will you survive, but you will also thrive in all your relationships with others. People will approach you. Opportunities will come to you. And some people will want to be like you.

CONCLUSION

Thank you for making it through to the end. Let's hope it was informative and able to provide you with all of the tools you need to achieve your goals whatever they may be.

The next step is to be on the lookout for those who may try to use some of these techniques against you. If you are not on the lookout, a dark manipulator may be able to use these tactics against you, and you may never know.

Now that we have gone through a number of nonverbal cues, it is worth noting that there are some cues that you may never see due to cultural differences. For instance, close proximity is considered aggressive in Japan. Constant eye contact also makes people very uncomfortable, whereas in Spanish and Arabic cultures, NOT maintaining a lot of eye contact is considered very disrespectful. For the majority of the nonverbal cues here, however, you shouldn't have any problems, just be sure to do a little research if you like to travel, so that you don't misinterpret a cue if you intend to go somewhere exotic.

Now that we have given you a larger sampling of the information that you need you will want to practice it. You will find a number of them readily in the workplace and at social venues that you frequent. Use this information to better arm yourself for dealing with Dark Psychology. Arm yourself as best you can with this information. It's the good stuff!

If you have made it this far in the book, congratulations. You have learned some of the most powerful and useful tools for manipulation and NLP. You are now equipped with all the tools you will need to not only be aware of people trying to manipulate you, but also to get people to do what you want. There is only one more thing to do: develop a strong sense of self.

As you go over these techniques and learn about what it really means to influence others towards your own ends, it is easy to get lost in the concepts. You may start to feel like you have been manipulated yourself. You may feel that in order to deploy these techniques, you will have to start to believe in untruths.

This is not the case and following this train of thought can be very dangerous. It can lead you to forget who you really are and what you really believe. When you do that, you not only become a kind of aimless wanderer in life but you also become a prime target for manipulation yourself. This is why it is infinitely important to develop a strong mentality and sense of self. Doing so will keep you from losing your original intent and identity. It will also ensure that you are not made a puppet in someone else's marionette theater.

Victim Versus Manipulator

It is important to know how to use these powerful tactics responsibly. We are not condoning that you go out and try to scam every person you know. These tactics should be used sparingly and only when you really need them. They can be used responsibly to help yourself get out of a bad situation or relationship. They can be used responsibly when you are in dire need of help but have no one willing to lend a hand. They can be used responsibly by remembering always that the "subjects" you manipulate are people as well.

Speaking of "subjects," we have used this word a lot in this book but it is crucial to know the difference between subject and manipulator or victim and manipulator. The lines between these two concepts can be blurred in your mind without you even realizing. When that happens you are easy pickings. A skilled manipulator will be able to spot you from a mile away and take advantage. It becomes of chief importance to step out of the victim role and be aware of yourself and your surroundings so that you are not the victim of manipulation yourself.

This is the perfect time to take an honest look at yourself through the lens of all the topics and techniques that we have discussed in this book to see if you are being or have been manipulated in the past. Be fearless in your memory and introspection. Has anyone ever used these techniques on you? Is someone in your life using these techniques on you now?

Take responsibility for your actions. Even if you are realizing now that you have or are being manipulated, don't wallow in regret. Don't feel sorry or bad about yourself. Realize that everyone has been manipulated at least once in their lives. The important thing is that you realize it now and can now take the step toward shedding the role of the victim. When you remain in the victim mentality – thinking that you are "so dumb" for letting someone manipulate you or that you will only repeat these mistakes – you remain an easy target.

Stepping out of the victim role and into the role of the manipulator is your first step in solidifying your identity and steeling yourself mentally. Own up to how you have been used in the past and move on from it. Just because it happened once or twice or three or even hundreds of times does not mean that it has to keep happening. Start thinking of yourself as a manipulator every day. Distance yourself from victim thinking and take control. Look at yourself in the mirror every day and say to your reflection "I am in control." It may feel silly at first but it is an effective way to program yourself out of victim thinking.

Developing a strong mentality will make it much easier for you to impose your influence on someone else and keep other people from doing the same to you. It is what you must do if you want to become a skilled manipulator. Learning the techniques is not enough. Manipulation is a mental exercise and keeping a strong mind will make you more successful at this exercise.

Stepping out of the victim role is just the first step. There is more you can do to fortify your mind and identity.

Meditation and Grounding

A strong mind is a grounded mind, but what does it mean to be mentally grounded? Being mentally grounded means that you have an unwavering point of reference to who you are at your core. Think of it like your own mental refuge to turn to when life gets too chaotic. In terms of manipulation, being mentally grounded will help center you from the lies that you may have to tell or the lies that you hear. It was stated earlier in this section that when practicing manipulation, it can be very easy to get lost or out of touch with your own reality.

That is where mental grounding comes into play. When you are mentally grounded you will never lose touch with your own reality and lose yourself in the many roles you may have to play when manipulating. It isn't always easy to find mental grounding though and it can be even more difficult to maintain. Before we get into ways you can become more mentally grounded, be aware that this is not a one-and-done practice. However you find best to mentally ground yourself should become a regular if not every day routine for you. Think of your mind like a car. When you manipulate, or even when you are just out in the world and interacting with others, you are putting miles on your mind. Every once in awhile, you need to change the oil and tune it up. For as long as you have a brain, you need to practice regular mental grounding.

So let's look at some ways to achieve a grounded mind:

- Meditation – Meditation is the practice of clearing your mind and focusing on your breathing. This is very difficult to do at first but the more you practice it, the better you will get at it and the more you will benefit from it. Try finding a quiet little spot where you can sit down on the ground or lay. This should be somewhere you will not be disturbed. Start with just 20 minutes a day in which you come to rest in this place, close your eyes, try to clear your mind and focus only on your breathing pattern. Focus solely on maintaining a uniform breathing pattern. When you feel more comfortable doing this for 20 minutes, increase it to ten more minutes and on and on in that fashion.

- Being Amongst Nature – There is a Buddhist parable called "The Sermon of the Inanimate." In this parable, a practitioner sat quietly in a forest and observed the nature around him; the trees, the grass, the rocks etc. He found that inanimate nature, by merit of being still has a lot to teach us. Being amongst nature is a good way to find your mental grounding. It doesn't have to be a forest. It could be a small park in your neighborhood. Just as long as you are more or less surrounded by natural things. Spend time here regularly and you will come to find that the needs and concerns of society are not the same as the needs and concerns of nature. The trees are not stressed about work. The rocks don't care about material matters like cars and clothes. Unfortunately we cannot be in this state of bare tranquility all the time but finding your own nature refuge can go a long way towards re-centering and refocusing on what is important and real in your life.

- Take Night Walks – Have you ever noticed that when you walk you think a bit clearer? Maybe you have taken a walk with someone and found that you have more to talk about while walking. There is a reason for that. When our bodies are active our blood is flowing more which means more blood flow to the brain. Try taking a walk at night when you know there won't be a lot of cars or other people on the street. Think about your day and your interactions. Evaluate them beyond the surface encounters and compare them to what you believe and feel. This just might help you get to the hearts of various matters better and realize where your grounding lies.

Practice Improving Your Frame Control

Mental grounding helps a lot in maintaining your frame because your frame is what you truly believe to be true and what you care about in life. You cannot maintain your frame without first finding your mental grounding. That is why it is important to practice grounding as often as possible. When you constantly remind yourself of your beliefs it will be that much easier to maintain your frame.

A strong frame is all about not wavering under criticism and pressure. You will be challenged a lot, especially when you are using any of the tactics you have learned in this book. Under this pressure you must be confident that what you believe is right and true. You can use any of the tips we have discussed for increasing charisma and confidence like standing/sitting up straight, speaking deliberately and maintaining intent eye-contact. Increasing your level of confidence will help you build a song self-frame.

Use these techniques and practices with patience, perseverance, care and awareness. Remember always that having a strong mind is the first step toward being able to sway anybody. Know that the only way to protect yourself from other manipulators is to have a strong mind. Keep in touch with your sense of self at all times. If you do all of these things and take to heart all of the techniques and tactics that you have learned in this book, you will find your definition of success in psychological wisdom and understanding.

The goal of this book is to keep you out on the lookout for the dark manipulators who may show up in your life. When you know some of the signs to watch out for, and you understand dark psychology, you can protect yourself and stay safe! You are the one who should be in control of your own mind. Don't let someone else take that away from you!

ANALYZE PEOPLE

How To Analyze People Guide. Discover The Secrets And Techniques Of Manipulation For Mind Control And Persuasion. Speed Reading Their Body Language And Behavior.

© Text Copyright 2019 – Jason Halpa

The content contained within this book may not be reproduced, duplicated or transmitted without direct written permission from the author or the publisher.

Under no circumstances will any blame or legal responsibility be held against the publisher, or author, for any damages, reparation, or monetary loss due to the information contained within this book. Either directly or indirectly.

Legal Notice:

This book is copyright protected. This book is only for personal use. You cannot amend, distribute, sell, use, quote or paraphrase any part, or the content within this book, without the consent of the author or publisher.

Disclaimer Notice:

Please note the information contained within this document is for educational and entertainment purposes only. All effort has been executed to present accurate, up to date, and reliable, complete information. No warranties of any kind are declared or implied. Readers acknowledge that the author is not engaging in the rendering of legal, financial, medical or professional advice. The content within this book has been derived from various sources. Please consult a licensed professional before attempting any techniques outlined in this book.

By reading this document, the reader agrees that under no circumstances is the author responsible for any losses, direct or indirect, which are incurred as a result of the use of information contained within this document, including, but not limited to, — errors, omissions, or inaccuracies.

INTRODUCTION

Much of basic common body language is the same all over the world despite religion and racial differences. Some examples of this are smiling when you're happy or scowling when you are sad or angry. The nodding of the head is almost completely universally used to indicate an affirmation of sorts. It is believed that this form of affirmation is a genetic predisposition because individuals who were born blind still use this form of body language even though they never learned to use it visually.

This then brings me to an interesting point about body language and whether it is a learned action or genetic action. This is a debate that is ongoing and is still being researched even up to this day. Some forms of body language can be traced back to animal ancestry and are believed to be purely genetic. This is the action of sneering at another person in anger or irritation. An animal's a similar action to this is done when preparing for an attack.

There are three basic rules for an accurate reading of somebody's body language. You must keep these three rules in mind when attempting to analyze any person for their body language.

1. Reading Clusters of Gestures Rather Than an Individual

You should never try to analyze or interpret a single solitary gesture separately from all of the others. You have to look at the entire picture. This means that you have to look at every action of the person's body and compare it to the rest of them. It is easy to remember this rule when you think of body language as just that: a language. As with any vocally spoken language, body language has its own "words," "sentences," and "punctuation." Attempting to understand somebody's body language through one specific gesture is like attempting to understand an entire paragraph from just a single word. You have to read each individual gesture as its own word and put them together to create sentences so that you can understand the language that someone's body is giving off. A common rule of thumb for this is the idea that someone needs at least three words to be able to create a proper sentence. As for body language, this means that you have to be able to compare at least three gestures that a person is giving off before you can begin to understand their innermost feelings and thoughts.

3. Searching for Consistency

This is especially important when trying to decide if somebody may be lying to you or not. Consistency is key in being able to tell if somebody is telling the truth. You have to consider the words that are coming out of their mouth in relation to what their body language is showing you. If an individual's words and body language are in conflict in a given moment, it is often best to ignore what is being said and focus instead on body language exclusively. Inconsistency between body language and vocal words is a strong sign of lying.

4. Context, Context, Context

Context is incredibly important when attempting to read a person's body language. You have to take into account an individual's environment, in addition to the signals that their body is giving off. There are lots of body symbols that have no meaning whatsoever when an individual is in certain situations. For instance, a person with arms and legs crossed tightly together on a cold winter's day is not necessarily a sign of feeling defensive—they are most likely just cold.

CHAPTER 1

WHY ANALYZE PEOPLE

Have you anytime looked at someone and thought you had them understood just from that look? Is it exact to state that you were right? Or then again would you say you were stirred up about some piece of their character? Despite whether you were right or wrong, you essentially tried getting someone, which is an ability that most of us would love to have. Everything considered, in case you can tell when your chief is feeling incredible, you understand when to demand a raise, right? When you understand your people are feeling awful you know, it is anything but a chance to unveil to them you scratched the vehicle. It is connected to appreciating what understanding people means and how it capacities.

The graph below shows the importance of nonverbal and verbal communication according to a survey conducted at the University of Michigan as of 2018.

What Is Reading People'?

When you look at someone and feel like you can condemn whether they are feeling extraordinary or a horrendous one, paying little heed to whether they are a wonderful individual or a mean one or whatever else using any and all means, you are getting them. At the point when all is said in done, understanding someone means researching them and it does not just should be a speedy look, and knowing something about them without them saying anything in any way shape or form. It is a tendency you get from looking and from viewing the way in which they stand, the way wherein they look around, the way where they move. There some different features that could play into your inclination and cognizance of them, yet the most critical thing is that they did not explicitly uncover to you whatever that thing is.

By and by, various people investigate someone and acknowledge they know something. You mull over inside 'charitable, they look sincere' or 'astonishing, they look upset.' These are instinctual suppositions and thoughts that we have when we see a person. As we speak with them, we may achieve new goals or even as we watch them over the room. Maybe you never banter with that individual, anyway you have examinations and considerations in regards to the kind of person that they rely upon what you have seen of them. You are getting them, and whether you are right or wrong is an assistant point.

For What Reason is Reading People Important?

For what reason would it be a smart thought for you to essentially disturb getting people? Everything considered, there are a couple of special reasons this can be a better than average capacity. In any case, at a most fundamental level, it reveals to you how you should approach someone. If they look neighborly, you might be also prepared to approach with a smile and a very much arranged welcome. If they look down and out, you might undoubtedly approach with a reason rather than basically stopping to make appropriate associate. If a friend looks upset, you may ask them what's going on or what happened. Understanding what they feel like just from a quick look can empower you to imagine whatever is going on essentially like that, and the better you get with the mastery, the better you'll be at talking with people.

In case you do not have the foggiest thought how to

scrutinize people in any way shape or form, you could wrap up interpreting something that they do or an action or an outward appearance mistakenly, and you may start to expect things about a person that is not correct. Maybe you see their face and accept that they are a perturbed person when they're basically furious with a condition. Maybe you think they look threatening, anyway they're basically perplexed with something that is going on around them. By making sense of how to scrutinize better, you'll have the alternative to push your life from numerous perspectives.

Understanding people can empower you to acknowledge who to approach with that unprecedented new idea (and when to approach) and who you ought to stay away from. It in like manner discloses to you how to familiarize something with them, paying little mind to whether from a precise perspective or dynamically fun and creative one. Before you know it, understanding people will be normal to you if you practice it routinely enough. Additionally, what's shockingly better is that you have no doubt been doing it for as long as you can remember and not despite contemplating it. That is in light of the fact that it is something that even kids will give a shot every so often, without acknowledging how huge it is.

Understanding People in Childhood

When you were an adolescent did you ever sit on a seat at the entertainment focus or on your porch and watch people walk around? You apparently did at some point or another, paying little mind to whether it was uniquely for a few minutes. Also, a short time later you look at the overall public and make stories. In the occasion that they're walking a canine, perhaps they're a pooch walker on their way to the entertainment focus. In the occasion that they're passing on an organizer case and walking quickly, they are late to a noteworthy social affair, clearly, that get-together may have been with outcasts in your young character, anyway, you get a general idea. You have successfully deciphered what you see of someone to make a story about them.

As you get progressively prepared, you use those proportional sorts of aptitudes to start understanding people extensively more and to some degree all the more accurately. Your cognizance of outward appearances and position start to develop to some degree more and before you know it you can look at someone and rapidly acknowledge what it is they are feeling at any rate, as a general rule. All things needed are a touch of producing for your childhood capacities and before you understand it you are en route to progressively significant accomplishment in your adult life.

Getting Help Reading People

Understanding people is a noteworthy ability to learn. For a large number of individuals, you probably look at is an 'acknowledge the main decision accessible' circumstance, is not that so? You accept on the off chance that I can scrutinize people, at that point extraordinary, yet if I cannot, well, no harm was done, is that not so? Everything considered, really understanding people energizes you a lot in your life and it causes you to be a prevalent individual as well, which is the reason it is a critical ability to have, paying little respect to whether you have a straightforward appreciation or an undeniably expansive one.

If you do not perceive how to examine people, it is a capacity that you irrefutably can learn. It is something that you can tackle for yourself by fundamentally coming back to those adolescent extensive stretches of making stories for the overall public walking around. And yet it is something that you can develop impressively further if you push yourself. The key is guaranteeing that you do not stop and do not desert the progression you are making. You may be bewildered precisely with the sum you can learn in a short proportion of time in case you move on these capacities, despite starting with people you certainly know.

For the people who are not sure where to start or how to wear down getting people, it is absolutely possible to get capable help with the strategy.

Starting with People You Know

It will, in general, be less complex to start scrutinizing the all-inclusive community you know before continuing forward to untouchables. These are people that you certainly know things about, and when you look at them, you can in all probability watch things that show those qualities. If your nearest friend is excessively bubbly and pleasant to everyone, you can undoubtedly look at them and jump on that trademark. Venture up to the plate and see them, see what it is about them that shows others they are bubbly and all around arranged and a while later quest for those characteristics in different people around you.

It moreover empowers us to move appropriately between our own one of a kind perspective and another. Unusually, social understanding relies upon information that cannot be truly observed at this point ought to be translated from moving toward information and our knowledge into the social world.

Moreover, continuously, confirmation proposes social cognizance incorporates reenactment, copying others' experiences as a way to deal with getting them. A real model here is the manner in which we experience other people's sentiments.

When watching someone's face we will, as a rule, duplicate her outward appearance, smiling when she does, glaring in comprehension. Such mimicry may not be obvious to the nice onlooker, yet minute muscle order can be distinguished in all regards not long in the wake of being exhibited to an energetic verbalization. Surely, even our eyes extend so as to the ones we are looking.

Research is beginning to exhibit this to be the circumstance.

Various people with mind hurt, oftentimes to the frontal folds of the cerebrum, develop excessively poor social aptitudes and social direct regardless of modestly incredible insight.

Basically, people with mental unevenness range issue seem to experience extraordinary difficulty with social information.

From a transformative perspective, it looks good that social discernment may have developed freely to non-social aptitudes.

Individuals are social animals relying upon interest and competition inside get-togethers to persevere. So the ability to see expressive motions and grasp the essentialness of social lead may be a transformative objective, realizing its improvement self-sufficiently of non-social information taking care of aptitudes.

Understanding the Brain

In some progressing work in my exploration office, we have found poor versatility and restriction can interfere with social understanding.

We requested a social event from adults who had persevered through genuine personality harm to finish a direct communication task: depict their "ideal" event resort. They were then drawn nearer to put themselves in the shoes of a substitute kind of event maker, for instance, a family with energetic adolescents.

When they had thought of their ideal inn, the speakers with mind harm could not delineate an event from someone else's perspective. Be that as it may, they did not have this issue when fundamentally gotten some data around two various types of event makers. The issue perhaps rose when self-contemplations were incited first.

Understanding social cognizance and how it might be exasperated in different kinds of mind issue holds remarkable certification for better assessment and remediation of social difficulties. It also assurances to open learning of how our cerebrums are wired to engage us to work in a social world.

More Imitation

Inside the mind itself, "reflect" neuron systems in the premotor cortex of the frontal projection are started when we watch the exercises of others. It creates the impression that we do not just reflect considerations, we furthermore reflect exercises!

Right when sound adults are set in fMRI scanners and got some data about the mental state of someone such as themselves, a comparative region of the prefrontal cortex is impelled as when they think about themselves. This additionally prescribes we appreciate others by reference to ourselves.

Facial mimicry can be blocked after mind harm notwithstanding the way that the reasons are still exploratory. If diversion clarifies social comprehension, there ought to be a type of control of the strategy so we are prepared to isolate between our very own experiences and that of others, and move between these adaptable.

CHAPTER 2

ANALYZING PERSONALITY PEOPLE

Personality analysis is a field that is constantly evolving and varied. There are varying schools of psychological thoughts and theories when it comes to studying an individual's personality. Some of the most popular personality analyzing schools include trait theory, social learning, biological/genetic personality influencer and more.

Personality refers to an individual's distinct characteristics connected to processing thoughts, feelings and emotions that eventually determine their behavior. It involves taking into consideration all the traits a person possess to understand them as an entity. Personality study also includes understanding the inherent differences existing between people where particular characteristics are concerned.

Here are some of the most common personality type classifications.

Type A, B, C and D

Type A personality people are at a bigger risk of contracting heart diseases since they are known to be more aggressive, competitive, ambitious, short-tempered, impatient, impulsive and hyper active. Type A personality theory was introduced in the 50's by Meyer Friedman and Ray Rosenman. These people are more stressed due to their constant need to accomplish a lot. They are always striving to be better than others, which invariably leads to greater anxiety and stress.

Type B people are more reflective, balanced, even-tempered, inventive and less competitive by personality. They experience less stress and anxiety, along with staying unaffected by competition or time constraints. A Type B personality person is moderately ambitious and lives more in the present. They have a steadier and more restrained disposition. Type B folks are social, modest, innovative, gentle mannered, relaxed and low on stress.

Later psychologists came up with other personality types, too, since they found the division into Type A and B more restrictive. They discovered that some people demonstrated a combination of both A and B Type traits. Thus, segregating people into only two distinct personality groups doesn't do justice to the classification. This lead to the creation of even more personality types!

Type C people have a more meticulous eye for detail. They are focused, curious and diplomatic. There tend to put other people's needs before theirs. They are seldom assertive, straightforward and opinionated. This leads to Type C folks developing pent up resentment, frustration, anxiety and depression. There is a propensity to take everything seriously, which makes them reliable and efficient workers.

This personality type also possess high analytic skills, logical thinking powers and intelligence. However, they need to develop the knack of learning to be less diplomatic and more assertive. Type C also needs to develop the ability to relax and let their hair down periodically.

Lastly, Type D personality people are known to hold a more pessimistic view of life. They are socially awkward and withdrawn, and do not enjoy being in the limelight. They are constantly worried about being rejected by people. Type D people are at a greater risk of suffering from mental illnesses such as depression owing to pessimism, pent up frustration and melancholy. Since the Type D personality doesn't share things easily with others, they suffer internally.

Psychoanalytic Theory

This theory is different from the regular personality classification theories in the sense that the analysis is based is not based on the responses of people about their personality, but a more in-depth study of people's personalities by glimpsing into their subconscious or unconscious mind. Since the analysis is based on a study on a person's subconscious mind, errors and instances of misleading the reader are eliminated.

In psychoanalysis, a person's words and actions are known to be disguised manifestations for their underlying subconscious emotions. The founding father of the psychoanalytic theory was Sigmund Freud, who was of the view that all human behavior is primarily driven by primitive instincts, passions, impulse and underlying emotions. He theorized that all human behavior is a direct consequence of the equation between our id, ego and superego.

Through the free association method that includes experiences, memories, dreams and more; Freud analyzed underlying emotions, thoughts and feelings that determine their attitude and behavior. Thus a majority of our behavior can be traced to our early childhood experiences that are still lingering in our subconscious mind, which we may or may not be aware of.

For example, if an individual demonstrates aggressive traits as an adult, it can be pinned down to the violence, harassment or bullying he/she experienced in their early childhood. Similarly, if a child comes from an environment where there were very high expectations from him/her and the parents were seldom happy with his/her accomplishments, he/she may constantly seek validation or acceptance from others. They may fear rejection.

Thus, a person's childhood experiences can help you determine their personality and read them even more effectively according to the psychoanalytic theory. The theory is still extensively used when it comes to helping people cope with depression, anger, stress, panic attacks, aggression, obsessive disorders and much more.

Carl Jung's Personality Classification Theory

Psychologist Carl Jung classified people on the basis on their sociability quotient into introverts and extroverts. Introverts are folks who are primarily inward driven, shy, withdrawn and reticent. They are more focused on their ideas and sensibilities than the external world around them. Introverts are known to be more logical, reflective and sensible by nature. They take time to crawl out of their box, and establish a rapport with others.

On the other hand, extroverts are outgoing, friendly, affable, social and gregarious people who live more in the present than worry about the future. They have a more positive and exuberant disposition, and are more than willing to accept challenges or changes.

After classifying people as introverts and extroverts, Jung received his share of brickbats from psychologists who believed that the classification was too restrictive to categorize every human being on the planet. Experts argued that a majority of people rarely demonstrated extreme introvert or extrovert tendencies. According to them only a majority of people possess extreme introvert or extrovert tendencies. Most people in fact possess a little bit of both, and their behavior differs according to the situation.

For instance, someone like me enjoys going out and spending time with people but I also value some time alone for reflection and contemplation every now and then. This neither makes me a hardcore extrovert or introvert but more of a combination of both – an ambivert.

Social Learning

This theory talks about how people pick up personality or behavioral traits from their immediate environment. It proposes that an individual's behavior is a result of their growing up conditions and environment. We pick up specific patterns and personality traits through our experiences. Social learning psychologists are of the view that all our behavior is learnt through our social experiences.

For example, if a person has been rewarded in a specific manner, he or she learns behavior through positive reinforcement and experiences. For example, someone throwing excessive tantrums may have learned through their experiences that drama gets them attention. Every time they want attention they know throwing tantrums will do the trick. At times, we don't have to experience something to learn behavior. Our mind is conditioned to use complex codes, information, actions, symbols and consequences. A majority of our observations and vicarious experiences drive our behavior, and help us imbibe specific personality traits.

Ernest Kretschmer's Classification

German psychologist Ernest Kretschmer's personality classification theory theorizes that a person's physical characteristics or personality traits determine the likelihood of a person suffering from mental ailments and their personality.

According to this personality classification, people are classified as Athletic, Pyknic, Dysplastic and Asthenic. Pyknic personality types are people who are round, stout and short. They demonstrate more extrovert traits such as gregariousness, friendliness and an outgoing disposition.

The Aesthetic personality types are people who have a

slender and slim appearance. They have a fundamentally introvert personality. These are folks who have strong, athletic and robust bodies, and demonstrate more aggressive, enthusiastic and energetic characteristics.

Briggs Myers Personality Indicator

There are multiple personality tests that determine an individual's personality type based on a psychological analysis. One of the most widely used personality analysis tests is the Briggs Myers Personality Indicator. It is a comprehensive report that analyzes people's personalities based on how they perceive the world and make decisions.

The Briggs-Myers Personality Indictor was created by Isabel Briggs Myers and Katherine Briggs. It is based on Jung's theory but expounds on it through four primary psychological functions or processes such as sensation, thinking, feeling and intuition.

The MBTI emphasizes on one of the four primary functions dominating over other traits. The personality indicator operates on an assumption that everyone possesses a preference for the manner in which they experience the world around them. These inherent differences emphasize our values, motives, beliefs and interests, and thus determine an overall personality.

There are around 16 distinct personality types based on this psychological personality analysis theory. The Briggs-Myers test comprises several questions, where test respondents reveal their personality through their answers. This test is also widely used in areas such as determining a person's chances of success in a particular role and compatibility in interpersonal relationships.

In Myers Briggs personality theory, a personality type is determined when there is a clear preference for one style over another. Different letters connected with individual preferences helps determine the person's Myers Briggs personality type. For instance, if a person reveals a clear tendency for I, S, T and J, they have the ISTJ personality type.

Extraversion and introversion – The first letter of the Briggs-Myers personality type is related to the direction of one's energy. If a person is externally focused or focused on the external world, they show a preference for extraversion. On the contrary, if the energy is inward directed, the person shows a clear inclination for introversion.

Sensing and Intuition – The second letter is concerned with processing information. If an individual prefers dealing with information, has clarity, can describe what they see etc. then they show a distinct preference for sensing. Intuition, on the other hand, is related to intangible ideas and concepts. Intuition is represented by the letter "N."

Thinking and Feeling – The third letter reflects an individual's decision making personality. People who show an inclination for analytic, logical and detached thinking reveal a tendency for thinking over feeling. Similarly, people who show a preference for feeling are more driven by their values or what they believe in.

CHAPTER 3

BODY LANGUAGES

While information regarding what characteristics a person desires people to see can be readily ascertained from that person's general appearance, information regarding what a person does not necessarily want to convey can be gleaned from that person's body language. This is because people are generally unaware of their bodily reactions to their environment, and people are even less able to control those reactions.

Body language will indicate the inner emotional state and characteristics of a person, such as frustration, fear, nervousness, joy, and honesty. The list can go on and on. These are aspects of a person that cannot usually be seen from their clothing or hairstyle. When a person's general appearance, voice, and/or body language are indicating different things, you should always go with what the person's body language is saying. This is because, again, people are unable to control their involuntary physical reactions.

While body language can reveal the otherwise unseen emotions of a person, it is important to remember that it could simply be indicative of a temporary mental state (i.e., depression), or some kind of physical issue (i.e., an injured leg or back), and may not be probative of any kind of permanent characteristic.

When analyzing a person's body language, as when analyzing anything else, consistency is key. As such, the more information you have about someone's character, the more useful the information gained from analyzing their body language will be to you. This leads us, once again, to the principle that you will need to identify patterns in someone's body language, as well as in their voice and general appearance, in order to draw accurate conclusions.

Practically speaking, body language can be separated into two general categories, those being "open" body language and "closed" body language.

"Open" body language is characterized by someone who is at ease, who directly faces those to with whom they are speaking and who maintain strong eye contact. A person with open body language will also not place their purse, arms, or anything else, in between themselves and the other person.

"Closed" body language can be illustrated by someone who crosses their legs or arms and faces either away from the person to whom they are speaking or be facing off to one side. A person with closed body language would also make sure something is in front of them, thereby forming a barrier between them and the person to whom they are speaking.

Whether someone is exhibiting open or closed body language could tell you something about whether that person is an introvert or extrovert, how comfortable they are in a particular situation, how interested they are in the conversation, how much they like the person to whom they are speaking, and maybe even something about their cultural background.

Interpretation

Body language is tricky because most body positions, postures, and movements can mean many different things or not mean anything at all, depending on the environment. In order to discern what body language signals are significant and which ones are not, you should learn how several basic emotions are generally expressed through various simultaneous movements. In other words, you should try and discern patterns of movements that typically accompany certain emotional states, rather than dragging yourself through the tedious, and often unreliable, practice of committing to memory hundreds of individual physical actions and what the meaning of those actions might be. Common emotions and the body language that typically accompanies them are discussed below.

EMOTIONS

Thoughtful or Focused

The states of either being thoughtful or focused are usually characterized by a person being noticeably devoid of movement. A person's stillness in this instance reveals concentration on either some unspoken string of thought (if thoughtful), or on what the other person is trying to say (if focused). Occasionally, a person who is focused or thoughtful may perform minor movements repetitively, such as tapping a pencil against a table top or twiddling their thumbs. A person who is thoughtful or focused will display this body language unconsciously, and this body language will be present and consistent for extended lengths of time.

Some of the other body language that is indicative of a person being thoughtful or focused includes:

- Holding the head in the hands
- Consistently staring at something
- Consistently maintaining strong eye-contact
- Furrowed brow
- Arms folded with vacant stare
- Looking up
- Laying the chin on fingers or hand
- General absence of movement
- Tilting the head
- Leaning back in the chair
- Scratching the head

Bored

People generally become bored when they do not want to be wherever it is that they are and they do not want to be doing whatever it is that they are doing. When a person is bored and wants to go somewhere else, the body will show signs that it, too, wants to go somewhere else. The tension between wanting to leave and having to stay causes people discomfort. Therefore, people who are bored will generally engage in some physical activity to distract themselves from that discomfort.

Some of the common movements associated with boredom include:

- Eye rolls
- Leaning backwards and forwards in the chair
- Wandering eyes
- Furtive looks at objects such as a watch
- Heavy sighing
- Staring into the distance
- Yawning
- Shifting their weight
- Foot tapping
- Twiddling thumbs
- Finger tapping

- Uncrossing and crossing arms

- Uncrossing and crossing legs

- Scribbling or doodling

- Playing with small objects such as paper clips, pens, coins, etc.

- Pointing the body away from the speaker

- Side to side head movement

- Preening clothes or fingernails

- Stretching

- Trying to do something else

- Holding the chin in the hand and looking around the room

When people are bored, they engage in some kind of physical activity in an attempt to stay attentive. If a bored person does not engage in these physical activities, they may fall asleep. Because of the necessary presence of physical activity, boredom is among the easiest emotional states to spot and among the most difficult to hide.

Some of the signs of boredom are the same or similar to those of someone who is attentive or thoughtful. The key distinction between the two is the absence or presence of movement. Remember that if a person is staring off into space and is completely still, they may be thinking something over. If that same person is staring off into space while fidgeting with something, odds are that person is bored out of their skull.

Angry

An angry person will express that anger by becoming withdrawn, aggressive, or defensive. Anger in the form of aggression is the easiest to spot, being characterized as it is by a flushed face, puffed out chest, a set jaw, tight lips, and a loud and forceful voice. However, many people try not to express their anger so outwardly, or they at least try to control that expression, and will then tend to become withdrawn or defensive.

Some common signs of the three types of anger include:

- Flushed face
- Sarcastic or feigned laughter

- Irritated movement of the arms
- Crossed legs
- Crossed ankles
- Crossed arms
- Finger pointing
- Firm posture
- Phrase repetition
- Lips that are closed tight
- Quick speech
- Quick body movements
- Fixed facial expression or grimace
- Shaking
- Clenched fists
- Set jaw
- General tension
- Quick, shallow, or short breaths
- Hands placed on hips.
- Invasion of personal space

Frustrated

The two forms of frustration are surrender and confrontation. Confrontational frustration is characterized by the person who is under the impression that they can fix whatever it is that is causing the frustration by approaching the problem directly. The signs of confrontational frustration can therefore mirror those that would otherwise indicate anger. The frustration of surrender happens when that irritated person realizes that they cannot fix whatever it is that is irritating them. Surrender frustration is characterized, not by signs indicating anger, but by signs of passive irritation.

Some common signs of frustration of the confrontational variety are:

- Direct and consistent eye contact
- Repetition of certain phrases
- Invasion of personal space
- Should shrugs
- Finger pointing
- Hand gesturing

Signs exhibiting the onset or frustrational surrender include:

- Over-emphasized movement
- Hands to head
- Scowling
- Sighing
- Quick exhalation
- Hands resting on hips

Signs that the frustration of surrender has been reached include:

- Hands thrown in air
- Shoulder shrugging
- Turning away
- Walking away
- Closing the eyes
- Rolling the eyes
- Head shaking

Although confrontational frustration can easily turn into anger, it is important that you not confuse the two and thereby throw off your analysis. It is also important that you do not mistake boredom for surrender type of frustration. While several bored signals mirror those of surrendering out of frustration, people who are bored are not necessary frustrated, just as those who have surrendered to a situation out of frustration are probably not going to be bored.

Depressed

Clinical depression is an animal all its own. Someone suffering from clinical depression may be entirely unable to function, suffer from eating disorders, find concentrating on anything almost impossible, and may disregard their personal hygiene. Clinical depression requires medical treatment. We will not here be describing clinical depression. What we mean here by "depression" is the average type of day-to-day depression that we all have felt at some point in our lives.

Depression affects almost every one of your body's functions, including your body language and voice. Depressed people move and speak differently.

Someone who is depressed will be lethargic and glum. They will be wholly unenthusiastic and tired. Thus, in addition to analyzing someone's body language when searching for signs of depression, remember to pay attention to that person's voice as well (discussed in detail later), as that is another avenue by which depression is sure to manifest itself.

Specific signs of day-to-day depression include:

- Lack of concentration
- Poor memory
- Intentional and slow movement
- Relaxed posture
- Increased appetite
- Decreased appetite
- Slow and quite speech
- Lack of focus
- Eyes downcast
- Isolation
- Diminished capacity to plan in advance

- Lack of attention to personal hygiene

- Lack of attention to personal appearance

Indecisive

Someone who is trying to make a decision between a couple of different options will ordinarily reveal that hesitancy in their body language. People stuck in this position will go back-and-forth in a very real and literal way.

Some signs of indecision include:

- Tipping the head from one side to the other

- Shifting weight back and forth in a chair

- Hands that open and shut

- Hand movements wherein one hand moves, followed by the other

- Looking at one thing, then another, and back again

- Mouth opening and closing without any words being produced.

Nervous

Being nervous, just like being bored, causes discomfort. And, again like boredom, in order to distract themselves from that discomfort, a nervous individual will move their body. Being nervous creates a lot of energy, and a nervous person will need to find something to do with all that extra energy.

Signs that are typical of nervousness include:

- Body tension
- Eyes moving back and forth
- Curling up of the body
- Rocking
- Side to side shifting of weight
- Uncrossing and crossing arms
- Uncrossing and crossing legs
- Tapping hands
- Tapping fingers
- Tapping feet
- Throat clearing

- Lip biting

- Nervous coughing

- Adjustment of, or fidgeting with, hair, jewelry, hands, pens, coins, clothing, fingernails, or any other small object

- Hand squeezing

- Nervous smiling (frequently and rapidly alternating between smiling and not smiling)

- Nervous talking

- Eyes downcast

- Shaking

- Biting finger nails

- Preening cuticles

- Sudden silence

- Upper body rotation from side to side

- Sweating

As you can see, nervousness comes with a great deal of signs, many of which are shared with other emotional states. However, nervous people will generally exhibit more than just one of the signs listed above. Therefore, when analyzing whether someone is nervous or not, look for two or three of these signs to be sure you are not misreading the situation.

Sexual Interest

There are thousands of signs of sexual interest that a person can give. Generally, any behavior that focuses on or emphasizes a person's sexuality could be a clue as to the level of that person's sexual interest.

A very short list of some of the more basic characteristics of behavior that indicates sexual interest includes:

- Slow blinks
- Stares
- Crossing legs (legs crossed towards you would indicate interest, legs crossed away from you would not)
- Uncrossing legs
- Tossing the hair
- Chest thrusted outward

- Hips thrusted outward
- Strutting
- Walking to emphasize curves
- Primping
- Wetting lips
- Winks
- Strong eye contact
- Over-emphasized smile
- Leaning backwards
- Leaning forwards
- Flirtatious smiling
- Close proximity
- Running fingers through hair
- Revealing clothing
- Self-touching (adjusting cuff links, smoothing the skirt, etc.)
- Touching the other (hand on shoulder, patting the hand, hand on knee, etc.

- Using an over-abundance of fragrance or makeup
- Over-dressing
- Deliberately looking the person over ("elevator eyes")
- Intense listening
- Trying to create intimacy, such as by whispering.
- Trying to get the person alone
- Frequently looking at the person
- Exposing the neck (such as by moving the hair)

Resentful

Resentment is usually the end result of jealousy or anger and will generally manifest itself as a cluster of behaviors, the object of which is to distance a person from the object of their resentment.

Signs associated with resentment include:

- Avoiding a person
- Avoiding looking at the person

- Any indication of anger

- Scowling

- Tensing the body

- Crossing arms

- Crossing legs

- Tightly closed or pursed lips

Defensive

Defensiveness is a response to feeling attacked, and will result in the person feeling vulnerable and somewhat awkward. As such, their body language will indicate a desire to circumvent the situation, either verbally or physically.

Many of the indications of a defensive person also apply to a person who is nervous, angry or secretive. Like everything else, the other clues you pick up will point you towards which emotion it actually is.

A defensive person may manifest mannerisms such as:

- Clenched teeth

- Clenched jaw

- Clenched or pursed lips
- Avoiding eye contact
- Body squarely facing person (sign of confrontation)
- Hands resting on hips
- Crossing arms
- Crossing legs
- Crossing ankles
- Abandoning the situation
- Refusal to speak
- Exhaling rapidly

Substance Abuse

Determining whether someone is abusing substances can be extraordinarily difficult because people will try and convince themselves that they are not seeing the signs indicating same, especially if the scrutinized individual is emotionally close to the observer. This is why it is important to stay objective.

Signs of substance abuse include:

- Baggy eyes
- Blood-shot eyes
- Eyes that are only partially open
- Exaggerated behavior (talking too loud, standing too close)
- Very fast speech
- Slurring words
- Rapid and sudden changes in mood
- Shaking
- Flushed face
- Smell
- Lack of personal hygiene
- Isolation
- Skinny legs with an oversized torso (indicative of alcoholism)
- Skinny person with a potbelly (indicative of alcoholism

- Lack of inhibitions

- Considerable inconsistency in behavior from one time to another

- Considerable inconsistency in general appearance from one time to another

How To Use Body Languages To Persuade

The Eyes

Firstly, the eyes. Our eyes operate greatly on their own accord- blinking when they need to and gazing where there is movement. While we can most often control where they look, they will sometimes operate on their own in interactions with others. The eyes will often be the first place to show how the person is feeling.

Our brain and our spinal cord make up the pairing that is known as the central nervous system. This pathway of neurons operates fully automatically- that is to say, with no help from our conscious mind.

The eyes are connected to this nervous system and are the only part of the central nervous system that actually faces the outside of the body. Because of this, the eyes are literally intertwined with what we are thinking and feeling, even more than we notice. The brain and the spinal cord give us life- they are responsible for initiating our movements, our thoughts, and our feelings. "The eyes are the window to the soul" got its origins in this fact of anatomy. That being said, it is very difficult to control the emotions and sentiments that people can see in our eyes as they come directly from the places within us over which we have no control. The eyes, therefore, are the first place to look when it comes to seeing someone's truth.

Eye contact is a big indicator of the intentions of a person. As previously discussed, the amount of eye contact someone is making is an indicator of their level of comfort. If someone is making and holding eye contact for a long period of time without looking away, they appear to be very comfortable to the point of seeming like they may have predetermined intentions.

If someone is avoiding eye contact altogether, they tend to seem very untrustworthy, almost as if they are trying very hard to hide something from you. We have all encountered an uncomfortable amount of eye contact, whether too much or too little, where it made us feel like something was not right. You may have been feeling unease but were unaware as to why.

Feeling someone's eyes staring directly into yours with no end in sight makes for a lot of discomfort while trying to catch someone's eye who is clearly making an effort to avoid yours makes for a very awkward conversation. If someone is making steady eye contact, looking away every now and then and then coming back to meet your eyes once again, they are probably feeling comfortable in the situation or conversation and are quite secure with themselves and their position. This amount of eye contact makes us feel comfortable in the other person's presence and feel that their intentions are pure.

Eye movement is also a type of communication that goes on. The eyes tend to go where the person wants to go. If someone glances at something, chances are they are thinking about it or wishing to go there. For example, if someone glances at a chair in the room, they are probably tired of standing.

If someone glances at the door, they would probably like to leave or may be late for something. If you see someone looking over at another table for the duration of your dinner date, chances are they are wishing they were with someone else.

Think of yourself in this type of situation.

On a date where you feel bored and unenthused, you would probably be searching wildly around the room for an excuse to leave or another person to daydream about. If your date is unaware of what your eye movements are demonstrating, they may keep droning on about the stock market for another hour or two.

While everyone blinks at slightly different rates, you can start to pick up on changes in blinking speed. Watch your partner next time they are sitting across from you and notice how often they blink. Picking up on this will alert you when there is a change in blinking speed. Blinking very often and quickly is said to be an indicator of thinking hard or of stress. What causes your partner to begin blinking quickly? This observation will give you some insight into what causes them stress and mental strain.

Facial Expressions

Subtle movements of the face can be picked up when examining another person closely. These subtle movements are said to happen instinctively when a person has a feeling of intense emotion. They are very difficult to fake as they happen quickly and subtly. These subtle movements can be very telling if we can learn to pick up on them.

The first involuntary facial movement is that of surprise. When genuinely surprised, a human face will drop the jaw, raise the eyebrows and widen the eyes. The second is fear. Fear causes the eyebrows to rise slightly, the upper eyelid to raise and the lips to tense.

The next is disgust, which causes the upper lip to rise and the nose to wrinkle. Anger causes the eyebrows to lower, the lips to come together and the bottom jaw to come forward. Happiness causes the corners of the lips to rise, the cheeks to rise and the outsides of the eyes to wrinkle. This wrinkling of the eyes is indicative of a real smile, as in a fake smile this does not happen.

Sadness involves the outside of the lips to lower, the inside of the eyebrows to raise and the lower lip to come forward. Finally, an intense feeling of hate causes one side of the mouth to raise. These expressions all take place so quickly that they are often missed. If you know what to look for though, you will notice them before they are gone. This will be one of the most accurate ways to analyze a person as they will likely have no idea that this has occurred on their face.

The face has a lot to say when it comes to body language, and with so many small muscles there are a lot of movements that occur unbeknownst to the person being observed. This is a great place to start when it comes to learning to analyze people.

Reading the language of the rest of the body can be better understood when done from the perspective of looking at an animal. Animals' main priority is always to protect themselves if a fight were to occur. They always have their vital areas covered when they are in a vulnerable position or situation and will open up when they feel safe.

Humans are similar in this way. Our vital areas are all in the middle of our body- around our heart and lungs. When we see an animal in a strange setting or around other animals that it may have to fight with it will be positioned in a way where nothing will be able to access its heart, its lungs or its stomach area. Thinking of humans in this way will be a great tool for analyzing them.

Use Powe Poses

Gestures and Facial Expression

You can read so much about someone by looking at their faces. From excitement, surprise, anger, happiness, confusion to sadness, all this is possible when you look at their face. Many people are conflicted because they try to protect another person's feelings. This is why they might say they are happy, but their face says something else.

From the facial expression, you can determine whether you can trust someone or not. In a split second, you can choose whether to trust them or not. If someone is assuring you with a sly grin on their face, it is wise to back off. Confidence and friendliness are often expressed with a light smile and slightly raised eyebrows.

Some people can read your face and tell whether you are intelligent or confident about what you are talking about. A simple question might throw you off your thought pattern and help them get a better perspective of you.

Gestures are direct. The signs associated with gestures

are obvious because some are universal. You can convey different messages from your gestures. They are part of body language that helps you put forward your message without saying something.

In terms of posture, it is always advisable to be assertive. An assertive posture is about confidence. Stand up straight, keep your shoulder and legs aligned, and make sure your weight is evenly distributed on your legs. An assertive posture is about confidence. It shows the person you are communicating with that you are sure of what you are talking about.

There is so much information displayed on your face. Awareness of this might shock you. Whenever you speak to someone, they will listen to your words but, at the same time, try to read your face because of the innocence and genuineness in it. You can mince your words or train as much as you can to present your case in a certain way, but your face will always tell a different story if you are lying.

Besides, by looking at your face, it is easier for someone to feel your emotions, especially if they are keen. While some people have mastered the art and can do it, not everyone can conceal their emotions. All this can be read from your face—your happiness, sadness, dismay, disappointment, elation, and so forth. A keen audience can tell your emotions, regardless of what you say.

Instinctive Cues

Trust your gut. You have heard this so many times. Does it work? It does. In fact, in most cases, you are wrong when you go against your gut. If you have a bad feeling about someone the very moment you meet them, there is a good chance you should trust that feeling and walk away.

Intuition and gut feelings can be accurate and help you get out of a dangerous situation. If you are meeting someone for the first time, you don't know anything about them, and neither do they about you. In your first chance meeting, it is always safe to trust in your gut.

The good thing about trusting your gut is that you don't have to read much into anything. All you need is to be relaxed, listen to what they have to say, and reflect on it. If it doesn't feel right to you, don't force it. Your gut feelings should alert you to monitor other observable cues about someone and use that as a credible way of determining whether they are lying or not.

Personal Vibes

Is it possible to feel a good or bad vibe from someone? It is true. Other than the visual and auditory communication, we can also communicate with people around us by giving off vibes. Vibes are about emotional signaling. The fact that we are social creatures means that naturally we are drawn to socializing and will often feel what someone is feeling by sharing in their vibe even if we are not physically feeling it too.

Take the example of talking to someone who says something that disgusts you. You will feel depressed and might lower your eyebrows or shrink in your seat. If they are keen, this will rub off on them too. Immediately, they realize that something is not right. This is how emotional signaling works. It is a good thing, too, because it allows you to understand each other and communicate faster without having to put up with different constraints in your environment.

In analyzing people, it is wise that you become aware of your environment, and the vibes people give off around you. This way, the vibes, and your gut feeling can always alert you when something is not right. The good thing is that some people are so evil, they give off a negative vibe around them that you cannot miss. Such are the people you need to stay away from.

Once you pick up on the vibe, you can easily trace the communication to other observable features like how their eyes are moving, the tone they use when talking to you, and so forth.

Your Hands

Have you ever watched a politician and how they use their arms and hands? The hand is often swept down in a cutting motion when they want to emphasize what they are saying and comes down emphatically to make each point.

Or have you watched how a comedian will open his arms to his audience with palms up, inviting his audience to share his incredulity at a ridiculous but hilarious occurrence he is describing? Creative people often wave their arms around, especially when they are getting excited about their current topic.

Research has found that babies who use lots of hand gestures at 18 months go on to be more intelligent in later life. We can say all kinds of things with our hands without ever opening our mouths, so we should get on and incorporate them into our lives as soon as possible.

Using our hands and arms comes naturally. Even blind people do it when speaking to other blind people. However, be aware that there are limits. You should not be waving your arms around like a windmill because that just becomes distracting and people cannot concentrate on what you're saying. So, let's get down to business and find out what we should be doing.

HANDS

Counting

Children learn to count using their fingers – and sometimes their toes – but it is often used in normal speech to emphasize what you are saying and helps others to remember. So, for instance, if you order three coffees in a busy café, and hold up three fingers at the same time, the server has a visual record as well as an audio one of how many you ordered.

Just a Tiny Bit

Holding your forefinger and thumb slightly apart indicates that you mean 'just a little'. You might do this to emphasize that you only want a very small amount if someone asks you if you want pepper on your food for instance.

Nothing to Hide

Holding both palms up indicates that you have nothing to hide and you are revealing that there is nothing in your hands. It is also an invitation for someone else or an audience to share something you are saying. This gesture could also be used to ask for compassion from someone else.

Stop Right There!

One palm up, pointing towards the other person(s), might be used to stop someone in their tracks when they are speaking. It might mean that you think that the person is under a misapprehension and it is an indication that you want to take back control in the conversation. It is the same gesture as a traffic cop might use to stop the traffic.

And, what's more......

This is a pointed finger in the direction of the person you are speaking to. But take care with this one because if it's done sharply and with a prodding motion, it can quite easily be perceived to be aggressive.

Whatever

Holding up your hands so that your palms face each other and loosely shaking them indicates that something can be one thing or another. It can represent flexibility and that there is nothing firmly fixed in place.

Making a Distinction

This is when you might raise one hand loosely to represent one point of view and the other hand then comes us as you home in on the other point of view. It's about delineating two points of view.

From Here to Here

Holding your hands facing each other and then moving them in or out can indicate growth or shrinkage.

Growth

Holding one palm facing downwards and then raising it indicates growth or shrinkage if used the other way of course.

And that includes you

This brings someone back to the conversation if you mind detect that their mind is wandering. It might mean, 'And I'm sure that you feel the same?' It gives grounds of commonality so that the person feels more attuned to what you are saying.

And I'm talking from the heart here

Holding both hands towards the chest or the heart means that what you are saying is heartfelt and that it is personally how you feel.

Let's go for it

Making a fist shows that you are about to make a determined effort. Watch the facial expressions when making a fist though because it can also mean that you're edging for a fight.

Let's put all that aside for now

Making a sweeping movement with your hands can indicate that you want to ignore what's gone before and lay out fresh information. Or it could mean that you want to amalgamate all the facts available.

Let's get cracking

This means that someone is eager to get started with something and shows enthusiasm. Alternatively, it could mean an anticipation of gain.

Now I feel confident

The gesture of clasping your own hands over your abdomen or crotch should be used if you want to feel more secure. It's used as a symbolic sign of protection. Watch out for others doing this because the higher that the hands are held, the higher the level of insecurity.

I'm the boss

When hands are clasped behind the back it normally indicates authority. Members of the English royal family often adopt this stance, but it could equally be used by an army sergeant or university lecturer. It shouts out that that person is confident because they are brave enough to expose their front body without feeling the need of protection.

ARMS

I'm trying to restrain myself

When someone is holding on to their arm behind their back, they are holding themselves back. They may find themselves becoming irritated and this is a way of keeping themselves in check against attack be that physical or verbal. It's done behind the back because the person doing it doesn't want to appear negative or aggressive to the other person.

United we Stand

Holding your arms out and then joining them together means that you are encompassing the other person(s) into what you are saying so that it unites you. Your fingers might intertwine to show extra solidarity. If you do this whilst facing someone, you might encircle your arms around them to say that they are part of your inner circle and that you trust them.

I am so bored

We are probably all very familiar with this one and it is represented quite clearly by crossed arms in front of the body. The body assumes a relaxed position because it feels disinterested and is switching off. It can also indicate a level of defensiveness, ostensibly protecting the main organs of the body. Watch out if the person's fists are clenched at the same time though because it can mean aggressiveness.

I'm safe

One arm across the chest with the hand clasping the other arm emulates when we were children and our parents hugged us. It provides us with comfort and reassurance.

I'm Waiting

Standing with your arms out with one hand on either side of your waist would indicate that someone is waiting with a reducing level of patience. Alternatively, it might also mean that someone is ready for the next step.

Of course, there are many more gestures, but this list

provides some of the most common and those that you should bear particular attention to. If you want to keep your thoughts to yourself, you better be sure to sit on your hands at the same time.

In the Western world, when we greet someone formally or perhaps for the first time, it is usual to use the handshake. This can be just as intimate as the French embrace because you are putting your palm into someone else's bare palm and may even pull them into your own personal space. The handshake evolved as a sign of greeting and whilst on the Orient they used a simple bow, in the West the handshake was used, palm meeting palm, to show that they were carrying no weapon and no evil intent. In ancient Rome, the greeting was made by clasping someone higher up on the forearm because they frequently carried daggers hidden near their wrists up their sleeves.

You might be meeting someone for the first time or using it as a greeting an associate or friend. Either way, it should be a firm grip and not last too long. When you shake the person' hand, look them in the eyes and have a slight friendly smile.

It all sounds rather straightforward but even a simple handshake can be adapted to take on many meanings. Some of those meanings have been allocated almost universally so that the initiator of the handshake will adopt a certain type of handshake to impress that assumption on the other person. In other cases, the assumption made about the other person is not necessarily complimentary but may indicate a weak personality, for instance.

There are many types of handshake, even though the action might sound quite straightforward and perfunctory. Outlined are the most common below.

Firm Handshake

This is as described above and would be preferable for new introductions or, indeed, for most situations. It shows no assumption of dominance or control but is about people meeting or greeting on equal terms.

Sweaty Palms

This might indicate a feeling of nervousness. If you're interviewing someone and their palm is damp, take this into consideration. If you come up a salesman with a sweaty palm, he is either desperate for the commission or he might not have that much faith in his product. Be sure to check it out thoroughly before committing. However, you should also be aware the 5% of the population suffer from excessive sweating that they cannot control and which is not a sign of nervousness.

Politician's Handshake

This is when the other person cover's your hand with their other hand so that it is encased between both of theirs. The hand grasping yours is firm. This handshake can be used between friends when it is indicates closeness between the two of you. This might even escalate into a sandwich of four hands if you are especially close or if someone is trying to achieve the illusion of it. Or it might involve the other person grasping your upper arm with their other hand, but this is normally only when a close bond exists between the two people involved.

However, when someone who does not know you very well adopts it, they are trying to emulate that closeness which is normally insincere. Don't be too ready to put your trust in them. A handshake is devised to keep someone in their place and keep a distance between two bodies.

Dead Fish

This is a limp shake and is normally given by someone you might regard as being wishy-washy, a bit of an insubstantial personality with nothing to bring to the table. This type of person is unlikely to be a people person.

Bone Crusher

This is used by someone who wants to assert their dominance in the relationship. They might use it to test the strength of the other person. However, it should be avoided as people who use this type of handshake are normally regarded as bombastic and overbearing.

Lobster Claw

This is when the other person's palm does not touch yours, but they put their fingertips to your palm instead. This shows a level of unwillingness to commit to being open with you and this type of person may have problems building meaningful relationships. They refuse to show too much of themselves and share information. Give them time to build their trust in you and don't try to rush them.

Finger Vice

This is when the other person grips your fingers instead of meeting palm to palm. It is an indication of assumed dominance and they want to keep you in your place and control you. They want to show their superiority over you most likely out of insecurity. Don't show any weakness but if it helps you get what you want you should treat them with respect.

Tea Cup

This is like a normal handshake, but the palms do not touch. It can indicate that the person is hiding something from you or not giving you all the information you should have to make a reasoned decision. If you are doing business with this person, check the facts before signing on the dotted line.

Dominator

This is when the person shakes your hand using a normal grip, but their palm is on top, facing the floor. This would indicate a show of dominance because your hand is on the bottom being forced into submission. If you want to let the other person they are in charge, adopt the stance of submission and the other person will feel a false sense of security in their power.

Queen's Fingertips

This is one that might be used between a woman and a man when the woman offers her hand face down as if she were expecting it to be kissed. It is normally a sign that the person prefers to keep more personal space between themselves and the other person, so she doesn't want the intimacy of a full handshake. It forces the other person to shake the fingers of the person offering their hand in this fashion and may indicate that the person doing so regards themselves as superior.

As can be seen from above, there are many types of handshake and the same person might use different types in different situations. None of them will give you a totally foolproof reading of another person but they are often a good indication of what you might expect as your relationship proceeds.

A handshake might also be used to say goodbye or seal a deal. Notice if the handshake is the same as the one the other person used to greet you. It may be that you've won them round and that initial handshake gave you the information about how to play it and get them to sign the contract.

Your Mouth

The Mouth

Another place to look on the face is the mouth. The mouth's subtle movements often go completely unnoticed by the person themselves. We will examine a smile for instance.

A genuine smile will include a change or movement in all parts of the face, this happens automatically and is not controlled by the person. A fake smile, however, will only involve the movement of the mouth into the desired shape of a smile and not involve the eyes or the upper areas of the face. These two types of smiles can tell a great deal about what a person is thinking.

A real and genuine smile indicates that the person is happy and interested, while a fake smile indicates that the person wants approval or acceptance. Another type of smile is one that includes the movement of only one side of the mouth. This type indicates that the person is feeling unsure or not convinced.

CHAPTER 4

EFFECTIVELY ANALYZING PEOPLE THROUGH THEIR WORDS

Everything that a person does or says reveals something about their personality. Actions, beliefs, and thoughts of people are aligned perfectly with each other in a way that they all reveal the same things concerning an individual. Just as it is said that all methods can lead to Rome, everything a person thinks or does can reveal a lot about their personality makeup and personality. The words that are spoken by a person, even if they appear to carry less weight, tell a great deal about a person's insecurities and desires.

No one doubts that the words we speak or write are a full expression of our inner personalities and thoughts. However, beyond the real content of a language, exclusive insights into the minds of the author are usually hidden in the text's style.

From our acts of dominance to truthfulness, we are revealing to others too much about us. You can quickly know the most important of all the people in the room by listening to the words that they use. Confident and high-status people use very few "I" words. The higher a person's status is in a given situation, the less the "I" words they will use in their conversations.

Each time people feel confident, they tend to focus on the task that they have at hand, and not necessarily on them. "I" is also used less in the weeks that follow a given cultural upheaval. As age kicks on, we tend to use more positive emotional words and even make very fewer references to ourselves. A study has also shown it that the higher social class a person is, the fewer emotional words he will need to use.

According to Pennebaker, style words include auxiliary verbs, prepositions, pronouns, articles, and conjunctions. He also goes ahead to explain the content words, which include regular verbs, nouns, and especially adverbs and adjectives. Here is the main difference between the style words and the content words. The content words are what someone is saying while the style words are how the words are said.

Women tend to use pronouns, social words, negations,

as well as references to the psychological processes as compared to the male. This could be a surprise, but men tend to use more big numbers, prepositions, and articles than women. But despite all that, the way women speak implies that human beings are more open and self-aware to the self-reflection. That is, according to Pennebaker, who also discovered that there are three main ways in which people speak when they are not saying the truth. He also discovered that the health of a person is likely to improve, not with the increased application of the emotion words such as joyful, happy, and sad, but with more use of the cognitive words such as understand, realize and know. Public figures who have the tendency of addressing press briefings tend to use more first-person singular each time they are prone to committing suicide or troubled. When people tell the truth, they are likely to use the pronouns of the first person singular more often than other times. When the levels of testosterone increase in people, they will tend to drop in their use of references to other people that they are talking to.

Another study has also shown it that people who talk about traumatic circumstances or decodes to share some moments of feeling down or painful truth are physically healthier as opposed to those who kept the experiences secret.

I earned another honorary degree.

The word clue in this sentence is "another." It is used to give a notion that the speaker has earned more than one previous honorary degrees. The person wanted to prove to others that he/she has earned at least one honorary degree. It is a smart way of bolstering the self-image of a person. The speaker may require the admiration of others to be able to show his/her self-esteem. Professional observers could exploit this kind of vulnerability by using flattery and comments that can help in enhancing the ego of the speaker.

I have worked so hard to achieve my goal.

The word clue in this sentence is "hard." It suggests that the speaker values goals that appear so hard to achieve. The sentence might also indicate that the goals that the person has made could be more difficult to achieve than the goals that he usually attempts to achieve. The word clue in this sentence also offers other suggestions. It also shows that the speaker can defer gratification or strongly believes that dedication and hard work tend to produce a better result. A job seeker that has the following characteristics stands higher chances of getting a job because the character traits could be attractive to the employers. It is because this is a kind of individual who would accept challenges and have the determination to be able to finish up tasks in a successful way.

I patiently sat through the public lecture forum.

The word clue in this sentence is "patiently'. It can be used in many hypotheses. It could mean that the person could have been bored with the public lecture forum. Perhaps the person was forced to talk on the phone or even use the restroom. No matter the kind of reason, the person has evidently preoccupied with other things apart from the main contents of the public lecture forum. Someone who patiently waits for a break before leaving a forum or a room is someone who obeys the social etiquette and norms.

A person whose phone rings and gets up immediately and leaves the room shows that they do not have strong rigid for the social boundaries. Those who have social barriers stand higher chances of getting job opportunities because they not only respect the authorities but also follow the rules to the later. Employers will analyze the characters of these people by listening to the kind of speeches that they offer.

On the other hand, someone who fails to follow the social conventions would stand a chance of getting a job that needs novel thinking. Someone who has the predisposition to act outside the social norms would make a good spy as opposed to someone who is disposed to follow the social conventions. This is because spies are usually asked to violate the social norms on a routine.

I opted to purchase that model.

The word clue in this sentence is "opted." It shows that the person weighs a few options before deciding to make the final purchase. At times, they could have struggled to some extent before making the final decision to buy what they wanted. The behavior trait showcased here is that this is a person who thinks through making the decision to buy something. The word "opted" can also be used to show that this person is not likely to be impulsive. Someone impulsive would likely use words such as "I just purchased that model'. The word clue in this second sentence is "just" and suggests that the person just purchased the item without giving it much though.

Based on the first-word clue of "opted," the listener can go ahead and develop a hypothesis that the speaker is an introvert. Introverts are the type of people who usually think before they decide. However, they tend to carefully weigh on each of the options that they have before giving their views and decision. Introverts, on the other hand, tend to be more impulsive. The use of the verb "opted" does not identify the speaker as an introvert in a positive manner, but it seeks to offer an indication that the person could be an introvert.

A detailed personality test needs a more definitive psychological assessment. However, an observer is still able to exploit a person if he is aware that the person tends towards the side of introversion and extroversion.

Extroverts are the kind of people who would get their energy from spending time with other people and look for stimulation from their surroundings. They also tend to speak spontaneously without having a second thought and use the trial and error methods more confidently. The introverts, on the other hand, tend to expend the energy that they got when they socially engage and seek some lonely time to perform other errands.

Introverts will usually look for stimulation from within and rarely speak without having a second thought. They carefully weigh the options that they have before making any decision. Before entering into any kind of business negotiations, knowing whether your opponent tends either towards introversion or extroversion can give a very strategic benefit. Salespeople should give their introverted customers to think about the sales proposals that they are presented to them.

The introverts tend to mull in the information that they got before they can come to a final decision. When the introverts are pressed to make impulsive decisions, they might be forced to say "No," even when they meant "Yes." This is because these people are not comfortable when it comes to making any immediate decision. Conversely, the extroverts can be pressed to certain levels to make quick decisions since they are more at ease when it comes to making impulsive decisions. In very rare cases do people show fully introverted features or entirely extroverted features.

The personality traits of a person tend to slide along a given continuum. There are also several people who show both the introverted and extroverted characters at the same time. In addition to that, those who are introverts appear to be comfortable with their environments and will usually showcase behaviors that are related to the extroversion behaviors. Extroverts can also display the introverted features at times.

What I did was the right thing.

The words clue in this sentence is "right." It is used to suggest that the speaker struggled with an ethical, moral, and legal dilemma and managed to overcome some degree of external and internal opposition to make a just and fair decision. According to the behavioral trait that is portrayed in this sentence, it is also very evident that the person has enough strength of character to be able to make the best and right decision even when pressed with several opposing views. The key here is to listen to what they are saying and let their words do the talking.

Open Communication

In most interpersonal interactions, the first few seconds are very vital. Your first impressions have a great impact on the success of future and further verbal communication with another person. When you first meet a person, you create an immediate impression of them; this is based on how they behave, sound, and look, as well as anything else you may have heard about them.

For example, when you meet a person and hear them speak, you create a judgment about their level of understanding and ability and their background. When you hear a foreign accent, for example, you might decide that you require to use simpler language for communication. You might realize that you need to listen more attentively to make sure that you understand what the person is saying.

Effective Verbal Communication

Effective speaking includes three main stages, that is, words that you choose to use, how you utter the words, and how you reinforce the words. All these areas have an impact on the transmission of your message and how the message is received and understood by the target audience.

It will be important for you to wisely and carefully choose the words to use. You will need to use different words in different events; even you are discussing a similar topic.

How you speak will include your pace and tone of voice. The pace and tone of voice communicate a certain message to the audience, for example, about your level of commitment and interest, or whether you are nervous about the audience reaction.

Active Listening

Effective listening is important for effective verbal communication. Ways that you can ensure that you listen more. These include:

- Be prepared to listen. Focus on the person speaking and not how you are going to reply to them
- Keeping an open mind while you avoid being judgmental about the person speaking.
- Always be objective

- Always focus on the objectivity of the message being conveyed

- Avoid distractions.

- Don't stereotype the person who's speaking.

Enhancing Verbal Communication

Techniques and tools that you can make use of to enhance the effectiveness of your verbal communication. These include:

- Clarifying and Reflecting. It is a process involving giving feedback to another person of your understanding of what has been conveyed or said.

Reflecting usually involves paraphrasing the message that has been conveyed to you by the speaker in your own words. All that you need to do is to capture the importance of the feelings and facts expressed, and communicate your understanding back to the speaker.

Reflecting is an important skill because:

- You are demonstrating that you consider the other person's opinions

- The speaker received feedback about how the message has been received

- Shows respect for, and interest in, what the other person has to say

- You can view what you might have understood the message properly

- *Questioning*. This is how broad we get more information from others on particular topics. It's an important way of clarifying aspects that are not clear or test your understanding. Questioning enables you to seek support from other people explicitly.

Questioning is a vital technique because it helps you to draw another person into a conversation or simply to show interest.

Types of Questions

Open question. These types of questions demand further elaboration and discussion. They help to broaden the scope of reply or response. These types of questions often take long to reply but give the other person a broader scope for encouraging and self-expression involvement in the interaction.

Closed question. They seek only two or one-word answer, often simply 'no' or 'yes.' They allow the person asking the questions to be in total control of the interaction.

CHAPTER 6

PERSONALITY AND BIRTH ORDER

Nope, the effect of birth order on personality type is not just pop psychology, BuzzFeed quiz-style talk. It is in fact based on consistent research and scientific principles. Chuck aside the entertainment and stereotypes, and you have a near accurate technique for determining someone's personality. There are plenty of psychological principles behind the amusing stereotypes that determine people's personalities depending on their birth order.

Why Does Birth Order Impact Our Personality?

According to some psychologists, birth order is as crucial as genetics in determining an individual's personality. It boils down to the nature versus nurture personality debate. Research has pointed to the fact that birth order can indeed influence our personality owing to the fact that the way parents relate to every child of theirs (based on his or her order of birth) is different. Children from the same household never assume the same role.

There is always a clear demarcation of roles and equations between the parents and children vary based on their birth order. For instance, if you are the oldest among siblings and assume the role of a caretaking sibling, no one else will fill that role. The others will then pick other roles, says an achiever or provider.

Parents are almost always directed by a different approach at the birth and subsequent upbringing of each child. The firstborn instills a sense of pride and paranoia in parents. If you are a parent, you'll understand how frightened you were at each potential injury of your firstborn. Similarly, the middle born is often bossed over or dominated by the firstborn sibling, who is already sufficiently acquainted with the ways of the world. The older sibling is viewed as wiser, responsible, and competent.

Compared to the firstborn, the other children are less likely to be micro-managed by the parents, thus changing the equation between them slightly. Parents are more exhausted and worn out by the time the later siblings arrive.

They most likely realize that their fears are unfounded

and that the baby doesn't really need to be micromanaged. Thus, parents turn slightly more flexible when it comes to disciplining and attending to later children. Therefore, middle and younger siblings learn to attract attention.

It isn't a biological process where just because you jumped out of your mother's tummy first, you are destined to be a leader. Rather, it is about how the parents treated the child depending on this birth order that leads to the child developing a specific personality.

Since the firstborn is more of an experiment for the parents, there is a greater tendency to be overly obsessed with minute details, thus leading the child to be a perfectionist. On the other hand, the youngest born child is born when the parents have already figured things out.

The youngest child is also competing for attention with older siblings, which makes him more of a people please and less obsessed with the idea of perfection.

The First Born

The firstborn child in a household is often believed to

be ambitious, dominating, and responsible. They are known to be natural leaders and often lead by example. These are the folks people often look up to for guidance and solutions. They operate with a deep sense of responsibility and are goal-driven.

Since firstborn children enjoy undivided attention, at least for some time from their parents, they are naturally used to being in the front or limelight. They feel like there's no competition and that they are born to lead. It can be seen as a byproduct of the attention showered on them in the absence of other siblings.

The firstborn child may connect more effectively with other firstborns than his or her siblings owing to the birth order. Parents often rely on their firstborns to assist with taking care of their younger siblings, which makes them responsible and reliable.

They are more often than not well-behaved, meticulous, caring, and conscientious. This comes from the idea that others rely on them. From childhood, they've been conditioned to believe that others are dependent on them for support and guidance.

It isn't surprising then that they turn out to be high achievers who constantly seek validation and appreciation from others. They also tend to have a dominating personality and are perfectionists by nature. The older siblings assume the role of a mini parent while also being insecure at the prospect of losing the parents' undivided attention.

The Middle Born

The general notion about middle born children is that they have a high sense of fairness and peace.

Middle children are generally understanding, adjusting, co-operative, yet competitive. They are likely to have a close set of friends, who give them the attention they've not got from the family. Middle children often receive the least attention and affection from the parents, which makes them turn outside the house for forging more meaningful relationships.

They are generally late bloomers and find their calling after much deliberation and experimentation. However, middle born people are often at the helm of powerful and authoritative careers that let them use their slick negotiation skills. This helps compensate for all the attention they probably didn't get as children.

The personality traits of a middle child are

diagrammatically opposite to the characteristics of the first and young child. However, they are unique, juxtaposed between siblings and this role makes them expert negotiators. They quickly learn to navigate their way through tricky and awkward situations. This equips them for entrepreneurship and other positions of authority.

Youngest Child

By the time the youngest child is born, the parents are fairly assured of their expertise as caregivers. They are no longer paranoid or hesitation about their skills as parents. This makes them more flexible and lenient towards the youngest child. There isn't a tendency to monitor every move of the child, which makes more independent. Younger siblings generally enjoy more freedom and thus become independent thinkers and decision-makers. The youngest and oldest children have few traits in common because they've both been brought up with a high sense of self-entitlement.

They've both been made to feel special based on their oldest and youngest positions in the household. Younger siblings have always learned to deal with their parents' divided attention. They are fairly adept at handling competition and aren't bogged by feelings of insecurity and jealousy. They operate with a sense of security and often know their place.

Since the parents are more flexible with them, youngest born people often tend to follow their hearts calling. You will find them in more creatively stimulating professions such as stand-up comedians, actors, painters, writers, and dancers.

The youngest born tends to take more risks, have an untamed spirit, and are often exceedingly charming. If someone tells you they are the youngest sibling in the family, they almost always know how to wriggle out any situation by using their charm. Don't forget to overlook the context though when you're analyzing people.

Sweeping judgments don't work very well when it comes to analyzing people. There may be several things to consider such as situation, setting, context, and culture. In your over-enthusiasm to read people, you may end up making incorrect observations by overlooking context.

The Lone Rangers

Yes, I know what you are wondering. What if you happen to be the only child and don't fit into any order of birth? Lone rangers or the "only child" is often more mature and confident. They tend to think beyond their years owing to the fact the lone rangers are almost always surrounded only by adults in the household. In the absence of siblings, much of their interaction is only with grown-ups of the household.

Having spent a lot of alone time, they become more confident, independent, solution-oriented, creative, and resourceful. Lone rangers have a lot in common with firstborn children. They also share the self-entitlement and feeling of specialness that is associated with the youngest siblings.

Is It Always True?

It may not always be true because parents are known to set extremely high expectations for the firstborn. When first born children do not meet their parent's expectations, they can become highly rebellious. There is a rejection of his or her role.

It is true that most middle born children are excellent

peacekeepers and negotiators because they neither have the rights of the oldest sibling nor the special privileges of the youngest sibling. Caught in the middle, they learn to negotiate their way through life and become exceptionally good peacemakers.

They are more emotionally connected to their friends, owing to the fact that they don't receive the desired attention from the family. They tend to become social butterflies who spend more time outside the house.

It is a known fact that parents aren't as stringent or careful about their youngest child since they are fairly experienced in raising children. They have already seen their older children grow with the required trial and error, and are hence more at peace. A majority of the time, parents are more financially independent by the time their youngest child is born. Thus, the overall feeling of contentment, security, and leniency towards them is high.

Sometimes, the youngest children don't fancy being the baby of their household. There is an increased need to be taken more seriously. This drives them to be more serious about their responsibilities.

Always pay close attention to how people refer to their

birth order while speaking about it. Do they appear more positive or negative about their position? This reveals a lot about whether their birth order has been a bane or boon while influencing their personality. Similarly, observe people's body language while they are speaking about their birth order.

Factors Impacting This Structure

Birth order is not a precise science for determining an individual's personality. It is a good practice to try and know more about an individual's siblings if you are trying to read their personality based on birth order. In addition to birth order, there are several other determinants of who a person turns out to be.

The Natural Elements

Genetics is the single most influential determinant of an individual's personality. About 50 percent of who we are is determined by our genetic make-up. A majority of our personality is influenced by natural, in-born factors.

Gender

Other than birth order, gender also influences who we

become or the roles we assume within our household. For instance, if the firstborn is a son, and the second born is a daughter, they will each have their own gender-based identity.

The daughter will not be bogged down by the pressure of living up to the boy's accomplishments and responsibilities. If the second child was a son, he would've probably experienced the pressure of living up to the older man's achievements. However, since it is a girl, the pressures are not as marked since she will have an identity of her own based on her personality.

Communicating With People Based on Their Birth Order

First Born

Firstborns on account of their undivided attention status, at least for some years, tend to be dominating, leading and controlling by nature. There are in fact two categories of firstborns. The first is the rule-abiding, responsible, and the compliant firstborn type who strives to be an example for their siblings.

The second category is aggressive and dominating leaders who know how to get things done owing to their perfectionist ways. Be a good team player, follow the rules, and demonstrate a caring approach towards the former category. Similarly, seek the expertise, and stick to perfect ways of the second type. The leaders enjoy being in control and issuing instructions, so you need to be a good follower while dealing with them. They derive a great sense of importance when people ask for expertise or guidance.

Middle Borns

Middle borns are often known to be rebellious by nature since they do not enjoy the special privileges of the first and last born. They often do not get the attention enjoyed by the firstborn or the special pampering received by the second born.

Showering them with special attention or offering genuine compliments is a great way to get into their good books. They tend to be either outgoing or lonely. Try to win the confidence of the lonely middleborns without pushing them to open up.

Give them their time and space, and you'll do well. Do not rush them into anything. Similarly, if you're negotiating with them, you better be excellent at the game because middleborns can be exceptionally gifted negotiators.

Handle the rebellious with gentle firmness. Be assertive yet polite while communicating them. They are good at compromising in any situation, which is why they also quickly take to peacemakers and solution providers.

Avoid confrontation and deal with them in a more sensitive, and accommodating manner. Learn to be more compromising and adjusting while dealing with them.

They may have issues with assertiveness, confidence, and self-esteem. Keep this mind while interacting with them. Boost their self-esteem while interacting with them, and you'll win brownie points with them.

Last Borns

Last borns on account of being "the baby of the family" generally become less self-reliant and independent compared to their siblings. They can often be unrelenting and stubborn. The best way to deal with them is to shower them with attention and affection. They are happy to take suggestions and advice because they aren't very independent thinkers. Don't try to negotiate with them as when they make up their mind, they are almost always sure.

CHAPTER 7

PERSONALITY TYPES AND PATTERNS

We use the different types of personalities to know the strengths of each person.

Let us look at the different kinds of people that you will come across.

Most people have a general idea of being shy, daring, outgoing, or charismatic. But this is not all when you understand the personality type you get to enjoy many benefits that include:

Knowing Other People's Preferences

Every person has his or her own preferences, and you can judge these by knowing the personality type.

When these people operate within the preferences, you get them to be more effective and efficient. However, operating outside the preferences requires more type and energy.

Knowing if you are within the boundaries can help you

improve efficiency, productivity, and even grow management skills.

Avoid Conflict

Understanding the type of person you depend on the personality type helps you avoid any conflict.

You get to diffuse them way before they come up. If you know that your personality makes you intense whenever a situation arises, you will adjust the behaviour so that you are more receptive to the issue.

When you are usually the one to accept responsibility even when you aren't the one that messed things up, you get o train yourself to become more analytical and take time to evaluate the situation before you handle it.

Helps You Appreciate Diversity

Once you know your personality type, you have the chance to interact with other people and appreciate how diverse they are.

When you are in a work environment, the chances are that at times you will hit a roadblock and end up failing to handle some situations.

When this happens, it is good to have a mind that will take up the issue on your behalf and implement it.

Find the Right Career

The personality type you adopt plays a huge role in the type of job that you are suited to.

It also affects how you handle the job that you are given.

The type of personality you have helps you find the right career that will give you proper job satisfaction. For instance, if you are an extrovert, you will find it hard to work in a position that requires you to work alone.

On the other hand, if you are an introvert, you will find it hard to work in a position that doesn't give you the chance to work alone.

Make Better Decisions

How you make decisions based more on what you see and past experience.

You know that when you take a certain decision, you will either end up with something good or you will lose out.

It also bases on sensing and intuition.

If you decide to make a decision based on sense, then you will engage all your fixe senses to gather information, analyze it then make the right decision.

On the other hand, if you use intuition to make a decision, you will most likely feel the situation before you can make a choice.

The only downside to analyzing issues before you make a decision is that you will tend to analyze the issues longer than necessary, which in turn makes the decision to take longer than expected.

The theory behind having a personality type is that we get born with it, and then we live with it before finally dying with it.

When faced with a situation, we have the chance to apply the personality type the right way spending on the scenario or experiences

> The personality types are based on Myers-Briggs theory that was developed by a partnership between a mother and daughter combination.
>
> Let us look at the combination pairs that make the theory applicable in all situations:

Extraversion and Introversion

This is concerned with the way you direct your energy.

If your energy is mostly directed towards dealing with people, situations, and things, then you are an Extravert (E).

On the other hand, if you direct your energy towards your inner world, then you are a perfect example of an introvert (I).

Sensing and Intuition

This looks at the kind of information that you end up processing.

If you are one to look at facts, analyze them, and then come up with a decision from the facts, then you are a sensor (S).

On the other hand, if you are one that makes your decisions without having to analyze facts, then you are intuitive (N)

Thinking and Feeling

This looks at your personality type, depending on your decision-making style.

If you base your decisions on the basis of logic, taking time to analyze and come up with the best approach, then you prefer Thinking (T).

If on the other hand, you prefer to use values, which means you make decisions based on what you see is important, then you are in for Feeling (F)

Judgment and Perception

This is the final pair that you can use to determine your personality type.

If you plan your life in a structured way, then you have a preference for Judging (J).

If on the other hand, you have a preference of going along with the flow, responding to things as they come along, then you are in for Perception (P).

Understanding the Scope and Limitations of Personality Analysis

At this point you may be thinking that if learning personality analysis is so advantageous, why doesn't everyone do it?

It may be difficult for the budding psychoanalyst to believe, but the biggest reason is that most people simply aren't interested in learning this skill, much less putting in the effort to master it. People in general are focused on their own lives and how they can affect change in their immediate surroundings.

By being willing to explore this field of knowledge, you are already well on your way to becoming a master of human psychology and personality analysis and will likely gain a huge leg up advantage in any social situation.

It must be mentioned, however, that this is also a skill that requires time and practice of careful observation of others. This isn't a skill that is going to all fall into place overnight, but with consistent observation of human nature, applied over time, you will find yourself becoming extremely perceptive of people's motivations and have a greater capacity to be able to manipulate and influence others to your advantage.

Luckily, we have compiled in this book some fantastic shortcuts to fasttrack you on your progress to becoming a master of human manipulation.

The other aspect of personality analysis to consider here is that you must be gathering data within a framework that allows to to most efficiently analyze and put to use what you are observing. Without a framework to understand your observations, you will be spending much more time trying to gain a foothold on any observations you have made, no matter how carefully or objectively.

By incorporating a framework in your analysis, you will be able to sift out the data that is most relevant to you and know what line of inquiry to take when dissecting someone's personality. After reading this book and applying what you have learned, you will be well versed in the personality analysis systems which will yield great and useful information.

Let's dive a little deeper into the two main aspects of analyzing people: the analysis framework, and cold reading.

The Analysis Framework

The first aspect of personality analysis is building a framework, or creating the foundation that you will need to be able to interpret data gathered from your observations.

When you look at a group of people, for instance, it can be overwhelming to consider the mass of collective experiences, thoughts, emotions, and behaviours that the group represents.

That's why it is so important to have a framework, a lens through which to understand other people's perspectives. The framework that you will develop will consists of a series of reference points for categorizing behaviours.

This framework will allow you to understand someone's personality intimately - so so that you can understand what they do 99% of the time. Knowing their patterns, and why they act the way they do now, you will be able to predict with a degree of accuracy what they are likely to do in the future. The key is understanding the why's behind their behavior.

By sorting people into various categories, you will begin to understand why they act a certain way, and their perspective will become clear to you.

Habits, tendencies, likes, dislikes...Their predominant desires, motivations, fears and consistent thought patterns will all become easy for you to read and interpret.

Another amazing thing about this type of analysis is

that once you are familiar with your target's personality (ie. have spent some amount of time with them observing their behavior) you can even do much of this analysis even away from the subject in question, without them even knowing about it, and without asking them questions that may be considered impertinent or that may give away your own motivations.

Cold Reading

This brings us to the second tool for personality analysis that we will be discussing in this book: cold reading.

Where the analysis framework is more of a scientific process of understanding social dynamics and theory, cold reading is more about the art of careful observation.

Cold reading is being able to understand what is going on in your target's mind at any given moment.

The skills that are relevant to developing cold reading abilities are:

- General body language analysis including

analyzing eye movements, gestures and voice intonation;

- Lie detection, and comparing & matching verbal and non-verbal cues;

- Understanding your own cognitive biases; and

- Developing your own intuition

That may sound complicated, and as if there is a lot of abilities that you need to put a lot of effort into learning. But after you understand the basics of body language and gain a handle on the information, you will find that all it takes is practice, and a little bit of patience, to become very good at cold reading.

Cold reading is essential to analyzing people effectively because it allows you to gather a very large amount of data on the other person, especially if you strive to maintain objectivity in your interactions.

Someone who is very good at cold reading will be able to pick up on all of the signals that someone is sending, whether they be conscious or unconscious, apply the principles of framework analysis, and be able to read someone like a book within the first few minutes of meeting them.

That is the beauty of cold reading. And you will be able to do just that if you practice these skills as well. Just remember that this ability comes naturally with practice.

Now that we have a handle on what we will be covering in this guide, let's jump into the first part - the analysis frameworks.

Where the outer world is concerned, most people present an outer self that is curated, and reflective of our best qualities. We present ourselves in a way that is accepted by the groups we are in. The outer self is also related to how people cope with the demands of work and life, and may be concerned with practical day to day and materially focused things. If someone is not aware of their outer world, they may be criticized for sharing views that are contrary to popular opinion, or they may not be considerate of others. On the other hand, if one is too focused on their outer world, there may be a disconnect between what they are truly feeling, or their motivations behind their actions.

The inner world, in contrast, is all about what can't be seen from the outside. The inner world relates to feelings, intuition, true emotions, spirituality, desires, fantasies, and inner purpose and motivation. Someone who operates effectively in their inner world will have strong self-awareness as well as an understanding of their own beliefs, values and life purpose.

It is helpful to be aware, therefore, that the persona that someone portrays is not always completely in line with what they are experiencing on the inside.

If we want to become good at analyzing people, it is almost always required to interpret the behaviors and external actions of the persona, to remove the mask that they wear to get to the true thoughts and motivations of the individual.

We will use this concept as we dive further into behavioural analysis in this book. It is always helpful to keep in mind that when someone acts a certain way, it may be a coping or defense mechanism, or a pre-programmed behaviour that is there to hide one's true feelings, mask one's true intentions, or even deflect from criticism. Many of the strategies we will learn are focused on peeling back the onion of someone's psychology and revealing the true intentions that lie beyond the facade of their external behavior.

As we cover analysis systems in later chapters, always keep in mind how the concept of the Inner versus the Outer worlds may be coming into play and influencing the way we are interpreting and analyzing people's behavior.

When engaging in a conversation, we typically don't pay attention to the movements of the lower body. Since our direct line of sight is from the chest up, we often miss the obvious signs of the legs and feet. Certain stances that occur within the legs can signify dominance, sexual attraction, and even anxiety. Let's consider a few common patterns to look for when attempting to analyze someone else.

Crossed Legs

Crossed legs could indicate defensiveness. Perhaps you are sitting in a meeting at work, and your colleague says something totally off-putting. You may find yourself slowly crossing your legs as a subliminal way of showing your disapproval. Defensiveness could be heightened when one hand is positioned on top of the crossed leg. This is almost like a taunting move, signaling combat.

Crossing the ankles or knees are signs of nervousness, anxiety, and fear. This stance is protective in nature, which indicates that someone is attempting to protect themselves from whatever source of fear they are encountering. It could also be a means to control actions during high adrenaline situations.

Pointing and Active Legs

If you are miserable at a party, likely your legs are pointed towards the door as you are ready to leave. Our legs inadvertently point to where our heart wants to go. This can be used to determine interest and attraction. The legs, even when covered, will almost always point in the direction they are interested in.

Legs that bounce continuously could mean two things: boredom and nervousness. When you witness a person continuously bouncing their legs up and down, they may be nervous about something. This bounce is like a protective blanket that distracts their mind from their jitters. In addition, when someone is growing restless and ready to go, they may move their legs rapidly. The bouncing or tapping of the legs can be likened to a compulsion carried out to make the irritation subside.

When both legs point in one direction, it could be a clear indicator of interest for the person. However, when one leg steps back, it could indicate that the person wants distance. They may be uncomfortable with the person, conversation, or situation at hand. This subtle movement could be their way of escaping something distressful.

Messages from the Thighs

The upper portions of the legs usually indicate sexual or suggestive invitations between men and women. In daily activities, men may sit with their thighs opened as a sign of dominance. This outward display of masculinity represents an "alpha male" mentality. With women, closed thighs are a polite sign of femininity. Many young girls are instructed to sit with their legs closed so as not to expose their private areas. This closed manner of sitting is graceful and emanates class. When opened, they express dominance and even a form of female rebellion. Since it is so common for girls to be taught to keep their legs closed, doing the opposite could indicate opposition to societal norms. In addition, it is also extremely flirtatious to sit with the thighs crossed and one sitting higher above the other. This could indicate interest.

The Feet

The feet work very closely with the legs to determine areas of interest. When the toes are pointed at a specific object or direction, this indicates where we want to go. This could be a subtle signal your body sends to your mind about certain situations. The feet are used to make a statement and could also be used as an accent to verbal cues. Stomping, imaginative kicking, or tapping are all means of gaining attention.

When toddlers throw tantrums, it's not only their flailing arms, crying eyes, and yelling demands that occur. Toddlers utilize their legs and feet to create loud noises to further emphasize their anger.

When it comes to interpreting the signs of the legs and feet, direction and movement are the two primary components needed for translation. Although we typically fret from glancing at the bottom half of a person, simple movements could be a key indicator as to how a person is feeling. It's imperative to understand the beauty of intricate movements in order to fully understand the inner workings of another person.

CHAPTER 8

THE ART OF ANALYZING HUMAN BEHAVIOR.

As suggested, studying people is not reserved for psychiatrists but any other person even though psychiatrists are best positioned to analyze people. Analyzing people requires understanding their verbal and nonverbal cues. When studying people, you should try to remain objective and open to new information. Nearly each one of us has some form of personal biases and stereotypes that blocks our ability to understand another person correctly. When reading an individual, it is crucial to reconcile that information against the profession and cultural demands on the target person. Some environments may force an individual to exhibit particular behavior that is not necessarily part of their real one. For instance, working as a call center agent may force one to sound composed and patient when in real life, the person acts the contrary.

Start by analyzing the body language cues of the

target person you are trying to read. Body language provides the most authoritative emotional and physiological status of an individual. It is difficult to rehearse all forms of body language, and this makes body language critical in understanding a person. Verbal communication can be faked through rehearsal and experience, and this can give misleading stand. When examining body language, analyze the different types of body language as a set. For instance, analyze facial expressions, body posture, pitch, tonal variation, touch and eye contact, as a related but different manifestation of communication and emotional status. For instance, when tired, one is likely to stretch their arms and rest them on the left and right tops of adjacent chairs, sit in a slumped position, stare at the ceiling, and drop their heads. Analyzing only one aspect of body language can mislead one to come up with a conclusion correctly.

Additionally, it would be best if you lent attention to appearance. The first impression counts, but it can also be misleading. In formal contexts, the appearance of an individual is critical to communicate the professionalism of the person and the organizational state of the mind of that individual. For example, an individual with an unbuttoned shirt indicates he hurried or is casual with the audience and the message. Wearing formal attire that is buttoned and tucked in suggests prior preparation and seriousness that the person lends to the occasion. Having unkempt hair may indicate a rebellious mind, and this might be common among African professors in Africa, for instance. In most settings, having unkempt hair suggests that one lacks the discipline to prepare for the formal context or the person is overworked and is busy. Lack of expected grooming may indicate an individual battling with life challenges or feeling uncared for.

It is also important that one should take note of the posture of the person. Posture communicates a lot about the involvement of an individual in a conversation. Having an upright posture suggests eagerness and active participation in what is being communicated. If one cups their face in the arms and lets the face rest on both thighs, then it suggests that one is feeling exhausted or has deviated from the conversation completely. Having crossed arms suggests defensiveness or deep thought. One sitting in a slumped position suggests that he/she is tired and not participating in the ongoing conversation. Leaning on the wall or any object suggests casualness that the person is lending to an ongoing conversation. If at home, sitting with crossed legs suggests that one is completely relaxed. However, the same posture at the workplace suggests that one is feeling tensed and at the same time concentrating.

Furthermore, observe the physical movements in terms of distance and gestures. The distance between you and the target individual is communicating communicates about the level of respect and assurance that the individual perceives. A social distance is the safest bet when communicating, and it suggests high levels of professionalism or respect between the participants. Human beings tend to be territorial as exhibited by the manner that they guard their distance. Any invasion of the personal distance will make the individual defensive and unease with the interaction.

For this reason, when an individual shows discomfort when the distance between communicators is regarded as social or public, then the individual may have other issues bothering him or her. Social and public distances should make one feel fully comfortable.

Allowing a person close enough or into the personal distance suggests that the individual feels secure and familiar with the other person. Through reading, the distance between the communicators will give a hint on the respect, security, and familiarity between the individuals as well the likely profession of the individuals.

Correspondingly, then try to read facial expressions as deep frown lines indicate worry or over-thinking. Facial expressions are among the visible and critical forms of body language and tell more about the true emotional status of an individual. For instance, twitching the mouth suggests that an individual is not listening and is showing disdain to the speaker. A frozen face indicates that the person is shell-shocked, and this can happen when making a presentation of health and diseases or when releasing results of an examination. A smiling face with the smile not being prolonged communicates that one is happy and following the conversation. A prolonged smile suggests sarcasm. If one continually licks, the lips may indicate that one is lying or that one is feeling disconnected from the conversation.

Relatedly, try to create a baseline for what merits as

normal behavior. As you will discover, people have distinct mannerisms that may be misleading to analyze them as part of the communication process. For instance, some individuals will start a conversation by looking down or at the wall before turning to the audience. Mildly, mannerisms are like a ritual that one must activate before they make a delivery. Additionally, each person uniquely expresses the possible spectra of body language. By establishing a baseline of what is normal behavior, one gets to identify and analyze deviations from the standardized normal behavior accurately. Against this understanding, one will not erratically score a speaker that shuffles first if that is part of his behavior when speaking to an audience.

Furthermore, pay attention to inconsistencies between the established baseline that you have created and the individual's gestures and words. Once you have created a baseline, then examine for any deviations from this baseline. For instance, if one speaks in a high-pitched voice that is uncharacteristically of the individual, then the person may be feeling irritated. If one normally walks across the stage when speaking but the individual chooses to speak from a fixed position during the current speech, then the person is exhibiting a deviation that may suggest that the individual is having self-awareness or is feeling unease with the current audience. If an individual speaks fast, but usually the person speaks with a natural flow, then the person is in a hurry or has not prepared for the task.

Correspondingly, view gestures as clusters to elicit a meaning of what the person is communicating or trying to hide. When speaking a person, will express different gestures and dwelling on the current gesture may make you arrive at a misleading conclusion. Instead, one should view the gestures as clusters and interpret what they imply. For instance, if a speaker throws the hands randomly in the air, raises one of their feet, stamps the floor and shakes his or her hands, then all of these could suggest a speaker that is feeling irked and disappointed by the audience or the message. As such, different aspects of body language should be interpreted as a unit rather than in isolation.

Then compare and contrast. For one to fully read the target person, try comparing the body language of the person against the entire group or audience. For instance, if one appears bored and other people appear bored, then you should conclude the tiredness of the person is largely due to the actions of the speaker for speaking longer than necessary. In other terms, the body language of the target person is not isolated. However, if you make a comparison, and it happens that the target person's body language deviated from the rest, then you should profile the actions of the individual accordingly. Making a comparison and contrast helps arrive at a fair judgment of the target person.

By the same measure, try to make the individual react to your intentional communication. Another way of managing to read a person is to initiate communication and watch their reaction. For instance, establishing eye contact and evaluating the reciprocation of the target person can help tell more about their confidence and activeness in participating in the interaction. When an individual ignores your attempts to initiate communication, the person could be concentrating on other things, or the person feels insecure. Initiating communication is critical where it is difficult to profile a person, and one wants to convincingly read the person.

Go further and try to identify the strong voice. A

strong voice suggests the confidence and authority of the speaker. If the speaker lacks a strong voice, then he or she is new to what is being presented or has stage fright. However, having a strong voice that is not natural suggests a spirited attempt to appear in charge and confident. A strong voice should be natural if the individual is feeling composed and confident in what he or she is talking about.

Relatedly, observe how the individual walks. When speaking to a target person, he or she will walk across the stage or make movements around the site where the conversation is happening. From the manner of walking, we can read a lot about the individual. Frequently walking up and down while speaking to an audience may indicate panic or spirited attempt to appear in control. Speaking while walking slowly across the stage from one end to the other end indicates that one is comfortable speaking to the audience. If a member of the audience poses a question, and one walks towards the individual, then it suggests interest in clarifying what the individual is asking.

It might be necessary to scout for personality cues. Fortunately, all people have identifiable personalities, but these can be difficult to read for a person not trained in a psychologist. However, through observation, one will get cues on the personality of the individual. For instance, an outgoing person is likely to show a warm smile and laugh at jokes. A socially warm person is likely to want to make personal connections when speaking, such as mentioning a particular person in the audience. Reserved individuals are likely to use fewer words in their communication and appear scared or frozen on stage when speaking.

Additionally, one should listen to intuition, as it is often valid. Gut feelings are often correct, and when reading a person, you should give credence to your gut feeling about the person. When reading a person and you get a feeling that the person is socially warm, you should entertain this profiling while analyzing the body language of the person. While considering gut feeling, you should classify it under subjective analysis, as it is not based on observable traits and behaviors but an inner feeling.

Expectedly, watch the eye contact. Creating eye contact suggests eagerness and confidence in engaging the audience. Avoiding eye contact suggests stage fright and shyness as well as lack confidence in what one is talking about. A sustained look is a stare, and it is intended to intimidate, or it may suggest absentmindedness of the individual. If one continuously blinks eyes while looking at a target person suggests a flirting behavior. An eye contact that gradually drops to the chest and thigh of the individual suggests a deviation of thoughts from the conversation.

Additionally, pay attention to touch. The way a person shakes hands speaks a lot about their confidence and formality. A firm handshake that is brief indicates confidence and professionalism. A weak handshake that is brief indicates that one is feeling unease. On the other hand, a prolonged handshake, whether weak or strong, suggests that the person is trying to flirt with you, especially if it is between opposite sexes. Touching someone on the head may suggest rudeness and should be avoided.

Finally, listen to the tone of voice and laughter. Laughing may suggest happiness or sarcasm. Americans are good at manifesting sarcastic laughter, and it is attained by varying the tones of the laughter. The tone of the voice tells if the person is feeling confident and authoritative or not. Overall, a tonal variation implies that the individual is speaking naturally and convincingly. A flat tone indicates a lack of self-confidence and unfamiliarity with the conversation or audience and should be avoided.

Distance in Communication

If one is talking to someone, the person violates your personal space, and you allow it, then it signals that you are okay to intimate ideas. Intimate ideas in this context include highly personal issues that one can talk with another person. For instance, if you walk and sit close and in contact with a woman watching television and she approves your behavior, then it is indicative that she is likely to allow you have a personal talk that may be intimate in nature. Such discussion may include your health challenges or mental health and not necessarily sexual issues. For this reason, one should carefully weigh the need to invade the personal distance.

Regarding children, violating personal distance will make them freeze due to feeling uncomfortable. If a teacher sits next to a student or stands next to a student, then the student is likely to feel uneasy and nervous. However, they are instances where the invasion of personal space is allowed and seen as necessary. For instance, during interviews or when being examined by a doctor, invasion of private space by the person with advantage is allowed. The panel during an interview may move or ask you to move closer, which may violate your personal space. A doctor may also stand closer to you, invading your personal space, but this is necessary due to the professional demand of their service.

As such, when one avoids personal distance, and the individual is expected to be within this space, then the individual may be feeling less confident or feeling ashamed. For instance, if a child has done something embarrassing, he or she is likely to sit or stand far from the parent during a conversation. For this reason, it appears that one should feel confident, assured, and appreciated to approach and remain in personal space when needed.

Additionally, staying in personal space during intense emotions may portray one as resilient, understanding, and bold. Think of two lovers or sibling quarreling, but each remains in the established personal space. The message that is being communicated is that the individual is confident that he or she can handle the intense emotions from the other person. For most people, they only allow their lover to stay in their personal distance when feeling upset because they trust that the person can handle the known behavior of the affected person. Since being in personal space places a person within physical striking range, most people will only allow trusted and familiar individuals into their personal space.

Equally important is that invasion of personal space is justified because it is part of professional demands. Think of a new teacher that is trying to help a student solve a mathematical equation. In this aspect, the teacher is a stranger because he or she is new to the school. By sitting or standing close to, the student, the teacher is invading the personal space, but the established norms in this context allow the student not to feel unease. For emphasis, this case is not unique as it aligns with stated expectations that people will welcome known or unfamiliar people in their personal space only if they trust them and, in this case, the student feels safe with any teacher. For this reason, the operationalization of distance in communication is mediated and moderated by established culture.

In most cases, one can start with public distance

before allowing the interaction to happen in personal or social space. For instance, as a student during tournaments, you could have initiated nonverbal communication with the student from the other college before suddenly feeling connected to the individual and allowing him or her to move into personal space as a potential girlfriend or boyfriend. At first, the target person saw you as a stranger but allowed you to make nonverbal communication within the public space. When the person felt the need to connect more with you and have given you the benefit of the doubt, the person allowed you to move through public distance and social distance to enter their personal space.

For instance, a lot can be learned from studying distance and space in communication. Being allowed into the social and personal distances implies that the person trusts that you will not harm them emotionally and physically. For the intimate distance, being allowed into this distance implies that the person trusts you so much and is confident that you can never harm them and that you share a lot. For instance, a mother holding her baby close enough to her signals that the baby is feeling assured of security and protection. When two lovers move, closer until their faces are almost touching suggests trust and confidence that the other person feels safe and protected.

Relatedly, if arguing with your child or lover and the individual moves farther from you physically, then it suggests that the person no longer feels safe with you being within their personal distance. Issues that can cause someone to expand the distance between you and them include the risk of violence from you and emotional issues. If you occasionally act violently, then chances are, your lover or children will expand the personal distance to social distance because this is where they feel safe due to your personality and character. It then appears that your prior behavior will also affect the distance during communication.

Nevertheless, they are other issues that cause individuals to extend the distance of interaction, and these include having a medical condition or having hygiene issues. For instance, if you are sweaty, then chances are that the other person may prefer to extend the distance of communication between you and them. Having oral hygiene issues may also make the other person move far away from you because the smell turns them off. For this reason, interpreting the distance between communicators should also include hygiene and health-related issues that impact this distance.

For instance, some medical conditions can make people maintain some distance from you or be closer to you physically. For instance, some conditions may attract uneasiness, and this includes epilepsy. People with epilepsy get seizures, and this can make people feel unease being closer to them because they inadvertently fall. On the other hand, having hearing issues or sore throat may make people move closer to you physically to facilitate effective communication. However, these are exceptions when analyzing space and distance as forms of nonverbal communication, but they should be taken into account where necessary.

In some cases, it is welcome to invade personal distance merely by circumstances. For instance, when attending a match in a full packed stadium or sitting to watch a movie in a movie theater, one will have his personal invaded due to the sitting arrangements. In this context, one may feel uneasy with this arrangement, but he or she has little control of the situation. While we value and seek to protect personal spaces, some situations make us allowing invasion of this space because it is beyond control.

Activity

1. Mark is talking to his girlfriend, and their noses are almost touching. Comment on what this means. Do you feel that the actions of Mark are appropriate? Why or Why not?

2. The following day, Mark is talking to his girlfriend while standing nine feet away. Comment on what this means.

3. An elderly person asks Mark to assist him in how to shop online using the smartphone. Richard is standing right next to this elderly person. Comment on what this means.

4. On Saturday, Mark argued with his sister. He was visibly angry, but they continued exchanging words while seated on the same sofa set. Comment on this distance and space in communication. Comment on the importance of trust and assurance for people who share this space.

5. Mark met his girlfriend while attending a football match. It all started when Mark threw a hard stare at her at the farthest end of the stand.

When the girl reciprocated the stare, Mark moved closer to her after the game and they walked holding hands. This is an example of allowing someone to transit from public distance to personal distance. Using analysis of distance and space in communication only, why do you think the girl allowed Mark to shorten the distance and welcome him into the personal space?

6. Nicole works as a nurse at the local clinic. When one of the patients asked for a nurse, Nicole moved close enough to the patient and touched his hand to examine it. What is the justification for this distance in this communication?

7. Nicole and her husband quarreled last night, and today they sat eight feet from each other while pretending nothing happened. Using the concept of space and distance only, suggest two reasons for this behavior?

8. As a new mother, Nicole holds her baby closer, making her nose and that of the baby touch while making sounds to the baby. Justify why this distance and space in communication is allowed?

9. Last month while seated on a bench in a public park, a stranger walked and sat right next to Nicole even though the bench had only Nicole. Nicole decided to stand up and walk away. Why do you think Nicole walked away? Use only the concept of distance and space to explain.

Major Components to Connectivity

There exist three critical components that determine a person's ability to connect with others successfully. They are; mindful observation, listening with intent, and useful feedback.

Linking with Other People Through Mindful Observation

What is a mindful remark? Just like most of us, you observe people and your surroundings at all the time, but what happens to other things apart from the stuff you discovered? How to apply what you have discovered to support your screening and adapt your behaviors and objectives? Normally, most people work with incredibly little of what they find to boost their calls. If they ever happen to be over-informed, they might find out what happens in declaring what normally does not sit well with the crowd. As a result, they quit conversing. Many people are essential in the making of extremely few modifications to increase their marketing and sales communications. Instead, they dialogue with a person who is definitely excited to participate.

In most cases, there is lack of monitoring and adjustment of verbal and non-verbal terminologies because many individuals never learned the skills on how to analyze people and they change their communication style to be very accommodating to match a person's personality. Remark forces help people to place what they discover to function and generate a livelier exchange of details.

To improve your remarks expertise, ensure to tackle the job like a pup! You heard that right, just like a pup. Pet dogs exhibit amazing interest in watching expertise. This simply means that dog trainers declare the very best approach to show a pup how to carry out the strategy by enabling them to see another puppy perform it and receive a prize. A dog's remark abilities will be excited that they ought to study better through observation, rather than spoken instructions. Who says that the same procedure is not applicable to humans?

Marsha's puppy is very observant; Hannah knows what she will be doing a time structured schedule in the items as she observes her own activity. For instance, if Marsha draws out her operating shoes or boots, Hannah is aware they will be heading to work. If Marsha holds her hair back into a ponytail, Hannah will suspect they will be going herding and working into the storage units. This means hanging on to a car door because Marsha definitely wears her mane in a ponytail when she and Hannah are herding.

The problem is that when Marsha decides to pull her hair into a ponytail, and she's not taking Hannah herding. Usually, Hannah is sure she's heading out to the herd, and she will commence to scratch and pester Marsha about why the turn was dragged. Hannah is very unremitting in her efforts to get Marsha to carry out what she needs as they might commence in the near future. Therefore, Hannah is sure of her potential in analyzing her owner and knowing that she will be standing at the storage door for almost an hour waiting for Marsha's method. Although Hannah reads all the signals, she failed to understand that the same signal could possess countless definitions.

The moral of the story is to caution you that

sometimes you can have excellent observation skills with this particular person. What you observe and affix a meaning is not a preference of what was expected. You can carry out the same issues; however, you lack the desired tools. Your connection does not get better; neither can your relationship. When this occurs, it implies there are modification issues. Stop supposing that the same analysis will apply to everyone. Make efforts for something leading to acquiring better sales and marketing communications. The crucial aspect to remember is that giving up will get you nowhere.

Sometimes you need to observe a little or a bit longer. Don't just look at the person as they communicate with you; watch their communication cues with others. Watch how others react to them. If the person with whom you are having issues and watching their body language is around the individuals they like, make efforts to pay attention to their tone as they speak with other people with whom they talk to in a pleasant way. Simply observe how various people respond to a person with whom you have problems with. How is their tone? What is their body language expressing? How will the ranking be? For confusing interactions, surface area findings are not necessarily enough.

Be mindful of your goals when observing your subject. What do you want from the relationship? Being aware means you can't always be focusing on all the things going on around others, but you need to choose one or two things to observe for some time until when you have a greater understanding of what they are saying with their gestures or expressions. After knowing what their moves will be on something else, you need to be mindful with the observation means with which you are determined to resolve the situation and improve the communication with that person.

Hearing with Intent

People observe others every moment; they listen to what they say very well. The disadvantage is that you can notice an individual, but if you are tuning in with a particular motive, you will not know what to do with what you have discovered. For example, you can hear an individual speak, but if you are not able to distinguish the person's dialogue level when they are conversing or the quantity in which they speak with a system in the discovery of their personality type, you hear a portion of the subject matter.

When playing with intent, you might have the

tendency of interrupting. This tendency system shows where you are heading to after the difference in communication shows that you have a tendency of speaking more than the person. In fact, you have a tendency to speak a lot; you are attentive to the motive of sense, which implies behind the phrases and between the lines.

Providing an Actual Opinion

There are times when providing effective opinions is a way of mimicking a person's price or quantity of conversation. Sometimes, useful opinions will mean implementing a relaxed open stance to reveal what you like to observe the other person do. There are occasions when useful opinions will mean modifying your personality characteristics so that you can avoid making the other person uncomfortable or angry. If your concept is garbled due to your body vocabulary, gestures, and expressions diverging from your words, you ought to provide clarity to the discussion by giving congruent opinions.

In a program, there are occasions where you avoid creating avenues for people to read your thoughts. Therefore, effective opinions will be those masking the way one experiences. It is not about hiding your thoughts, but handling them. It is not about how effective you or anyone else seem, but how you generally show every sole assumption and sensing. There are situations when you want to bury your thoughts a little bit to ensure devices don't present you or set you in any insecure opportunities. In such a circumstance, powerful remarks do NOT unveil what you never wish another to discover.

Practicing these three major factors for connectivity, and other folks might be linked to you. Nevertheless, they might give more support to your thoughts and ideas. It is an approach to acquiring what you wish without mental outbursts and unreasonable requirements. You can maintain your approach since you are a remarkable communicator. You acquire the support from others since they like you; with this, you can quickly get to them. You can attain achievements in your personal and professional lifestyle because you hook up with others and they with you, this include all the results of the few approaches you have discovered from these web pages. Do you have an apparent tendency? Then you've just used the three critical elements to connectivity: mindful statement, listening with intention, and providing useful opinions.

Word Clues You Need to Know

"I Labored Hard to Accomplish My Dreams"

The clue in this sentence is labored hard, and it shows that the person's dreams were difficult to accomplish. Perhaps it took him longer and harder to accomplish this particular dream as compared to the other goals he has accomplished. When we delve deeper, you will discover that the word clue labored suggests the person holds the belief that dedication and hard work can produce great result.

"I Bagged Another Contract"

The word clue is another, and it reveals that the speaker or writer has won so many contracts and this is just the latest accomplishment. From the above sentence, you can deduce that the speaker wants everyone who cared to listen to know that he won so many awards. He is trying to bolster his self-image by appearing successful. To an astute observer, this person seems self-conscious about what others think. More so, he needs the adulation of others to boost his self-esteem. Others who noticed this character weakness might try to exploit it for their personal gains.

"Jim and I Remained Friends"

The word clue in this sentence is remained. From the sentence, you can deduce that the speaker and Jim have gone through trying times. Perhaps the fabric of their friendship has gone through different difficult situations. They probably weren't supposed to be friends under normal circumstances. The speaker is trying to defend why she remained friend with Jim. The speaker doesn't feel convinced about her choice and, therefore, feels the need to defend her decision.

"I Patiently Sat through the Meeting"

Here, the word clue patiently holds a plethora of hypotheses. For instance, the speaker might be bored with the lecture but felt obligated to sit through it for various reasons. Perhaps the speaker had to use the restroom but felt self-conscious or trapped from standing up to go the restroom. You could also deduce from the statement that she might have had an urgent appointment somewhere else.

Gauging from this statement, we can accurately say the speaker is someone who adheres to social etiquette and norms, irrespective of other pressing needs. Those with no social boundaries would have left the lecture to attend to any other issue that needs their attention. People with social boundaries like the speaker would make good employees since they know how to follow the rules and respect authority.

Conversely, those who leave during the lecture to attend to other pressing needs are perfect candidates for jobs that require out-of-the-box thinking.

"I Decided to Buy That Dress"

The modifier or world clue here is decided. It indicates that the speaker weighed several options before settling for that particular dress. This statement shows us that the speaker is not impulsive. Rather, she weighs her options and takes the most logical step. More so, there's a high chance our speaker is an introvert since introverts tend to weigh their options before taking a step.

It's not a sure analysis, but a hypothesis about the speaker's personality. Conversely, an impulsive person would say, "I just bought that dress." The word clue just represents an impulsive decision.

"I Did the Right Thing"

The word clue, 'right', suggests that the speaker

struggled with a moral or ethical dilemma before arriving at the decision. This verbal statement suggests that the person has a solid strength of character to make the best and just decision in the face of overwhelming opposing views.

CONCLUSION

The body is a fascinating group of systems that work coherently to expose our innermost emotions. From a simple glimpse of the eyes all the way down to the positioning of the toes, the body is honest. Mastering the art of analyzing others begins with a comprehensive understanding of yourself. Even different inflections of the voice can change a sentence in its entirety. In addition, the art of touch can mean the difference between attraction and repulsion. Learning how to analyze others assists with social connection and your ability to understand what others are truly saying. The beauty behind the human connection is that there are universal mannerisms that give off social cues open for interpretation. A simple shrug of the brows paired with a crossing of the arms signals a sign of discontent. A slight lean inward can give you the signal that your date is legitimately into you! These subtle cues are intricate in nature, but the magnitude is revolutionary. By mastering these techniques, you will have this unwavering gift that is easily applicable to your everyday life. You will be able to seek the truth and defend yourself against possible threats. One of the key secrets to mastering the art of analyzing others is keying in on your observation skills. The entire body works in conjunction with the brain to send and expel certain messages that define emotions, often leading to subconscious visual cues that may give away the true thoughts and feelings of a given individual without their even realizing what they are doing. Inside, you will find dozens of different ways to pick up on those cues for fun and profit. By being observant and truly reading the behaviors of others, you will be able to emphasize this gift to meet your needs. We encourage you to implement these practices into your daily life to further analyze yourself and truly be able to read others.

The next step is to practice these tips throughout your daily life! By doing so, you will gain a better understanding of yourself and human behavior as a whole.

www.ingramcontent.com/pod-product-compliance
Lightning Source LLC
Chambersburg PA
CBHW071800080526
44589CB00012B/622